A Christian counselor explores the most
common conflicts of marriage

Questions
COUPLES ASK
behind closed doors

JAMES OSTERHAUS, PH.D.

TYNDALE HOUSE PUBLISHERS, INC.
Wheaton, Illinois

To Helene and Jerry,
who have kept their promise to
each other all these years.
Thanks.

OTHER TYNDALE–AACC BOOKS

Family Shock: Keeping Families Strong in the Midst of Earth-shaking Change by Gary R. Collins, Ph.D.

Intimate Allies by Dan B. Allender, Ph.D., and Tremper Longman III, Ph.D.

"Why Did You Do That?" Understand Why Your Family Members Act As They Do by Wm. Lee Carter, Ed.D.

High-Maintenance Relationships: How to Handle Impossible People by Les Parrott III, Ph.D.

Psychology, Theology, and Spirituality in Christian Counseling by Mark R. McMinn, Ph.D.

Counseling Children through the World of Play by Daniel Sweeney, Ph.D.

AMERICAN ASSOCIATION OF
AACC
CHRISTIAN COUNSELORS

The American Association of Christian Counselors is an organization of professional, pastoral, and lay counselors committed to the promotion of excellence and unity in Christian counseling. The AACC provides conferences, software, video and audio resources, two professional journals, a resource review, as well as other publications and resources. Membership is open to anyone who writes for information: AACC, P.O. Box 739, Forest, VA 24551.

Copyright © 1996 by James Peter Osterhaus

Cover photography copyright © 1996 by Bill Bilsley

Scripture quotations are taken from the *Holy Bible,* New International Version®. Copyright © 1973, 1978, 1984 by International Bible Society. Used by permission of Zondervan Publishing House. All rights reserved. The "NIV" and "New International Version" trademarks are registered in the United States Patent and Trademark Office by International Bible Society. Use of either trademark requires permission of International Bible Society.

Editor: Vinita Hampton Wright

Cover Design: Beth Sparkman

Library of Congress Cataloging-in-Publication Data

Osterhaus, James P.
   Questions couples ask behind closed doors : a Christian counselor explores the most common conflicts of marriage / James P. Osterhaus.
     p. cm.
   Includes bibliographical references.
   ISBN 0-8423-5103-5 (pbk. : alk. paper)
   1. Marriage—Psychological aspects. 2. Marriage—Religious aspects—Christianity.
3. Interpersonal rellations. I. Title.
HQ734.0745 1996
306.81—dc20   96-28518

Printed in the United States of America

02 01 00 99 98 97 96
7   6   5   4   3   2   1

CONTENTS

ACKNOWLEDGMENTS

Books spring from our head and from our heart. As a writer, I find it difficult to trace all of the influences that have been brought to bear on my head and heart as I have worked. I wish to acknowledge and thank the most obvious, realizing that there are literally hundreds of men and women who have shaped my thinking over the years, to whom I owe so much.

First, I say thank you to my wife, Marcy, who permits me to set up my computer on the kitchen table and work at these projects when she would rather I busy myself with other, more practical things.

Second, I say thank you to Jim Denney, who has been my word-smith on this project and on others. Not only is he adept at fashioning ideas into understandable sentences, he also brings much of his own intelligence and feeling to the work; and I count it an honor to have him as a friend and fellow laborer.

Third, I say thank you to Tyndale and her editors, who have given encouragement and practical helps that have sped this project along.

Fourth, I say thank you to my partner, Joe Jurkowski, who has been the most instrumental in guiding my thinking about couples.

Fifth, I say thank you to Bill Reardon, a true friend, who has permitted me to bounce many ideas off his well-travelled brain.

What Does a Healthy Marriage Look Like?

Rick and Teri came to me with a question that was causing them considerable pain and confusion: What is a healthy marriage supposed to look like? What does "healthy" really mean?

It was not difficult to see why they felt confused. Rick's parents were divorced when he was ten. "There was this gigantic tug-of-war going on all the time," he recalls, "and I was the rope. I just wanted to love both of my parents, but they wouldn't let me. They always made me choose between them. Now I'm married with kids of my own, and I'm scared that my marriage may be falling apart. How am I supposed to build a healthy marriage when I don't know what one is supposed to look like?"

"Unlike Rick's parents," says Teri, "my parents never got a divorce—but I sometimes wish they had. Maybe my childhood memories would have been happier if they had split up." Teri remembers going to bed many nights and pulling blankets and pillows over her head, trying to shut out the sound of her parents' fighting. But it wasn't until recently that Teri realized that she was putting her own daughter through the same misery she had gone through as a child.

"Rick and I were in the middle of a fight. I don't remember what we were arguing about—something small and inconsequential, as usual. Suddenly, right in the middle of it all, our four-year-old, Katie, got between us and put her hands on her hips and shouted, 'Stop it!' at the top of her lungs. Well, that stopped the fighting, all right. Rick and I looked at Katie, and there were tears streaming down her face. That's when it hit me that we just can't go on like this. I want to have a healthy marriage so we can raise happy, well-adjusted kids. The problem is I don't know what a healthy marriage is."

"What is 'healthy'?" is just one of many questions couples ask me over and over again in my counseling practice. Some of the typical questions include:

How did we end up together, anyway? Rod and Amy are in my office because their fourteen-year marriage is in trouble. They seem to have nothing in common anymore—if they ever did. Rod feels that Amy's fiery, often angry, personality is like fingernails screeching on the blackboard of his soul. For her part, Amy feels that Rod is an under-motivated underachiever who needs to be pushed and prodded and lashed in order to accomplish anything. Looking back, they both wonder what they ever saw in each other and why they ever got married—and both admit that they wouldn't marry each other again if they had it to do over. Sitting in my office, they wonder aloud, "How did it happen? How did two such obviously mismatched people ever find each other and fall in love?"

Who leads? "This is our third year of marriage," says Michael, "and I kept hoping things would get better. But Kristy seems to get more stubborn and unyielding all the time. Since she's a Christian, I just assumed Kristy would understand that a wife is supposed to be submissive."

As you would expect, Kristy has a different point of view. "When I married Michael, I loved him for his strong personality," she says. "I'm a tough cookie myself, and I needed to marry someone who was a match for my personality. But something happened after we got married—Michael went into this 'Me Tarzan, you Jane' routine. I mean, I want a partner, not a boss. Most of the conflict in our relationship centers around the question, 'Who leads?' How do we resolve this issue?"

Neil and Lori face an array of problems. At age thirty-three, Lori has decided to go back to school for her master's degree, and that means she has less time and energy for their relationship, for their sex life, and for their children. As if these pressures weren't enough, Lori also has to put up with continual criticism from Neil's parents, who accuse her of neglecting her family. Lately, it seems that every conversation

Neil and Lori have turns into a fight, and they have no plan for dealing with these recurring conflicts.

So Neil wants to know, "**Why aren't we close anymore?** Lori says she needs this master's degree, but what about the kids' needs? **What about my needs? What about our sex life?** Isn't that important?" And Lori asks, "**Why do we keep having the same arguments over and over? How do I get Neil's parents off my back? How do we resolve these conflicts?**"

These are the kinds of questions I hear over and over again from Christian couples who come to my office for counseling. Many of them know what the Bible says about marriage, about loving one another and forgiving one another. Yet their relationships are distorted, their emotions are confused, their lives are in pain, and their marriages are in danger of breaking apart.

Why?

THE NOT-SO-OBVIOUS QUESTIONS

Many of us who are Christians already have a spiritual foundation for our marriage. But somewhere along the line we have not acquired the practical skills and insights we need to resolve differences, to meet each other's needs, to balance closeness and individuality, and to experience the true intimacy for which marriage is designed. Often, we depend upon spiritual processes, such as prayer and Bible study, to solve every problem. What we don't realize is that behind the broader questions—"What is God's purpose for marriage?" "Why is adultery wrong?"—lie the not-so-obvious, everyday questions: "When you said that, what did you mean?" "Why do you have such a strong emotional reaction when I do or say such an insignificant thing?"

So many couples come to me hesitantly and reluctantly—and often with a sense of guilt and failure because they can't seem to resolve their problems even though they hold strong Christian beliefs. We close the office doors and shut out the world, and we talk and try to listen to one another.

Here are two people struggling to love each other, struggling to honor the marriage vows they have made to each other. In the secure privacy of the counselor's office, they face each other, and they face their own pain—and they voice the questions that go right to the core of the marriage relationship.

Usually these questions are *not* "What does God say about my role in this marriage?" or "What does the Bible say about divorce?" Rather, they are the recurring deep, troubling questions about feelings, hidden thoughts, unspoken expectations, unexpressed needs, forgiveness, and sex. And they are also the everyday, practical questions about communication, arguments, in-laws, resentments, old issues that keep resurfacing, decision making, blending stepfamilies together, and personality differences.

Often, one partner will share these questions and emotions, and the other partner will look up in surprise and say, "I never knew you felt that way!" And real communication begins—sometimes for the first time in years.

Obviously, no book can take the place of a therapy session with a trained marriage and family counselor. But in this book, I have tried to gather together the questions I most often encounter in my own counseling practice—questions that often reveal the hidden dynamics of a relationship and lead to a major breakthrough in communication and understanding. I have also collected those principles and insights that have produced healing and transformation in so many couples who have walked into my office. This book is built on a foundation of biblical Christian values, but the emphasis is on those hidden issues and questions about practical, everyday matters that can quietly, devastatingly undermine a marriage relationship:

- Why do men and women feel, behave, and communicate differently?

- Why are my spouse and I out of sync emotionally and sexually?

- Why do my partner and I do and say things that sabotage our relationship and our happiness, even when we don't want to?

- Why are my spouse and I continually bumping up against new issues, emotions, and problems at different stages of our relationship?

- Why does my spouse's behavior often seem exasperating, irrational, and inexplicable?

- How can my partner and I become more aware of the hidden and unconscious dynamics in our marriage relationship so that we can make conscious, constructive changes?

As we explore the answers to these and other honest yet difficult questions about marriage, the answer to the big question—What is a healthy marriage supposed to look like?—will come into focus. This book is designed to give you the hands-on, practical tools and communication strategies so that you and your marriage partner can experience the rich and rewarding relationship God intended for marriage.

THE JOURNEY AHEAD

As you read stories of couples who are much like you and your spouse, as you learn new insights and workable principles, and as you work through the question-and-answer exercises at the end of each chapter, you'll find yourself becoming more conscious of your own motivations and of the dynamics that make up your marriage relationship. If both you and your partner read and work through this book together, I'm convinced you will discover new channels of communication and new levels of honesty and realism opening up in your relationship.

Even if your spouse does not read and work through this book with you, there are still many useful insights *you* can gain to enrich and strengthen your marriage. Wherever you and your partner may be in your life together—newlywed, thirtysomething, fortysomething, middle-aged, second or third time around, blended family, or golden years—the next fifteen chapters will enable you to acquire powerful insights, skills, and attitudes to help you build a healthy and happy relationship.

I encourage you to think of these chapters not so much as a book to be read but as a journey to be walked and an adventure to be lived. It is a rewarding journey—the journey of two people spending a lifetime together, growing in love toward each other. By reading this book, you have chosen to move forward, deliberately and consciously, along this lifelong path with your spouse.

Not everyone makes this choice. Unfortunately, I have seen many couples—including committed Christian couples—simply give up without making a real, honest effort to save their relationship. They conclude that the work of building a healthy marriage is just too hard. Or the process of self-examination and change is too painful. But I believe there is a better future in store for you because you have chosen to do whatever you have to do in order to make your marriage better. You have chosen to move forward in the journey of marriage.

And you have already taken the first step.

Is
This Really
Love?

The worst relationship I ever saw was a "marriage made in heaven."

Nathan and Sarah had been married about a year. How did they meet? "God brought us together," they told me. They met in the singles group at their church. They had a brief, whirlwind courtship and were married in the belief—and practically the *religious conviction*—that they were not only "in love" but they had been selected by God before the beginning of time to be joined together in holy matrimony.

Yet only a few months after this "divinely appointed" wedding, they were at each other's throats. "The Bible says I'm supposed to be the head of the household," said Nathan. "But Sarah won't respect my leadership. She spends money when I tell her we need to save. She won't let me watch football on Sundays because she thinks it's a sin. And she often refuses sex when I want it—she just tells me, 'Take a cold shower and pray about it.'"

"I've had it up to here with his so-called leadership!" Sarah countered. "He's always bossing me around, and he doesn't respect my Christian convictions! He doesn't want a wife; he wants a little harem girl to cater to all his wants, but he doesn't care about my needs one little bit!"

"Did you love each other when you got married?" I asked.

"Of course we did. God brought us together," they both insisted.

"Then where did the love go?" I asked.

There was a long, confused silence. "I don't know where the love went," Nathan finally said, "but it's gone. All the romantic feelings I had for Sarah were gone not long into our marriage. I don't feel anything for her now but anger."

"I keep wondering," said Sarah, "why God allowed us to feel such an intense love before our marriage, then allowed it to die afterwards."

THE HAPPY MARRIAGE: ONE LOVE OR THREE?

The irony of this relationship is that both Nathan and Sarah knew the Bible and were committed to living by it—yet neither of them had any real understanding of *what the Bible says* love is all about. As both a noun and a verb, *love* is perhaps the most overused word in the English language. Most of our books, films, and plays are devoted to the theme of love. Roughly 95 percent of popular music either sings the praises or bemoans the pain of love. We invest a significant part of our lives and our energy searching for love. But like Nathan and Sarah, few of us really know what love is.

Amazingly, the English language offers remarkably little versatility in matters of love. Instead of giving us a spectrum of words to express the many nuances of love, our language gives us a spectrum of meanings and only one poor, overworked word.

The ancient Greeks and Hebrews—in whose languages the Bible was originally written—appear to have been wiser in matters of love than we are. They had many words for love, and each word had a specific connotation. The Hebrews used the word *hesed* to denote "covenant-love," which is rooted in loyalty and faithfulness to a promise or covenant. This form of love is expressed in commitment.

The Greeks had a parallel word for the Hebrew concept of *hesed;* their word was *agape.* Although you find this word used only a few times in classical Greek literature, it is lavished throughout the Greek New Testament. Agape-love seeks the good of another person not because of emotional attachment or because that person has earned the right to be loved but simply because a prior commitment (a promise) has been made. Agape-love does not derive from the fact that the other person is lovable or valuable. Rather, it actually creates value in the person being loved.

There is no single word in the English language that corresponds to the Hebrews' *hesed* or the Greeks' *agape*. It takes a minimum of one or two sentences in English to convey what a single word instantly connoted to the ancient Hebrews and Greeks. And that defect in our language is a cultural tragedy because our difficulty in expressing the concept of covenant-love cripples our ability to practice the concept in our everyday lives.

In this culture, we usually use the word *love* to mean passion; passion was expressed by the word *eros* in ancient Greece. *Eros* derives its power and electricity from the object of love. Eros says, "I love you because you are so lovable."

While passionate love—the physical component of a couple's relationship—is the most exciting dimension of the relationship, it is also the most dangerous. Passion is highly possessive, an actual physical craving of two people for each other. Passionate eros-love leads to physical arousal and to the intense desire to unite and fuse with the loved one—a desire to penetrate and be penetrated. Passion develops quickly and is much like an addiction. Once a person becomes accustomed to a given level of passion, greater and greater levels of stimulation are required to produce the desired sensations of arousal and satisfaction.

We also have the capacity to love in a third way, with a kind of love the Greeks called *phileo*, which would be translated "friendship-love." Like eros-love, it is rooted in emotions. But whereas eros-love feels intense attraction and desire, phileo-love is motivated by feelings of fondness, of wanting to cherish and nurture another person.

All three of these loves—agape, eros, and phileo—must be dynamically present if a marriage is to be healthy. Passion is essential: The two marriage partners must want each other and must physically bond with each other. Friendship is essential: The two partners must cherish, nurture, and protect each other. Unconditional agape-love is essential: The two partners must accept, forgive, and seek the best for each other, choosing to honor promises and commitments—even when, emotionally, they want to escape the relationship.

Perhaps the best way to understand these three forms of love is to recognize that each form of love involves a different dimension of our humanness:

FORM OF LOVE	DIMENSION OF OUR HUMANNESS	RESULT IN THE RELATIONSHIP
Eros	Body	Sexual Satisfaction
Phileo	Mind/Soul	Friendship, Intimacy
Agape	Spirit Fellowship	Commitment

Phileo and eros, which are feelings-centered forms of love, are not sufficient to hold a marriage together over time. Marriages need the added strength of committed covenant-love—agape-love—in order to endure. Feelings, unfortunately, have a habit of changing. But if we have love that is rooted in promise and commitment, we can go on loving even as our feelings go through natural periods of ebb and flow.

ZAPPED!—OR TRAPPED?

Annie is getting married. Her fiancé is a handsome, successful young man named Walter. They are happy together, making plans and building a life together. Then one night, while Annie is driving alone in her car, listening to the radio, she hears a caller on a late-night talk show. The caller is a lonely man taking care of his young son all by himself after the tragic loss of the wife he deeply loved. He describes the magical, mystical kind of love he had with his late wife. As Annie listens to this man tell his story on the radio, she realizes two things: (1) She does not have this magical, mystical kind of love for her fiancé, Walter, and (2) she is intrigued with an anonymous caller on a radio show. Problem: How can Annie, who lives in Baltimore, find this unknown man who lives on the other coast, in Seattle?

That's the premise of the hit romance film *Sleepless in Seattle,* and the rest of the film is about getting these two people—Annie Reed (Meg Ryan) and Sam Baldwin (Tom Hanks)—together so they can meet and fall in love. I "love" this film (there's that word again!). It's a funny, romantic urban fairy tale. But I also believe this film could ruin a lot of marriages! Why? Because it promotes a hopelessly unrealistic image of love!

When Sam and Annie first meet face-to-face, their eyes lock, and the air crackles with energy—not just sexual energy but a spiritual energy. Here are two souls whom the stars have literally decreed should be partners for life! (Throughout the film, the stars are actually depicted as astrologically arranging events and pulling these two unwitting lovers together.) Love, according to *Sleepless in Seattle,* is a kind of heavenly magic that zaps two people and inexorably draws them into a dreamy world of consuming passion and complete bliss. The perfect, just-right person for you is out there, says this film. Your dream lover's name is written in the stars, and if you want to live happily ever after, just keep searching until you find Mr./Ms./Miss Right.

But love isn't about being magically zapped, nor is it about living happily ever after. It often feels that way, especially in the early stages of a relationship. The passion of eros-love feels not only sexual but also transcendent, spiritual, and eternal. That's why the passion of eros-love has inspired so many films, books, and popular songs. That's why, for example, pop diva Mariah Carey sings about a "vision of love," a dream that she "visualized" and which "sweet destiny" has brought into being, a love "that heaven has sent down to me."

The result of this kind of magical thinking about love is that people feel they are "in love" only as long as the passion, the magic, the transcendent emotions last. As long as two people feel they are "made for each other," life is one big honeymoon. But as soon as this haloed image begins to fade and problems and practical realities begin to emerge, these two people with their Technicolor concept of love begin to think, *Hey, what happened to the magic? Oh, no, I must have made a mistake! This person isn't my dream lover after all!*

It happens in every marriage, without exception: The day arrives when love's illusions are replaced by disappointing (and downright annoying) realities. When two people wake up and discover that they have not been magically zapped by "sweet destiny," and when they begin to feel more "trapped" than "zapped," they start to panic. All too often, even among Christian couples, this is the moment when one or both partners begins looking for a back door: desertion, separation, divorce, an affair, or even an "emotional divorce," in which both partners maintain the outward fiction of a marriage while living in emotional isolation from each other.

Real love is not about discovering that "dream lover" who is so perfectly attuned to your soul that "two hearts beat as one." Real love is often set in motion by passion and/or friendship, but hearts have to learn how to beat together, and people become dream lovers with time and practice.

DOES THE PASSION HAVE TO FADE?

Does all this mean that marriage is nothing more than a few months of passion and excitement followed by years of drudgery and toil? No! The good news is that passion and excitement don't have to fade from a marriage! In fact, all healthy marriages are passionate marriages. I know couples in their seventies and eighties, couples who have celebrated golden wedding anniversaries, who are still as passionate as many couples in courtship. Couples who manage to keep passion in their relationships are the couples who have learned that it takes covenant-love to preserve the ardor of eros-love.

When two people love each other in a committed way, faithfully keeping their marriage vows, they create a nurturing environment for passion. By agape-loving each other, they actually make each other more desirable as a source of passion, pleasure, and excitement. Why? Because agape-love creates value and lovability in the person being loved. Agape-love also creates security; both people know that there is no "back door" or Plan B.

GETTING PAST THE STARS IN OUR EYES

But how many couples go into marriage realizing that the foundation of a healthy, long-lasting marriage must be a covenant-love? As a psychologist who has spent hundreds of hours doing premarital counseling, I've found that hardly anyone does. For almost every couple contemplating marriage, love is something that occurs in the emotions rather than in the part of them that makes choices. Each partner views the other as the only person in all the world who can excite the senses and stir the hormones until Gibraltar crumbles into the sea. So one of my objectives in premarital counseling is to throw a bucket of cold water on those airbrushed romantic images.

Premarital counseling is different from every other kind of counseling I do. Why? Because so often couples don't feel a need for premarital counseling. They are not coming because they have a problem, so there is no sense of urgency. They are not motivated to listen to my counsel or even to examine their own relationship honestly. They come because they have been referred by their pastor as part of a requirement for a religious wedding ceremony. It's not easy to get through to people who have stars in their eyes.

"What do we need counseling for?" they ask. "We've found each other! What more is there to talk about?" So while I'm trying to talk to them about their issues and histories and values and personalities and motivations, their minds are off dealing with the *really* important aspects of marriage—the color of the bridesmaids' dresses, the flowers, and the honeymoon arrangements.

"How do you two plan to get along with each other for the next fifty years?" I ask.

"Well," they dreamily reply, "that just falls into place. After all, we love each other!"

I'll let you in on a secret: The most important tool in a psychologist's black bag is anxiety. If people aren't anxious, counseling usually fails. A couple of starry-eyed lovers don't see clearly enough to be anxious about the right things—if they're anxious at all! But people who are anxious and upset are motivated to work and to change and to listen. So I usually try to stir up a little anxiety.

I start by giving the couple a personality inventory, such as the

Taylor-Johnson* test, which reveals a lot about basic personality traits, beliefs, habits, compatibilities, and incompatibilities. After scoring the test, I might sit down with them and say, "It's clear to me that you two are looking at each other through rose-colored glasses. This tells me that you haven't seen the real person you're marrying. This tells me that each of you is in love with an image you have invented in your own mind."

Sometimes I can cut through all the violin music that's playing in their heads long enough to get across the fact that love is much more than what they see and what they're experiencing now. Unfortunately, many about-to-be-married couples aren't buying. They're convinced that they are really in love and that this love is the "real thing." Phil and Renee are a classic case.

MUTUALLY ASSURED DESTRUCTION

Phil was a truck driver. Renee was a graphic artist. As instructed by their pastor, they came to me for premarital counseling. They sat in my office, casting longing glances at each other, squeezing each other's hands, calling each other pet names. We did the Taylor-Johnson test, and I learned that in each other's eyes, Phil and Renee were more flawless than Ozzie and Harriet and more passionate than Romeo and Juliet. Yet the test also revealed that they were totally unrealistic about each other and they had a totally unrealistic view of love. They were as hopelessly mismatched as any couple I had ever met.

Moreover, they were both powerful personalities, accustomed to getting what they wanted on demand. I had a feeling that their first disagreement would look a lot like nuclear war: "mutually assured destruction." I never got through to them; but they did their required three appointments, and then they were gone. I was relieved to learn that they would be moving to the Midwest immediately after their wedding. When their passion disappeared and reality set in, I wanted at least six states between me and the war zone.

The fact that most couples enter marriage with so many misconcep-

For further information on the Taylor-Johnson materials, write to: Psychological Publications, Inc., 290 Tonejo Ridge Ave., #100, One Thousand Oaks, CA 91361-4928

tions about the real meaning of love is tragic—but not hopeless. I know a lot of couples who have learned about covenant-love in time to prevent lasting harm to their marriage.

So, *is* this really love? In the early stages, what two people feel for each other is rarely the promise-keeping kind of love that "real love" depends upon. But real love can be learned, nurtured, and practiced if both partners are serious about the process and patient with each other.

If you are passionate about someone, is that enough? If you are not passionate, you have something to be concerned about (for more on this, read chapter 11). But, no, passion is not enough to make a lasting love. The key is not leaving the person you're passionate about but learning how to develop the friendship and agape-love that will allow that passion to flourish over time.

Will mere friendship hold a marriage together? A good marriage can't survive without friendship. But friendship without passion or covenant-love will lose its ability to feel that fondness and to nurture the other person.

If you and your partner are willing to look honestly at the love you have and then work to develop the love that's missing, you will come to possess something far better than "movie love." And you will be able to say with confidence that, yes, *this really is love.*

Is This Really Love?

These Take Action sections will work most effectively if you and your spouse each have a journal. Write your honest responses in your own journals. Then compare notes with one another and discuss what your separate responses mean to your relationship. At the end of your discussion, you can agree on goals, commitments, or small projects you want to work on together—and record these in your journals also. (To save time and space, one of you could be the "secretary" and use your journal to keep track of the goals you set together.)

1. **Complete this statement (or write out the completed statement in your journal):**

   I have derived my concept of what love is from

   _____

   Examples: my parents and upbringing, movies, TV, books, popular music, conversations with friends, courtship experiences, the Bible

2. **On a scale from 1 to 10, where 1 equals "Not at All Important" and 10 equals "Very Important," rate yourselves in the following three areas:**

   _____What role does phileo-love (friendship) play in our marriage?
   _____What role does eros-love (passion) play in our marriage?
   _____What role does agape-love (covenant) play in our marriage?

3. **Circle the correct responses, or write the statements in your journals.**

   My spouse and I are (comfortable/uncomfortable) expressing friendship-love to each other. We express this love in the following ways:

   _____

   _____

Examples: We enjoy spending relaxing and fun times together; we share common interests and pastimes; we confide in each other as best friends.

Note: We will explore the phileo-(friendship) aspect of your relationship in greater detail in chapter 10: "What Is Real Intimacy—and How Can We Develop It?"

My spouse and I are (comfortable/uncomfortable) expressing passion-love to one another. We express this love in the following ways:

_____

_____

_____

Examples: We are comfortable touching and kissing each other; we are satisfied with the frequency of our lovemaking; we are satisfied with our sex life overall; our sexual expectations match and complement each other's.

Note: We will explore the eros (passion) aspect of your relationship in greater detail in chapter 11: "How Important Should Sex Be?"

I (feel/don't feel) spiritually close to my spouse. I feel this way for the following reasons:

_____

_____

_____

Examples: We can talk about spiritual matters; we sometimes pray together; we enjoy attending church and other spiritually oriented group functions together; each of us understands fairly well what the other person believes about God, the afterlife, sin and forgiveness, etc.

I (have/have not) demonstrated Christlike covenant-love for my spouse during the past week in the following ways:

_____

_____

_____

Examples: I have treated him/her with the honor due a child of God; I have been understanding and forgiving when he/she has made a mistake or failed in some way; I have prayed for him/her; I have encouraged him/her on the basis of what God has said about who we are and how he will help us grow into Christlikeness.

My spouse (has/has not) demonstrated agape-love for me in the past week in the following ways:

_____

_____

_____

2

How
Can I Be
Married and Still
Be My Own
Person?

Will and Gail had been married more than twenty years. "Will hides behind his job during the day," Gail complained, "and he hides in his workshop at night. I never see him, and he refuses to talk to me! I don't have anyone else to talk to, I never get out, and I just want to have a little fellowship with my husband. But he shuts himself out of my life! Is it any wonder that I'm depressed?"

"I no sooner walk in the door," Will countered, "than she's all over me with things she wants to do, things she wants me to do, things she wants to discuss with me! I work hard all day; I'm tired; I just want a few minutes to relax before dinner—and instead, I'm overwhelmed with all these demands! I just can't take it!"

"Will," I said after a few moments' reflection, "I think you're too close to your wife. You need more distance in your relationship."

Gail hit the roof. "What?!!"

Even Will seemed surprised. "I do?"

"Yes," I said. "Until you put a little more space between yourselves in this relationship, you'll never be able to truly help and support Gail in the marriage."

Gail was stunned. "But that doesn't make any sense! I just told you,

Will walls himself out of my life as it is. How much more distance can he put between us? Should he move to another state?"

"What I'm suggesting," I explained, "is that by putting some healthy space into the relationship, Will can be even more available to you than he is now. The way things are now, he runs from you because you cling to him, and the more he runs, the more you cling—and you will never be able to enjoy his friendship and receive his support as long as you keep clinging and he keeps running. When two people 'become one,' as the Bible says, that doesn't mean that their individuality disappears."

"But isn't that what Christian marriage is all about?" asked Gail. "The two becoming one?"

"In a healthy marriage," I replied, "there must always be two intact, distinct personalities—even though these personalities are united in marriage. If those two personalities become too close, if they absorb each other and try to meet all of each other's needs, they will smother each other. Will sensed that this was happening in your relationship, and he ran and hid to keep from being smothered. Each of you needs outside interests, your own friends and activities, your own life apart from each other. Then, when you come together in a committed relationship, you can give yourselves to each other, confident that you remain intact as individuals."

Gail seemed dubious, but Will said, "It sounds like a paradox—but it also makes sense." We hammered out an agreement whereby Gail would become involved in outside activities such as volunteering at the church-run thrift shop. She made friends, developed new interests, and within a few months, the entire dynamic of their relationship had improved.

AN EMOTIONAL FENCE

A boundary is anything that marks a limit or border. The term implies a restriction and a defensive barrier. Boundaries say, "Certain people, certain actions, certain intrusions are not permitted here. This is who I am; this is how I should act; this is how you should act toward me. Anything that falls outside of these limits is not allowed." Boundaries draw clear, healthy distinctions between one individual and another. They are like fences with a gate—and you have the key to the gate; you decide whether or not to let anyone else within your boundaries.

An emotionally healthy couple is a well-bounded couple. Each partner within the marriage needs a boundary around himself or herself, a sense of personal individuality and identity. Each must be able to say to the other, "This is who I am as opposed to you. These are my thoughts, my feelings, my desires, my goals." These within-the-marriage boundaries enable both partners to feel that their unique needs, abilities, and convictions are recognized and respected by the other partner. These inner boundaries protect the identity, security, and individuality of both partners.

When you talk to a married couple with healthy boundaries, you should be able to distinguish differences between them—different likes, goals, interests, wants, needs, ideas, convictions, and so forth. There are always real distinctions between people with healthy boundaries. If you find a couple who are virtually identical in every way, it is very likely that they do not have adequate personal boundaries.

When there are clear boundaries within the relationship, it is easier to build clear boundaries around the relationship. On the basis of mutual trust and respect, both husband and wife are able to cooperate together to maintain a clear boundary between their own bonded relationship and the outside world.

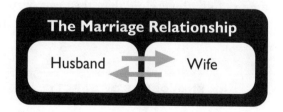

The Outside World
Parents, Siblings, Friends, Associates, Etc.

The Marriage Relationship

Husband   Wife

Now, while it is important for each partner in the relationship to have individual boundaries and individual "space" within the relationship, we should be aware that it is not unusual for couples to experience unusually intense bonding—and some confusion of personal boundaries—in the early stages of the relationship. In the emotional hothouse of the courtship and honeymoon phase, it is normal for couples to seek such an intense emotional amalgamation that they will say to each other such things as, "You are me, and I am you." Soon, however, the relationship should cool down to a point where each partner sees the other partner as a distinct individual.

We should also be aware that it is possible to take boundaries too far. The couple that maintains completely separate finances, sleeps in separate bedrooms, and routinely takes separate vacations has erected walls of isolation instead of protective boundaries. Many couples live in a state of "emotional divorce"—they live under the same roof, but they do not share any genuine emotional or intellectual intimacy. If you want to be married and still be your own person, you have to seek that delicate balance continually—two well-bounded individuals, distinct but not too separate, joined but not totally lost in each other—two partners—unique in their intellect, creativity, ability, and viewpoint, but joined at the heart for life.

When a poorly bounded man and a poorly bounded woman come together, they create a relationship in which there are continual encroachments and trespasses against each other's personhood, and the relationship that results is painful and dysfunctional. But when a well-bounded man meets a well-bounded woman, they create a safe and nurturing enclosure where their relationship can thrive and grow. The paradox of marriage is that when two people join to become one, both become more fully themselves than they ever were when they were alone. That is the beauty and mystery of marriage as God designed it to be.

AN ENCLOSURE OF SAFETY

Boundaries enable us to maintain our selfhood and individuality within the confines of marriage. The boundary a healthy couple builds around the marriage relationship serves a double purpose: It keeps some things out while keeping other things in. A well-bounded couple recognizes that certain people, certain actions, certain words are off-limits. A person with clear boundaries does not flirt or respond to flirting with people outside the relationship. A person with clear boundaries does not act disloyally toward a spouse by criticizing, ridiculing, or embarrassing him or her in front of others. A person with clear boundaries does not reveal secrets of the marriage relationship—sexual intimacies, family struggles, and so forth—to other people (except, when appropriate, to counselors or support groups). Boundaries create zones of protection and safety within and around the marriage.

Healthy couples are comprised of people who have left their respective families and have established clear physical and emotional "out-of-bounds" lines between themselves and their childhood families—and between themselves and the rest of the world. When children become adults, their parents must release old emotional claims on them. When a parent is insecure, however, he or she tends to cling to the child; this, in turn, causes that adult child to be hindered in taking responsibility for himself or herself. The adult child must step away from the grasp of the parent. Unless both partners in a marriage are able to separate effectively from their respective families, they will be unable to establish a boundary around their marriage—and they lay themselves open to continued interference from dysfunctional family members. Patti and Johnnie are a perfect example of this.

Patti came from an upper-middle-class family and married a young man named Johnnie. While it's true that "opposites attract," Patti and Johnnie had almost *nothing* in common. "I was attracted to Johnnie because he was different," Patti recalls. "He was different from me, different from my background—and he was *really* different from my parents! I mean, they hated him! Johnnie really set my dad's teeth on edge. The more my folks told me how wrong he was for me, the more I wanted to be with him. It was really a rebellion thing. My parents never let me have a life of my own, never let me make my own decisions, never gave me any privacy or freedom—so to me, Johnnie symbolized freedom from my parents and my upbringing."

Unfortunately, Patti discovered that by marrying Johnnie, she had not gotten rid of *one* set of intrusive parents—she had actually added a *second* set: Johnnie's parents! Johnnie's mother didn't hesitate to drop by unannounced, walking in the back door without knocking. She would proceed to hint about how Patti should cook, sew, clean, and care for her son Johnnie (her "hints" were about as subtle as a Scud missile!).

What's more, Johnnie's brothers and sisters were constantly borrowing things without permission—gardening tools, videos and CDs, clothing, even Patti's car. "When I married Johnnie," Patti said bitterly, "I *never* imagined I'd be marrying his whole annoying family! We don't have any privacy! I might as well have stayed home with Mom and Dad!"

Indeed. In fact, Patti's mother and father were every bit as intrusive as Johnnie's family. "I know that husband of yours doesn't provide for you," her father would say, pushing a wad of money into her hands, "so here's something to get you through the month." If Patti refused it, he would just go down to the bank and deposit it directly in her checking account. Patti's mom, meanwhile, made a habit of stopping by every now and then to make sure that Patti kept a clean house— "You know how messy your room at home always was!" She would run her finger on the tabletops, checking for dust, and even rearrange Patti's furniture. No subject was off-limits to her mother's prying curiosity—not even Patti's sex life.

Through counseling, Patti discovered that a large part of her problem with parents and in-laws was that *neither she nor Johnnie had any boundaries* in their family relationships. Both families considered Patti and Johnnie to be children who were just "playing house" and who hadn't really moved away from home. Since "we're all just one big happy family," there was—in the minds of Patti's parents and in-laws—no need to give Patti and Johnnie any privacy. Patti and Johnnie urgently needed to draw some clear boundaries between themselves and their families of origin.

TYPES OF BOUNDARIES THAT KEEP A MARRIAGE HEALTHY

Patti and Johnnie's boundaries had been trampled in more than one area of their lives. There are at least four major boundaries that are necessary for the good health of a marriage:

Control boundaries. As an adult, you have a duty and a right to make your own decisions regarding your career choice, your finances, your friends, your marriage, your leisure time, where you choose to live, and how you choose to live. If you like, you can ask for the opinions and counsel of other people regarding those choices, but no one—not even a parent—has the right to manipulate or control you. When other people try to control you, it's time to lay down some boundaries.

Emotional boundaries. A person with healthy emotional boundaries is able to say to family members, "My sense of well-being doesn't depend on you, and yours shouldn't depend on me. I care about you, but I can't be the answer to your emotional needs, and I can't allow you to intrude into the private places of my marriage." Family members who do not have boundaries between themselves are said to be "enmeshed." They unconsciously consider other family members to be extensions of themselves, so they do not see that it is wrong to intrude on the lives of these other family members.

Parents who are emotionally enmeshed with their children have trouble letting go. They do not recognize the maturity and separate personhood of their children. At the same time, however, the adult children of enmeshed parents have some responsibility for the lack of emotional boundaries. Often, in the painful or confusing dealings they have with their parents, they unconsciously allow or invite intrusions because it is emotionally comforting to remain a child in some ways.

How do you draw emotional boundaries where they have not existed before? By communicating clearly and positively. It's not necessary to say, "I need to pull back from you." Instead, say, "I think it would be healthy for both of us to find more time for our own goals and our own interests. You and I have taken too much responsibility for each other's happiness and well-being, and I would like to see us have a more balanced relationship."

If there are specific areas of intrusion to be confronted, address them firmly yet graciously. Stay focused on the issue, and avoid accusing or bringing up side issues and past grievances. Be firm, yet positive: "Mom, I know you love me, but I don't want you to ask me questions about my sex life or rearrange my furniture anymore."

Time boundaries. If you have a parent who continually calls or visits and monopolizes your time, you need a firmer time boundary in your relationship. These boundaries may take the form of ground rules: "Mom, please call first before coming over to visit." "Dad, please call only at certain times." "This isn't a good time to talk; could we talk later?" "I only have ten minutes to talk right now." Avoid making phony excuses for ending a conversation. Just tell the truth: "Time's up, Mom. I've got to get this laundry done. Call me tomorrow morning, and you can finish telling me about Aunt Sophie's funeral."

Financial boundaries. Sometimes the financial needs of parents can strain the resources of their married kids—and sometimes it's the other way around. Parents occasionally use money (either consciously or unconsciously) as a way of controlling their adult children. Whenever you accept money from your parents, you incur a debt (often a debt of being emotionally dependent or controlled, as well as a financial debt). Such debts diminish our sense of self-esteem and maturity.

One sign that we have achieved full and healthy adulthood is that our financial life is completely separate from that of our parents. This doesn't mean that one side can't help the other with an occasional gift or loan. But the normal situation is for finances to be completely separate—and that means financial boundaries.

Having healthy financial boundaries means (1) we don't expect our parents to continue providing for us; (2) we prefer to put off purchases and make do with less rather than to be dependent on others; (3) we accept sacrifices in order to maintain our independence; and (4) if we find we are not succeeding financially, we take the necessary steps to solve the problem ourselves: a new or extra job, cutting back on spending, putting away the credit cards, getting counseling to change overspending habits, and so forth.

Remember, you have no obligation to impoverish yourself on your parents' behalf, nor are they obligated to impoverish themselves or endanger their retirement in order to bail you out. If you or your parents have trouble with spending, saving, investing, or indebtedness, seek professional help and counseling. Your pastor or counselor can usually provide help or direct you to the resources you need.

WHAT ABOUT THOSE IN-LAWS?

Jokes about in-laws—and especially mothers-in-law!—have been standard material for stand-up comics since the beginning of time. But the fact is, for many married people, the subject of in-laws isn't funny at all. In-law problems frequently drive wedges of conflict and hurt between marriage partners. Common problems include:

Marriage Partners Who Have Made an Incomplete Break with Their Families of Origin

According to the Bible, when two people marry, they leave their parents and are united to each other (see Gen. 2:24). In practice, however, one marriage partner often continues to feel a greater allegiance to his or her parents than to the spouse. Sometimes, even though the husband and wife sincerely want to be loyal to each other, their parents make demands on their loyalties that cause them to side with the parents against the spouse.

Unexamined Attitudes and Assumptions Held Over from the Family of Origin

These old mind-sets—which I call "baggage"—may include beliefs, habits, expectations, traditions, and values that have been absorbed from the parents throughout childhood and adolescence.

For example, Jack just naturally assumes that it's OK in all families for family members to clip their toenails in the living room and leave the clippings in the carpet—after all, that's why God invented Hoover vacuum cleaners. His parents always did it; he always did it. It doesn't even occur to him to clip his toenails in the bathroom over a wastebasket, in private, as his wife, Cindi, always does. But the first time she comes into the living room and sees one of Jack's toenails go flying into the deep, plush pile of her brand-new carpet, she lets out a scream that can be heard for blocks.

Couples need to unpack their family baggage, sorting through all the attitudes and assumptions they have absorbed from their families of origin. They need to agree on which pieces of baggage are worth keeping and which should be discarded. Unfortunately, many couples never go through the baggage-sorting process. They just assume that they were brought up in the right way—and that their spouse's habits and attitudes are weird or wrong.

Intrusive, Insulting, or Controlling In-Laws

A parent-in-law who thinks it is OK to interfere in your marriage at any time, for any reason, can be a very painful cross to bear—and a very dangerous bear to cross! I've counseled couple after couple who have been tormented by an in-law's bullying, meddling, advice giving, and sharp-tongued criticism. I've seen couples brought to the brink of divorce (or pushed over the brink!) by such controlling personalities. In such cases, I encourage couples to do the following:

Recognize that you are an adult and as an adult, you are fully equal to that parent. You do not have to be intimidated or bullied by a parent or parent-in-law. You are free to ignore the advice or criticism of others, including the people who parented you or your spouse.

Discuss in-law problems honestly with your spouse, and state clearly and firmly that you expect your spouse to align himself or herself with you. The two of you must cooperate if you are to head off the in-law's controlling or meddling behavior.

Declare your independence—respectfully, firmly, and clearly. When an in-law tries to interfere with some area of your life, state your case simply, calmly, and confidently: "That is an area of my own privacy, and I choose not to discuss it with you." Don't get drawn into an argument; just close the subject. If the in-law persists, avoid getting drawn in. Just restate your position: "As I said before, I choose not to discuss that with you." If the in-law still pursues the matter, simply stop responding. There is nothing anyone can do or say to move you if you remain silent. Eventually, the in-law will tire of the game and recognize that you are invulnerable to any attempts to attack or control you.

In some very extreme cases, an in-law will be so difficult, so intrusive, so obnoxious that the marriage relationship itself is threatened. In such cases, possibly all the couple can do is limit contact—or cut off the relationship with that in-law altogether. Before God, you are now a marriage partner first, someone's child second.

CREATING AND MAINTAINING A SAFETY ZONE

In every marriage, there are adjustments and accommodations to be made in relating to our spouse's parents; we must learn to deal with annoying habits, different styles of relating and ways of doing things, unwelcome intrusions, differences in values and beliefs, friction, conflict, or emotional outbursts.

Our goal is to make these adjustments and come to a place of mutual acceptance. We may have to work through some issues with our in-laws, eyeball-to-eyeball. We may decide to let other issues go in order to keep the peace. Ultimately, if all goes well, we will come to a place where we have established a mutual zone of inclusion and acceptance along with a set of commonly agreed-upon and recognized boundaries.

Every couple should be able to say, "Here are the boundaries. Inside this boundary line is our zone of privacy and safety. This is who we are as a couple, and no one else, not even parents, are allowed in without an invitation. Over here, outside of this boundary line, is our zone of inclusion and acceptance. That zone defines who we are as an extended family, a community of parents, siblings, in-laws, and so forth." It's not healthy for a couple to dig a moat around their relationship, completely closing out parents (unless the parents are destructive, abusive personalities). But neither is it healthy for a couple to have a lowered drawbridge that parents and other extended-family members can use anytime of the day or night to intrude into the couple's safety zone.

When everyone in the larger family understands where the boundary lines are—and when everyone respects those boundaries—then that extended family becomes a rich and rewarding network of connections and relationships. In-laws can often become loving resources and repositories of emotional support and spiritual strength. Couples experience security and stability because the larger family becomes the kind of caring, safe community God intended it to be.

For additional insight into dealing with past or present conflicts with parents and in-laws, see my book *Family Ties Don't Have to Bind* (Thomas Nelson Publishers, 1994). In chapter 14, we will look at some of the special issues that come with blended families.

How Can I Be Married and Still Be My Own Person?

1. Read Genesis 2:24. According to this verse, what two steps must a couple take in order to become "one flesh"? Write them down. Have you and your spouse taken both of those steps?

2. Think back over your marriage and finish these statements:

   Some of the baggage from my family of origin that I've already unpacked is

   _____

   Some of the baggage I wish my spouse would unpack and discard is

   _____

   Ask each other what kind of baggage each of you would like the other to unpack and discard.

3. On a scale from 1 to 10, where 1 equals "War Zone" and 10 equals "Safety Zone," how do you rate your marriage? Do you feel that your marriage is free from intrusions by in-laws and others? Or is it under enemy attack? Or somewhere in between?

4. Think (or write) individually about what you see as the biggest problem or issue you currently face with your in-laws. Do you feel that your spouse aligns with you and supports you, or do you feel that your spouse maintains an allegiance to his/her family of origin and aligns against you? What steps could your spouse take to alleviate this problem or issue with your in-laws?

   Compare notes with your spouse and make a covenant together to be more supportive of each other in dealing with in-law problems.

5. Be brutally honest with yourself: In the blanks below, or in your journal, list your priorities in the order in which they actually occur in your life.

Husband's Priorities

1: My relationship with _____
2: My relationship with _____
3: My relationship with _____
4: My relationship with _____
5: My relationship with _____
6: My relationship with _____

Wife's Priorities

1: My relationship with _____
2: My relationship with _____
3: My relationship with _____
4: My relationship with _____
5: My relationship with _____
6: My relationship with _____

Spend time together, praying specifically for your parents and siblings and your spouse's parents and siblings. Pray that God would heal any broken relationships and that he would change lives that are twisted by anger and bitterness. Ask God to bless the people in your spouse's family who have hurt you, and ask him to give you the grace and strength to forgive them.

6. Have you truly separated from your family of origin? How well defined are the emotional boundaries between you and your parents? To find out, take the brief Emotional Boundaries Test that follows. Check *T* (true) or *F* (false) on this page, or write in your journal the statements that are true about you.

	WIFE'S RESPONSE	HUSBAND'S RESPONSE
I often feel guilty about spending too little time with my parent or parents.	T___ F___	T___ F___
When I see or sense that my parent or parents are hurting, I feel responsible and feel that I need to do something about it.	T___ F___	T___ F___

	WIFE'S RESPONSE	HUSBAND'S RESPONSE
My parent or parents rely on me as a source of happiness and emotional support.	T___ F___	T___ F___
My parent or parents discouraged me from moving away from home.	T___ F___	T___ F___
My parent or parents frequently shared intimate confidences and secrets with me.	T___ F___	T___ F___
I feel closer to one parent than the other.	T___ F___	T___ F___
I have been my parent's best friend.	T___ F___	T___ F___
I often share information with my parents (about my social life, finances, career decisions, and so forth) that is really none of their business.	T___ F___	T___ F___
One of my parents preferred my company to that of his or her spouse.	T___ F___	T___ F___
One of my parents told me or conveyed to me that I was his or her favorite or "special" child.	T___ F___	T___ F___
My parent(s) did not want me to date or marry.	T___ F___	T___ F___
One of my parents seemed overly interested in my sexuality and my body.	T___ F___	T___ F___
I often find myself explaining or defending my parents to other people.	T___ F___	T___ F___

If you scored four or more "True" answers in this quiz, there is a strong likelihood that the emotional bond between you and your parent or parents is too close to be healthy for you and your other relationships (this is called "enmeshment"). You need to define clearer boundaries with your parent(s) in the emotional dimension of your relationship.

7. On a scale from 1 to 10, where 1 equals "Never" and 10 equals "All the Time," how much do you allow other people to control you?

   Name a specific area of your life in which you have allowed someone else to control you during the past week. What could you have done differently to maintain a healthy boundary in that area?

8. On a scale from 1 to 10, where 1 equals "Poor" and 10 equals "Good," how well have you done in separating yourself from your family of origin so that you can be your own person in your marriage?

   What is a specific area of your life in which you have allowed a family member to intrude across the boundaries of your marriage during the past month? What could you have done differently to maintain a healthy boundary in that area of your life?

9. On a scale from 1 to 10, where 1 equals "Very Dissatisfied" and 10 equals "Very Satisfied," how satisfied are you with the level of individual boundaries in your marriage? In other words, how satisfied are you with the zone of safety and secure personhood you have in your marriage? To what extent do you feel your spouse respects your individuality—your thoughts, your personality, your beliefs, your convictions, your abilities, and your feelings?

10. Which statement describes the present state of the boundaries between you and your spouse?

	WIFE'S RESPONSE	HUSBAND'S RESPONSE
There are no boundaries at all between us; we're totally enmeshed with one another.	_____	_____
We have established the boundaries that we need; there's good balance between our togetherness and our life as individuals.	_____	_____
There are too many boundaries between us; we are more isolated than we are united.	_____	_____

In what specific area of your marriage do you feel you need stronger, clearer boundaries? What would you like to do differently in order to maintain a healthy boundary between you and your spouse?

3

What
Would It Take
for You to Trust Me?

Such a big house, and so many rooms. And in every room she entered, people looked at her strangely.

"Have you seen my husband?" Clarice asked a group of strangers standing by an obsidian-black fireplace at the end of the large white-walled room. The strangers looked at each other, then back at Clarice, shaking their heads and smiling oddly. No—not smiling, smirking. There was a glint of wicked amusement in their eyes. They had seen Bill, but they were lying to her.

She went to another room, another large white-walled room with a black piano. Whose house was this? She couldn't remember, but it reminded her of the office where Bill worked. "Have you seen my husband?" she asked a group of strangers grouped around the piano. They all turned to stare at her. One of them, a man seated at the piano, was playing a familiar song faintly. None of the strangers answered her.

"I said," she repeated, "have any of you seen my husband? I can't find him anywhere."

The man at the piano cocked his head and asked, "Have you lost your husband?" Then he began to snicker as if he had just said something enormously funny. The others around the piano laughed at his private joke. Something about the way he stressed the word "lost" filled Clarice with panic. Had she lost Bill? Where was he?

She hurried into another room, and another, and another. Each room had people in it, and all of them denied knowing where her husband was. Yet all of them seemed to know exactly where he was, and they were lying to her about it.

Finally, she came into another room—a white room with a black leather couch along one wall. On the couch were two people—her husband and a woman—locked in a passionate embrace. She shouted his name: "Bill!"

Slowly, Bill turned his head toward her. She had expected him to jump up from the couch, to look guilty, to make some lame excuse. Instead, he just smiled naturally at her, with his arms still wrapped around the woman. "Hi, Clarice," he said. "What do you want?"

"What are you doing with this woman, Bill?" asked Clarice. She looked at the woman who shared the couch with her husband. The woman seemed familiar, yet for some reason Clarice had trouble seeing the woman's face, as if her features were out of focus.

"Oh, didn't I tell you?" said Bill. "I'm with her now. You and I aren't together anymore."

Clarice tried to scream. No sound came. She tried harder as she backed away from her husband and the woman with the out-of-focus face. Still no scream came out. Now she knew why strangers snickered and smirked at her. Now she knew why she had felt a mounting sense of dread and fear as she had gone from room to room, searching for her husband. The horror of losing Bill washed over her like a black tide. Finally, she was able to scream . . .

And scream . . . and scream.

A light came on. The bedside lamp. She heard Bill's voice. "It's OK, honey, you're dreaming! You're just dreaming! It's OK, I'm right here!"

She opened her eyes and saw Bill's face hovering over hers. They were in bed together, and she had just awakened. Vaguely she wondered if the woman with the out-of-focus face was in the room with them. And then the anger boiled up in her.

"Don't touch me!" she screamed, shaking Bill's hands off her. "Get away from me!"

"But it was just a dream!" Bill objected.

"You were holding that woman!"

"What woman?" asked Bill in bewilderment. "I wasn't holding any woman! I was asleep! And so were you! You dreamed the whole thing!"

"Get away from me!"

Bill got out of bed and spent the rest of the night on the couch. Clarice was still mad at him when he left for work the next morning.

That evening they talked about her dream, and she became angry all over again. But the more they talked, the clearer it became that Clarice had been plagued by fear and anxiety for weeks, in both her waking and dreaming hours. It had all begun when Bill had gotten a new secretary. She had never met the woman, but she had heard others describe her as a "knockout." Though Bill had never committed adultery with his secretary or any other woman, though he had never given Clarice any cause to doubt him, Clarice was haunted by suspicion and distrust.

Her unfounded feelings were ripping at the fabric of her marriage relationship. She needed to learn to trust Bill, or their relationship would be hindered and eventually seriously damaged.

TRUST: FOUNDATION FOR A HEALTHY RELATIONSHIP

Trust is built upon commitment, upon the ability to make and keep a promise. Trust is the foundation upon which a solid relationship is built—and it is also the protective canopy beneath which a relationship unfolds. The two crucial ingredients of trust are as follows:

Predictability. In order to trust one another in the marriage relationship, we must be able to foresee each other's behavior with a certain degree of reliability. For example, you must be reasonably assured that the person you married is not a bigamist, an axe murderer, a mobster hiding out in a federal witness-protection program, or a playboy (or playgirl). You could not feel safe if your spouse fell into one of those categories. You could not be sure what such a person might do to disrupt your marriage or your life.

Dependability. In order to trust one another, you have to be able to rely on each other. You have to be assured that this person is available to you in times of need or crisis. You have to know that this person keeps agreements, respects your boundaries, and cherishes you. You have to know that this person is able to make and keep promises.

The ingredients of predictability and dependability draw from past behavior to create certainties regarding the future. That's one reason it is so important to know a person well before you get married. When you have a certain depth of experience with another person, you can rely on your knowledge of that person to predict how he or she will react under certain circumstances. There is a safe level of predictability and dependability in a relationship that has had time to grow rich and deep.

A DAMAGED CAPACITY FOR TRUST

Many people find it hard to trust even when their spouses are perfectly trustworthy and committed to their marriage vows. I've counseled many couples whose marriages were being torn apart by suspicions and doubts—even though it was clear to me that the person under suspicion was completely innocent and trustworthy. Unfortunately, some people come into a marriage with a severely damaged capacity for trust.

Adult experiences can play a major role in determining our ability to trust our spouse. Charlie, for example, continually watches Andrea. He closely monitors every check she writes, demands to know where she's been whenever she comes home a little later than expected, and has even listened in on her phone calls from time to time. Why? Because Charlie was married once before. His previous wife drained their joint bank accounts and was carrying on an affair shortly before she walked out on him. If he doesn't soon learn to trust Andrea—who has been perfectly faithful and trustworthy but is getting tired of Charlie's paranoid behavior—he is going to tear their marriage apart with his suspicions.

In most cases, however, a diminished ability to trust is the result of childhood experiences. For most of us, the ability to trust is learned in our earliest years. But some people grow up with a stunted ability to trust because of hurts inflicted on them at an early age by parents or other primary caregivers (stepparents, foster parents, other adult role models and authority figures). Childhood wounds that can hinder one's ability to trust include:

An unhealthy relationship with a smothering parent. Despite the stereotypes of the overinvolved "smothering mother," there are smothering dads as well. A child who experiences smothering parenting is a child who is overprotected and overindulged. Such children are never allowed to experience the normal disappointments, frustrations, and problems that are a part of growing up and developing character. They are never allowed to make their own decisions or take normal childhood risks. They never learn to trust their own feelings and perceptions because Mommy or Daddy is always there to smother those feelings and reinterpret those perceptions: "You don't really feel sad; you just need a piece of pie, and you'll feel all better!"

Because smothering parents are so overprotective, they often teach their children to view the opposite sex with suspicion and distrust: "Watch out for girls, Son. They're all just after your money." Or "Just stay away from boys, honey. They only want one thing from you."

An emotionally deprived childhood due to an emotionally distant parent. Emotional distance can take many forms. Most alcoholic parents are emotionally unavailable to their children. So are most depressed or mentally ill parents. Some parents are emotionally distant from their children simply because that's the kind of people they are: cold, self-absorbed, and emotionally sealed off from others.

A child can become hindered in his or her ability to trust simply through a lack of something as basic as parental touch. Children need to receive physical affection—a hug, a pat, a loving touch on the hand or face—from both their mother and their father. When parents touch their children, they invite their children to bond with them emotionally. The parent who does not touch his or her child actually communicates a silent message of distance and rejection to the child. Though the child may have no conscious awareness that he or she failed to receive parental touching in childhood, the hidden and silent pain of that message of rejection will be carried by the child into adulthood as an inability to trust others.

An emotionally deprived childhood due to parental absence. A mother or father may be absent because of death, divorce, or illness. Children often take these events very personally and even feel responsible for them. Sometimes there is anger, either open or repressed, which may seem illogical from an adult point of view but which is very real to the child: "Why did Daddy get cancer and go away to heaven?" or "I hate my parents for getting a divorce!"

Sexual or physical abuse. The most extreme damage to a child's ability to trust occurs when a parent, stepparent, or other primary caregiver violates that child's boundaries by engaging in sexual abuse or violence against him or her. This is the most egregious violation of trust imaginable. A child has a right to feel safe and protected, emotionally and physically. Abuse violates the core of a child's being, making him or her feel unsafe, unprotected, and incapable of ever trusting anyone again.

HOW FEAR AND TRUST ARE RELATED

A person who is unable to trust is a person haunted by fears. The person who grew up with a smothering parent is haunted by a fear of engulfment, of being smothered by excessive, destructive "love." I place the word *love* in quotes because it is really not an authentic form of love focused on the well-being of the other person. Rather, the smothering parent has a selfish obsession with the child, treating that child as a possession to be preserved rather than as a person to be respected, nurtured, and (when mature) set free to live as an individual. The child who lives under a parent's smothering love becomes an adult who fears engulfment in adult relationships. This person tends to create distance and barriers whenever another person—especially a spouse—appears to come too close and threatens to smother him or her with excessive "love."

The person who grew up with a distant or absent parent is haunted by a fear of abandonment, of being left alone. As adults, such people tend to probe and pester their partners for reassurance that they will not be abandoned. For reasons that we allude to in chapter 5, those who fear abandonment tend to be attracted to those who fear engulfment—and vice versa. This sets in motion a dynamic where one partner is continually seeking reassurances and trying to edge closer to the other partner; that partner, meanwhile, is wary of engulfment. One side advances, the other retreats, the first side advances even more aggressively, the other side retreats even more frantically, and the fears on both sides are stoked to a dangerous fever pitch, resulting in megaconflict.

The person who grew up with an abusive parent is haunted by a fear of invasion—either sexual invasion or violent invasion. As adults, such people live in fear of the dangerous or unpredictable behavior of others, especially their spouses.

The key to calming all these fears and conflicts, of course, is trust. Once trust is cemented into a relationship, those fears evaporate.

HOW DO WE BUILD—OR REBUILD—TRUST?

As we will see in chapter 5, it is a normal tendency to unconsciously use the marriage relationship as a place to work out the unresolved conflicts of childhood. So, if you had an emotionally smothering parent, a distant or absent parent, or an abusive parent, there is a very good chance that you will seek out a marriage relationship with someone who symbolically represents that parent, and you will try to resolve your old conflict with that parent through your present spouse. In time, the pain of the marital conflict (which is merely a replay of childhood pain) will become so intense that you will take some sort of action to end the pain. For example, you might choose to

- read a book on marriage, such as this one, hoping to gain some useful insights

- seek marriage counseling, hoping that a counselor can resolve the problems (or at least point the way to a resolution)

- end the relationship—a very common approach, unfortunately, especially among those who do not know how to break the cycle of conflict or who do not want to take on the hard (but rewarding) work of making the relationship healthy

What can we do to build or rebuild trust in a relationship? How can we put an end to fears and insecurities—both those that arise from childhood and those that stem from adult experiences?

First, Both Partners Must Decide That They Want to Trust and Be Trusted.

A willingness to trust another person cannot and should not be built upon a wish or a dream. It must be built upon the reality that the other person is trustworthy. If trust has been broken, then it must be slowly, painstakingly rebuilt. The person who has betrayed trust must be willing to be held accountable, to submit to outside limits, to open his or her life for inspection so that damaged trust can be restored. There are various ways in which the trust relationship of marriage can be broken, the most common being the betrayal of trust that takes place when one partner in the marriage has an affair. For specific, practical insight into restoring trust after adultery has occurred, see chapter 15.

Second, Both Partners Should Make Sure That Old Issues and Wounds Are Flushed Out and Dealt With So That They Can No Longer Hinder the Present Relationship.

The partner who is haunted by fears of engulfment or abandonment, who was raised by smothering, distant, absent, or abusive parents, should deal with those powerful emotional issues. That person needs to resolve old hurts and forgive the offending parent or parents in order to get on with life. Professional counseling may be required in order to gain the insights and healing to resolve those issues. For insight into dealing with past or present conflicts with parents, see my book, *Family Ties Don't Have to Bind* (Thomas Nelson Publishers, 1994).

Third, Both Partners Should Recommit Themselves to the Original Promise They Made on Their Wedding Day.

Moreover, both partners should commit themselves to becoming people who are uncompromisingly truthful and who make and keep promises. Truthfulness goes hand in hand with trustworthiness and reliability; if we are not truthful, trustworthy, and reliable, we will not keep promises—and we will not earn anyone's trust, especially the trust of people who are closest to us and know us best. We put a promise into words, and in order for the promise to be trustworthy, our words must be backed up by consistent, honest behavior.

In today's world, being honest and trustworthy is not easy. People all around us tend to place a very low priority on truthfulness and keeping promises. In fact, one recent survey of Americans reported that fully 91 percent of respondents lie regularly and only 31 percent believe that honesty is the best policy.*

The Bible has much to say about honesty, about integrity. "Therefore each of you must put off falsehood and speak truthfully to his neighbor, for we are all members of one body" (Eph. 4:25. See also Eph. 4:15; 1 Pet. 2:12; Ps. 86:11; Prov. 6:19; 8:7; 12:19; 30:8). Lies and broken promises destroy trust, generate fear, drive marriage partners apart, and shatter the foundation of the relationship. Christian couples should strive to overcome these all-too-common problems. Yet we find ourselves caught in dishonest patterns. We need to take certain steps and build up our personal integrity; we want to be trustworthy people in our community in general—but especially to our marriage partner.

HOW PROMISES AFFECT OUR LIVES

A promise is a declaration of intentions. It's a statement of assurance regarding what one will or will not do. A promise looks to the future and is intended to overcome the unpredictability of tomorrow. Promises reach ahead in time to create certainty and security.

Human society is impossible without promises. We make promises in every arena of our lives, even in the most mundane circumstances and transactions. Unless certain assurances are in place in our business, social, and marital relationships, chaos results. On any level, the more that's at stake in a relationship, the more formal the promise must be. In our own culture, the solemnity of a promise ranges from a casual statement ("Hey, no problem, consider it done") to a handshake, a sworn oath, or a written contract.

James Patterson and Peter Kim, *The Day America Told the Truth* (New York: Prentice-Hall, 1990), p. 45.

Promises bind us together; without them, all human relationships would soon dissolve. As we look around us, it seems that society is unraveling right before our eyes. The reason? Fewer and fewer people place a premium on keeping promises. Why do we see such growth in the number of attorneys in our society? One reason is that the precious commodity of trust is deteriorating in our society. As fewer and fewer people demonstrate a commitment to keeping their word, they need more and more attorneys to make sure covenants are kept.

The commitment of a promise is foundational to a marriage. A strong marriage bond is foundational to a family. The family is foundational to the community, to the nation, and to the society at large. When the promise that binds and secures the family begins to crumble, all our other institutions are threatened with collapse as well, for they are supported on the foundation of the family.

We derive much of our sense of who we are from the promises we keep. The promises we make largely define our relationships. When a person demonstrates integrity by making and keeping promises, we learn that this is a person we can trust.

An antisocial personality is by definition a person who cannot keep promises. The antisocial person ignores legal, financial, social, and family obligations. He is totally untrustworthy because trust is the result of promises made and kept. He breaks relationships and bleeds society. The more people demonstrate a willingness to disregard promises, the faster society weakens and dies.

Human freedom comes alive in the secure confines of a promise. The boundaries of a promise give us the freedom to truly be ourselves. A promise says, "This is the protected enclosure of our relationship. You can feel safe with me. You can reveal yourself to me because I will never betray your trust in me." Within the secure boundaries of a promise, we can relax, drop our guard, and release our wariness, becoming vulnerable, open, and intimate.

A network of promises, faithfully kept, delineates the boundaries of the playing field. Only when we know the rules of the game and the location of the goals, yard lines, and sidelines is the game of life comprehensible and fun to play.

True freedom is not the absence of a master but having the right master. The antisocial, promise-breaking person is not a person without a master but a person whose master is him- or herself. This person is a slave to his or her most basic drives and impulses and has little true freedom or purpose in life. Only a committed promise keeper has the power to set a course in life and stick to it.

If you have found it difficult to be a truthful person who makes and keeps promises, here are some practical suggestions:

In your daily devotional life, commit yourself in prayer—not just once but every day—to being truthful and trustworthy throughout that day. Make your commitment to truthfulness one day at a time. Ask God to convict you whenever you are on the verge of telling even a "little white lie." Commit yourself to a zero-tolerance policy toward dishonesty in your life, and ask God to help you keep that policy.

For men: Become involved in a Promise Keepers men's group through your local church. This organization is devoted to building Christian character qualities in men—qualities such as integrity, honesty, commitment, and reliability.

Become involved in an accountability group such as a small group Bible study, a support group, or a men's or women's fellowship group. Find a group of people who believe as you do, who struggle in some of the same areas you do, who desire to be honest and open with one another about those struggles, and who hold each other accountable on a regular basis (preferably weekly). Share the fact that you struggle with being honest and trustworthy, and ask your friends in the accountability group to check in with you on a regular basis regarding your progress in that area of your life. Invite them to ask you tough, challenging questions and to pray for you about your issues.

"Blest be the tie that binds," says the old hymn. When you promise, you bind. Whatever you bind, you tie up and make secure. When you enter into a marriage vow, you obligate yourself to certain conditions for the benefit of your marriage partner, and your partner does the same for you. The marriage vow binds two people together in a relationship, making them feel safe and protected. When we make and keep promises, we declare ourselves to be reliable and unchanging, even in the face of unpredictable events and circumstances. We eradicate fear. We generate trust. We build a healthy, durable, strong relationship.

What Would It Take
for You to Trust Me?

Take turns responding to the following questions and statements:

1. **Complete these statements:**

   My greatest fear in our marriage relationship is abandonment/
   engulfment/invasion/other.

   This fear affects the way I interact with my spouse in the following
   ways:

   _____

   _____

   My spouse's greatest fear in our marriage is abandonment/
   engulfment/invasion/other.

   This affects the way he/she interacts with me in the following ways:

   _____

   _____

2. **On a scale from 1 to 10, where 1 equals "Never Keeps
   Promises" and 10 equals "Always Reliable," how would your
   rate yourself as a person who is honest and keeps promises?**

3. **Talk about a specific situation in your life in which someone
   broke a promise to you. How did that incident affect your
   ability to trust the other person? Explain.**

4. **Describe a specific situation in your life in which you broke a
   promise to someone you cared about. How did that broken
   promise affect the relationship? Explain.**

5. Describe a specific situation in your life in which you experienced a greater sense of freedom as a result of binding yourself to a promise. What do you think was the source of that sense of freedom?

4

Am I
Supposed to Be a
Mind Reader?

"We've been married six years," Jay said in exasperation, "and I still don't know what Shannon expects of me. Take last month. We were on vacation, having the time of our lives on St. Croix. We had saved for years to take a Caribbean vacation, and it was finally happening. Everything was perfect—the flight, the hotel, the beach, the food, the weather—everything.

"Then, during the last three days of our stay, something went wrong. To this day, I don't have a clue what happened. All I know is that Shannon started giving me the silent treatment—answering in words of one syllable, if she answered at all; sitting through a fabulous dinner without saying a word; giving me icy stares. And whenever I tried to find out what was bugging her, she'd just say, 'Nothing.' But she said it in that tone that means, 'Figure it out for yourself, you dumb geek!' I finally decided to do my best to ignore it and wait for her mood to blow over. It eventually did—about a week after we got home! No matter what was bothering her, she should have been willing to talk about it. Giving me the cold shoulder was just plain stubborn and selfish."

"Stubborn!" Shannon exploded. "Selfish! What about you, Jay?"

"Well, what about me?"

"I waited and waited for you to apologize, and you never did."

"Shannon, I would have loved to apologize! I begged you to tell me what I did wrong so I could apologize! But you refused to tell me!"

"You knew what was bothering me!"

"I didn't!"

"You mean to tell me you don't remember telling me I was fat?"

For a moment, Jay was completely speechless. "Shannon, what in the world are you taking about? I never said you were fat!"

"Oh, yes you did, Jay, and you remember it as clearly as I do!"

"Shannon, I don't remember any—oh, wait a minute!"

"Ah-hah!"

"Do you mean out on the beach when I asked you about the bathing suit?"

"Don't remember, eh? You pointed to that sleek, slinky Vogue model in the white two-piece and said, 'Why don't you look like that anymore?'"

"I did not! I said, 'You have a bathing suit like that at home. Why don't you wear it anymore?' I wasn't implying you were fat!"

"Same thing."

"It is not! My gosh, is that what this is all about?"

That's what it was about, all right. And Shannon's expectation was that Jay should know—as if by mental telepathy—why she was angry and what he should do to make up to her. Jay and Shannon had stumbled into one of the most common potholes of marriage: hidden expectations.

BEING CLEAR ABOUT OUR EXPECTATIONS

We all have expectations of our marriage partners. Some of these expectations are on the table. These are called *spoken expectations*. Some examples of spoken expectations:

"I'd like you to be more friendly and outgoing when my parents come to dinner."

"I'd like you to take responsibility for taking out the trash and cleaning the bathrooms once a week."

"I'd like you to demonstrate more spiritual involvement and have a greater leadership role in our family devotions."

But many of the expectations we have of our spouses are *unspoken expectations*—the kind that Shannon had of her husband, Jay. These are much more difficult to deal with than the spoken kind because people are not mind readers. Some examples:

"If he loved me, he'd just know I want to go out to dinner tonight."

"I shouldn't have to tell her what I want. If she doesn't know after twenty years of marriage, she just doesn't care about how I feel!"

"I want him to be able to enjoy all the things I do and to enjoy them just as much as I do. I mean, he should want to share these interests with me. Is that too much to ask?"

When these expectations are not expressed verbally, openly, and clearly so that they can be discussed and negotiated, the stage is set for conflict—because one way or another, these expectations will be expressed! They will most likely be expressed in a negative, destructive, and hostile way: the "silent treatment," subtle "digs" and sarcasm, open attacks and criticism, or hostility that is "stuffed" for a while until it explodes unexpectedly sometime later.

Uncommunicated, unrealistic, and unreasonable expectations are dangerous to a marriage. These expectations lurk just below the surface, creating a minefield of hidden agendas that the other partner finds impossible to fulfill. Until these agendas and expectations are forced to the surface, they will continue to garble communication and create wariness and distrust in the relationship.

Our goal should be to identify and express those unspoken expectations we have of our spouse. Many people, for example, have unspoken expectations about sex. They find it a little embarrassing talking about what they would like their partner to do during lovemaking. As a result, many people end a sexual experience with the thought, *If he/she really cared for me, I wouldn't be lying here feeling hurt and unsatisfied.* It would save so much unhappiness if they would only turn their unspoken expectations into spoken requests: "I'd like you to take sex slowly and gently; I want you to spend time holding me and talking before the intercourse begins."

In the case of Shannon and Jay, Shannon eventually did give voice to her unspoken expectation as the two of them sat in my office. But in many cases, these unspoken expectations remain unspoken—and the person at whom those expectations are directed never gets a chance to know what is expected. There are simply unexplained conflicts, fights, and blowups—and one partner (if not both) is left wondering, *What have I done this time?*

Unconscious Expectations

A third kind of expectation is the most difficult of all: *the unconscious expectation.* Our unconscious expectations are tucked away in our storehouse brain (for more on the storehouse brain, see chapter 5). One of the most common forms of unconscious expectations is to have a mental (and largely subconscious) image of an idealized spouse. Without even realizing it, you may have entered into marriage in the belief that your spouse would meet all your emotional and sexual needs, would provide you with nonstop intellectual stimulation and excitement, would provide for you or cook for you or maintain your house for you, would build up your ego, would be patient with you, and on and on. You selected and married your spouse to attain all these attributes because these attributes represented your image of what a spouse is supposed to be.

After the marriage, however, your spouse behaved in ways that did not conform to the idealized image in your mind. You became frustrated, impatient, and angry when the reality of this person contradicted your unconscious expectations of how he or she was to behave. Meanwhile, he or she has been undergoing a similar process of disillusionment about you—and the stage is set for conflict. Because neither of you fully understands why you are frustrated with each other—your expectations are, after all, unconscious—you continually find yourself in conflict for seemingly irrational or trivial reasons.

Many of our unconscious expectations are simply the baggage we carry into the marriage from our family of origin. Tim's dad always ordered Tim's mom around, and she always accepted this treatment and scurried around, trying to make the old man happy. Now Tim is married, and he can't understand why his wife stands up to him and says no when he gives her an order. Tim is convinced there's something wrong with his wife. It never occurred to him to consider that maybe his unconscious expectations are out of whack and that he has brought certain assumptions into the marriage that are simply not valid.

Barry comes home from work and talks about some problem at the office. Sheri listens patiently as Barry talks—then she begins suggesting solutions to his problems. Barry gets aggravated. "Stop trying to fix my problems!" he growls. "I can run my own life, thank you very much!" Sheri is bewildered. "I just wanted to help," she laments, very hurt, "like my mom always helped my dad!"

Sheri's parents ran a mom-and-pop store, so it was natural that they would discuss business problems together. Sheri expected that Barry would feel the same. But Barry sees Sheri's offer of solutions to his problems as interference in his business life. He wants to be able to share with her his struggles at the workplace, but he wants to solve his problems on his own.

Unconscious expectations are often conflicting and inconsistent. For example, you may want your spouse to become more independent and confident, and you may often criticize him or her for not being assertive enough; yet at the same time you may become frustrated when your spouse holds views that conflict with yours! The inconsistency in your expectations may not even be apparent to you until it is pointed out.

MONITOR AND READJUST

The goal of an emotionally healthy couple is to bring hidden expectations out into the open on a regular basis, to make sure that all unspoken expectations are spoken and that all spoken expectations are fairly and mutually negotiated between both partners. Here are some suggestions for monitoring and readjusting your own and your spouse's expectations:

Set aside time on a regular basis or as the need arises to communicate honestly about your mutual expectations. It is best not to attempt this immediately after a conflict since the act of discussing expectations can be stressful and could renew the conflict if tensions are still running high.

Practice being a good listener. When your spouse proposes an expectation that you find unacceptable, avoid immediately countering or objecting to that expectation. Consider: Is this expectation reasonable or unreasonable? Can it be modified to the satisfaction of both parties? Can we come up with an alternative?

When stating your expectations, use "I" statements. "I need more time to myself" or "I want you to be more romantic" or "I would like you to help more with the children." Avoid "you" statements, which are threatening and confrontational—"You need to do such and such."

Consider writing out a "Contract of Expectations" between yourself and your spouse. Give the contract an expiration date—say, six months or a year from now. Then, on that expiration date, come together and renegotiate the deal. A contract may include some or all of the following:

- A statement of mutual faithfulness, devotion, fidelity, and support.

- Spiritual expectations: "I expect Joe to lead the family in evening devotions on a consistent, nightly basis." "I expect Sandra to support me in prayer as I struggle to launch this new business."

- Emotional expectations: "I expect Sandra to treat me with respect, without name-calling or criticizing me, either in private or in front of the children." "I expect Joe to turn off ESPN every night at nine, so that I can have twenty minutes or so to talk to him about things that are important to me."

- Sexual expectations, including the recognition of needs, a goal for frequency (if frequency has been a problem), and steps for improvement or exploring new sexual techniques.

- Practical expectations, such as household chores, taking care of the children, finances, and so forth.

Sometimes, in the process of actually articulating and negotiating our expectations, we begin to see that some of those expectations are not realistic or reasonable. So, in the process, we discard some expectations, we modify others, we make trade-offs and compromises, and we mesh our expectations with those of our partner. The result is a mutually satisfying, bonded, stable, caring relationship that grows and thrives over the years.

Am I Supposed
to Be a Mind Reader?

1. How open are you with your spouse? In a few sentences, describe the areas of your life in which you have maintained open, clear communication with your spouse.

2. How has your spouse disappointed you in the past few weeks? Refer to a specific situation or situations.

   Now ask yourself: Have I openly communicated my expectations to my spouse regarding that situation in which he/she disappointed me?

3. In this chapter, we have seen three kinds of expectations: spoken expectations, unspoken expectations, and unconscious expectations. Below is a chart on which you may list your expectations of your spouse and identify them as either spoken or unspoken (we will deal with unconscious expectations in the following exercise). Here are some examples:

   "I expect my spouse to meet all my emotional needs."   *Unspoken*

   "I expect my spouse to help get the kids washed and dressed on Sunday mornings so we can get to church on time."   *Spoken*

   "I expect to have great sex with my partner every day."   *Unspoken*

   List your statements in the spaces below, or write them into your journals, then discuss them together.

HUSBAND'S EXPECTATIONS

Expectation   **Spoken or Unspoken**

_____

_____

_____

_____

_____

_____

_____

WIFE'S EXPECTATIONS

Expectation   Spoken or Unspoken

_____

_____

_____

_____

_____

4. But what about unconscious expectations? How do we become aware of our unconscious expectations? The following exercise is often very helpful in bringing people's unconscious expectations out into the open.

Take a sheet of paper and write a few paragraphs entitled "The Ideal Spouse." Write quickly and write what comes easily to mind. Allow a limited amount of time in which to complete this exercise—say, five minutes—and don't mentally edit as you go. Just let it flow out of you, honestly and spontaneously. Be specific, not general. When you are finished, you will probably be surprised at all the unconscious expectations you have already placed on your spouse. Finally, ask yourself, "How many of these expectations are reasonable? How many should I discard? How many should I clarify? How many should I turn into open, clear spoken expectations?"

5

How
Did We
End Up Together,
Anyway?

"How does that corny old song go?" asks Terese. "'Some enchanted evening, you may see a stranger . . . across a crowded room.' That's literally how Scott and I met."

"We were at an Amy Grant concert," recalls Scott. "Terese was there with a couple of girlfriends, and I was there with a date. My date and I went through one turnstile, and Terese went through the next one. Our eyes met for just a couple seconds, but it was electric, you know?"

"Electric, yeah!" adds Terese. "It was like that! Instantaneous! And then we were separated from each other, just like that."

"Terese and her friends just melted into the crowd, and I didn't think I'd ever see her again," Scott continues. "But all through the first half of the concert, while I was sitting with my date, watching Amy Grant perform, all I could think about was this beautiful girl I had seen for just a few seconds. Well, at the intermission, my date went to the ladies' room, and I went out to get some Cokes at the concession stand—and there she was again!"

"I was getting some snacks for my girlfriends and me," Terese interjects. "And Scott came up and talked to me. And it was so clear that something was happening between us. I'd never felt anything like that before. It was so exciting. I don't remember what we talked about—just chitchat about the concert and stuff. Oh, and he asked me what church I went to. But we didn't exchange names or telephone numbers or anything. I had no idea who he was, and he had no idea who I was."

"But I knew where she went to church," added Scott. "So the next Sunday, I went to the same church. I introduced myself, we began dating, and the relationship just moved really fast from there. We were together almost every moment, and we were married six months after we met."

Stories like that of Scott and Terese—spontaneous romantic combustion—are the exception rather than the rule. Much more common is the experience of Kent and Melina, a couple who met at U.C. Santa Barbara. Kent was a sophomore, Melina a freshman. "It wasn't love at first sight, exactly," Melina recalls. "Kent was a friend. We both had lots of friends; but we were both serious about our studies, and we weren't interested in romantic attachments. Kent and I were good friends all through college. We studied together sometimes. We socialized on weekends, went to the beach or to movies or concerts together, often in a group. We never considered it dating, just friends hanging out together."

"In fact," adds Kent, "I was dating someone else during my senior year. I really expected to marry my girlfriend, Julie—but then she was killed in a car accident. I tell you, I was absolutely devastated. And it was during this time, as Melina really stood by me as a friend, that I began to fall in love with her."

"You hear about it all the time," Melina puts in, "that lovers so often start as friends. And that's the way it was with Kent and me, in the early part of our relationship. As Kent and I talked and cried together after his loss, our friendship just flowered into romance. We both felt it growing, and at some point we just felt it was right that we should marry."

Romance—this mysterious spiritual/sexual/intellectual attraction between a man and a woman—sometimes takes place with the explosive suddenness of a lightning bolt, and it sometimes emerges slowly, steadily, almost imperceptibly out of a rich, warm friendship. And yet, whether your marriage relationship came about like a lightning bolt or a gentle flowering, there were certain psychological and emotional forces involved. Most of these forces are hidden and unconscious. And they continue to exert tremendous influence over the day-to-day issues of your relationship.

It is so important that you understand how and why you were attracted to your spouse. As you understand that process and what goes on behind it, you receive information that helps you function as a couple. But, more immediately, you can see that there were real reasons for the attraction between you. And there are real reasons you seem so mismatched a few months or years into the relationship. How did the two of you end up together? The process of your attraction was nothing short of amazing.

WHAT DID I EVER SEE IN YOU?

I hear these exasperated questions all the time in my counseling practice: "We're so different! What did I ever see in him, anyway?" Or "We have absolutely nothing in common! How could I ever have been in love with her?" In fact, there are a number of ingredients that go into this mysterious mix we call "romantic attraction."

There are, of course, the obvious features that attract the sexes: physical beauty, youthfulness, and other physical attributes that suggest to us on an unconscious level, "This woman would make an excellent lover and childbearer" or "This man would make an excellent provider." We also tend to select partners who are similar to us in economic/social class, intellect, values, and attractiveness.

But there is an even more fundamental and all-pervasive answer to the question "How did I select this person as my spouse?" Most people don't like to hear the answer, but it applies to some degree to almost every marriage relationship: You selected this person by searching for what you didn't get as a child—and by turning to an insufficient source to attain it. Many problems that arise in marriage are due—at least in part—to an unconscious drive on the part of one marriage partner to be "reparented" by the other. It turns out that there's a lot more truth than anyone realized in the old song "I Want a Girl Just like the Girl That Married Dear Old Dad."

When I suggest this idea to couples in counseling, I frequently meet with resistance: "No way! I don't want anyone to 'momma' me or 'daddy' me! I'm an adult! I entered into marriage for adult reasons, because I'm mature enough to take on the adult responsibilities of marriage." On one level, the conscious level, this is probably true. But within each of us there is a hidden, unconscious component of the brain that exerts a powerful influence over our feelings, our thinking, our decision making, and our behavior.

I HAVE THREE BRAINS—AND THEY'RE ALL ATTRACTED TO YOU!

The human brain is an amazing piece of equipment, and it is fascinating to explore its design and functioning. God designed your brain to achieve a wide variety of functions—from such higher, human functions as thinking, imagining, and creating to the more basic functions such as surviving and procreating. Your brain is not merely a single organ but a complex assemblage of different structures, each performing a specific, specialized task.

It may be an oversimplification, but I find it useful to think of the brain as consisting of three main divisions:

The survival brain: made up of the brain stem and the limbic system, centered beneath the cerebral cortex.

The logical brain: the left hemisphere of the cerebral cortex.

The storehouse brain: the right hemisphere of the cerebral cortex.

Each of these divisions plays a unique and crucial role in communication. If we understand how these different segments of the brain affect the way we communicate and interact with our marriage partner, we will be able to clear away much of the misunderstanding, miscommunication, and distrust that damages our relationship. We will also be able to better understand how and why we selected the person we did and how those factors continue to affect the marriage.

The Survival Brain

The function of this part of the brain is very basic, even primitive. The survival brain, located underneath the reasoning areas of the brain, does not think, reason, or analyze. It scans, in a wary sort of way. Its primary function is to protect you from danger. It continually examines the environment in light of one question: Is it safe?

The survival brain receives the bulk of its input from your eyes. When it comes to safety, vision dominates the other senses. As you look into another person's eyes, you may feel as though you have direct contact with that other person. Someone has rightly called the eyes "the window to your soul." Ever notice how people who make no eye contact or who stare too long into your eyes or whose eyes dart back and forth make you anxious? Your survival brain is sending you a message (which may or may not be accurate) that this is a person to be wary of. People's eyes communicate fear, sadness, arrogance, irritability, and a host of other feelings—and the survival brain has an uncanny (though imperfect) knack for reading those emotions.

The survival brain also checks posture, movement, appearance, facial expression, and many other factors to determine whether the people around you are safe or threatening. It uses the sensory input of the ears to listen for safety. Your survival brain is finely tuned to the voices of others and can pick up subtle mood changes, even from the inflection of only one word. (Did you ever notice how much you can pick up about a person's mood just by hearing their hello when they answer the phone?)

The Logical Brain and the Storehouse Brain

After the survival brain finishes its work of safety assessment, the higher levels of the brain take over—the two hemispheres of the cerebral cortex, surrounding and mounted over the survival brain like two halves of a walnut. Each hemisphere (half) of the cerebral cortex has its own function.

The left side is the logical brain. It is the side that takes in language and processes it to make sense of the verbal messages it receives. The logical brain breaks messages down for analysis and reaches logical conclusions based on the information given.

The right side is the storehouse brain. It is more of a synthesizer than an analyzer. It does not use logic and words, but images and symbols. The storehouse brain is more imaginative and intuitive. Whereas the left side is objective, the right side is subjective. I call this part of the brain "the storehouse" because this is where images and symbols are stored throughout life, to be used as a guide to reality and relationships.

Our relationships are largely made up of messages (both verbal and nonverbal) that we send to each other: "I love you." "I need something from you." "When you do such and such, I get angry." Whereas the left, or logical, brain looks at the *content* of a message, the storehouse brain looks at the *context* of the message. The storehouse or right brain synthesizes all the messages coming from the senses by way of the survival brain. The storehouse brain takes into account the circumstances of the encounter with the person and makes a determination about the relationship that exists between you and the other person.

A SIMPLE MEETING ISN'T SO SIMPLE AFTER ALL

Now let's combine all three parts of the brain and see how they function together. Let's say you are an unmarried young man attending college and a friend introduces you to a young woman at the campus coffee shop. You sit down across from each other at a table and begin to talk. Here's what takes place from your brain's point of view.

Survival brain. This wary, unreasoning portion of your brain receives visual and auditory impressions of this young woman. She smiles. Her eyes sparkle. She is physically attractive. Her voice purrs. Your survival brain sees no threat; in fact (since many of the brain's sexual functions are centered here), your survival brain becomes sexually stimulated in a mild, harmless, but very pleasant way. Your survival brain signals your higher brain centers that it is safe—indeed, it is desirable—to remain in this person's presence.

Storehouse brain. Over the years, this right-hand side of your cerebral cortex has stored up thousands of symbols and images, many of them related to your primary caregivers in life. Your brain seeks the comfort of familiarity, so it compares input of opposite-sex acquaintances with the master template of the opposite sex that is recorded in the storehouse brain: the image of Mom. Those opposite-sex parent images formed by years of time spent with Mom are powerful symbols of what feminine companionship is all about. Here, in the storehouse of the right brain, are all the symbols of what a wife and mother are supposed to be—symbols of nurturing, caring, competence, joy, love, affection, and every other womanly quality.

Logical brain. The left hemisphere of your brain analyzes the content of what this pleasant young woman says. Being verbal and logical, it interprets her words into meaning. The logical brain is the part of our brain with which we think we think. No, that's not a typo. We *think* we think with our logical brains, but we actually think with our *whole* brains. Our storehouse brain also affects our thinking, modifying the meaning of the young woman's words with an overlay of symbols and impressions. And our survival brain affects our thinking, continuously scanning the young woman for safety and sexual desirability.

In the process of attraction and spouse selection, all three parts of the brain function together. The logical brain is attracted to her wit, her intelligence, her friendliness. The storehouse brain is attracted by how familiar and comforting she is to be around; something about her voice, her mannerisms, and her eyes remind us of our idealized image of The Perfect Wife. The survival brain finds her sexually attractive and safe. If these favorable impressions continue to accumulate over several months of courtship, there is a good likelihood that a point will come where you, as an eligible young man, will say, "This is the woman for me. I want to spend a lifetime getting to know her."

The process of attraction is virtually the same for a marriageable young woman. All three parts of her brain are engaged, building up impressions and memories that point to a certain young man as "the man for me." Her image of Dad, stored as symbols in her storehouse brain, will form a large part of the template of manhood by which she makes her selection.

NEGATIVE ATTRACTION AND HOW IT WORKS

It is important to understand, however, that it is not only the positive traits of our parents that shape our attraction to a given man or woman as we choose a person to marry. We are also attracted by the negative traits of our parents as we find them in potential spouses. Why? Here are two reasons:

These traits are familiar. As illogical as it seems, people tend to prefer familiar situations, even if painful, to new and unknown situations. So if your dad was an alcoholic, you might have a tendency to select an alcoholic husband because living with an alcoholic would be a familiar situation. Don't ask the storehouse brain to be logical; logic is the function of the left brain, not the right. As a result, people are often drawn into painfully illogical situations by their storehouse brains.

We are trying to recreate the past. Our symbolic right brain—our storehouse brain—continually tries to heal the wounds of childhood, to resolve childhood conflicts, and to compensate for the emotional deficits of childhood. The symbolic storehouse brain confuses the image of the parent with the image of the potential marriage partner and says, in effect, "Here is someone like Mom (or Dad). This person is anger-prone, violence-prone, and abusive, just like my parent. If I marry this person, I can carry on the struggle I began in childhood—a struggle for love and acceptance. And this time I will win."

And so it goes. Children of alcoholic parents marry alcoholic spouses with numbing regularity. Children of abusive parents find themselves paired with abusive spouses (and even a succession of abusive spouses) with amazing frequency. Children of unloving, unfeeling parents marry emotionless, uncaring spouses again and again. The symbols stored in the storehouse brain propel us in the direction of a potential spouse who unconsciously reminds us of our parents.

Consciously, we tell ourselves that this prospective spouse is kind, thoughtful, compassionate, considerate, the answer to all our prayers. But the storehouse brain thinks, "Here is my parent all over again. Here is a symbolic approximation of the person I struggled with throughout my formative years. If I can just recreate my upbringing, then perhaps I can attain what was denied me in childhood: security, affirmation, love. Finally, I have a chance to get what I never got as a child."

At this point, you may be thinking, *This stuff doesn't apply to me! My parents weren't abusive. They weren't alcoholics. I never felt deprived of love or security. I was never psychologically damaged as a child.* The fact is that, even if we never underwent a shattering childhood trauma because of abuse or alcoholism in the family, all of us—even those of us who were raised by the best of parents—experience emotional deficits, psychological scars, shame, pain, and unmet needs.

Even though we consciously look for positive traits in a prospective spouse, on an unconscious level we are attracted by both positive and negative traits. Our storehouse brain transfers the feelings and symbols we had for our parents (both positive and negative) onto the spouse, heightening those traits that match the parental traits, while ignoring those traits that do not match. Once the storehouse brain is satisfied that the original situation, with all its struggles and stresses, has been restored, it is ready to carry on the old struggles of childhood.

"I DID NOT MARRY MY FATHER!"

Carrie and Tom have been married fourteen years. Though they both profess to love each other, they have endured a relationship that is frequently punctuated by arguments and periods of mutual withdrawal that seem to have no solution. In the last couple years, however, the level of conflict has increased dramatically—and the increased pain of their relationship has finally driven Tom and Carrie into counseling. In their first counseling session, Carrie explained what she thinks initially attracted her to Tom.

"I was having a lot of struggles with my father," she recalls. "He was so opinionated, so stubborn, so controlling—and he really disapproved of Tom. I'm not saying I married Tom just to get back at my father—I truly did love Tom—but I saw Tom as a real contrast to my father, and my going with Tom just sent my father up the wall! So, in my nineteen-year-old rebellious mind, that made Tom all the more attractive."

Over several additional counseling sessions, however, a different picture of Tom and Carrie's relationship began to emerge. Although Carrie had pictured Tom as a night-and-day contrast to her father, many striking similarities between Tom and Carrie's father became apparent:

- Both came from strict fundamentalist religious backgrounds.

- Both had very strong and similar views on a number of subjects: Both men strongly distrusted doctors, lawyers, and other professionals; both were fascinated by guns and were involved in gun owners' organizations; both were fascinated by conspiracy theories and were suspicious of the government.

- Both had limited educational background (Carrie's father left school after the eighth grade; Tom did not complete his senior year of high school).

- Both considered women to be inferior to men in status and intellect.

At first, Carrie was reluctant to acknowledge any similarities between her husband and her father—even though most of the similarities had emerged from statements she herself had made in counseling. When it was suggested to Carrie that she had unconsciously selected Tom in order to continue and resolve her childhood conflicts with her father, she went ballistic!

"I did *not* marry my own father!" she shouted, her eyes flashing with rage. Such an angry response, of course, is often characteristic of denial, when a person *consciously* rejects a concept that he or she *unconsciously* recognizes as a painful truth. It was deeply embarrassing to Carrie to confront the possibility that she had married Tom for an array of hidden and totally mistaken reasons.

"I didn't say you married your father," I replied. "Of course you didn't. You married a man who is very much a distinct individual, and you were attracted to him for a number of reasons. You were aware of some of those reasons, and you were unaware of others. The more you become aware of the hidden factors that attracted you to Tom, the more clearly you will be able to see him and relate to him."

After a number of counseling sessions, Carrie did in fact begin to see that many of the things about Tom she found so exasperating were also the most hated aspects of her father: rigidity, a judgmental attitude, his controlling behavior. She realized that she could become unreasonably enraged with Tom whenever he made a disparaging comment about doctors or when she would find him in his den, oiling and cleaning his guns. And then she flashed upon the fact that such incidents reminded her of her father saying and doing those very same things!

Carrie and Tom were able to begin resolving their conflicts, but it took some concentrated work from both of them.

Carrie began to recognize those moments when the unconscious, unreasoning parts of her brain confused her image of her father with her image of Tom. She had to separate them into two distinct people in her mind. When a phrase or mannerism of Tom's reminded her of her father, she had to determine to separate this present situation from her memories. It was not acceptable to judge her husband's behavior on the basis of her father's behavior. Nor could she assume that Tom's motivations for saying or doing certain things were the same as her father's motivations would have (or had) been for saying or doing those same things. Carrie needed to see Tom as he actually was—not as a symbol of her past struggle with her father.

Tom came to realize that certain aspects of his manner and behavior hit sore spots from Carrie's past, and he had to do some adjusting. And some of his behavior genuinely hurt Carrie, and he had to change that behavior. He learned that he needed to respect her as an equal and that his controlling behavior had to end. And Tom realized, too, that he reacted to Carrie—although to a lesser degree—according to some of his own issues from early life. He, too, was continuing childhood struggles in his relationship with his wife.

Although we most often confuse the image of our opposite-sex parent with the image of our spouse, sometimes we are dealing with the image of the same-sex parent—or even both parents at once. The storehouse brain will, in fact, place any "primary caregivers"—stepparents, foster parents, grandparents, aunts and uncles, or whom-ever—in the place of the symbolic parent.

So, while we don't consciously go looking for these people in our relationship with our spouse or potential spouse, the images are always there, underneath the surface. This is why it is so important for potential marriage partners to explore one another's family history. This is why we never marry only a husband or a wife but, in a sense, that person's family. Family histories and issues can be painful to reopen and examine, but whether we like it or not, they have a continuing influence on our current relationships, especially our marriage.

WHY "OPPOSITES" ATTRACT

Shanna was an only child who grew up not merely sheltered but *smothered* by her mother's love. Her mother coddled her, excused her mistakes, and never let her try anything—much less fail or get hurt. Shanna was not permitted to change, to grow, or to form attachments outside her family. She was home schooled and was not allowed to play with neighborhood children or go away to camp. In fact, she was rarely out of her mother's sight.

Part of Shanna grew up fearing the perils of the outside world, as her mother persistently portrayed them. But another part of Shanna rebelled at the way she was kept a prisoner in her own family, and feared being swallowed up by her mother's possessive love.

Jack's upbringing was the opposite of Shanna's. His parents main-tained an emotional and physical distance from each other, from Jack's two sisters, and from Jack himself. The rules of his family were unspoken yet very strict: "You don't bother me, and I won't bother you. Stay out of my space. Mind your own business." So Jack grew up sensing an enormous emotional neediness in his life—a deep hunger for human connection and for someone who would share his need to love and be loved.

When Shanna and Jack grew up, they found each other and got married. This might seem paradoxical—a union of two people from such different backgrounds—but it happens all the time. It happens for a reason often oversimplified by the phrase "opposites attract." But opposites do attract for a reason, one clearly illustrated in the story of Shanna and Jack.

After having been emotionally smothered, Shanna, understandably, possessed an excessive resentment of control, intrusion, or involvement by other people in her life. Emotionally cold and distant, she was often antagonistic in conversations with other people. Shanna enjoyed being thought of as "different" and was quick to take offense toward people who tried to get too close to her or make emotional demands on her.

Jack, by contrast, exhibited what psychologists call "a dependent personality," characterized by an excessive and childlike desire to have others provide for him, meet his emotional needs, and interact with him. Because his parents were so emotionally distant and unloving, Jack had very low self-esteem, and he tended to cling emotionally to others. Being alone made him very anxious and agitated, so he had an intense drive to "fuse" emotionally with another person. He tended to behave submissively, and his feelings were easily hurt by Shanna's criticism or emotional distance, which he interpreted as abandonment—much as he had felt emotionally abandoned by his parents. In classic victim style, he put up with Shanna's angry outbursts and her contentious, argumentative conversational style—but he didn't like it. In fact, it was extremely painful for him.

Do you see what brought these two people together? Consciously, Shanna wanted to escape the emotional clutches of her smothering mother—yet unconsciously, she found Jack, who was needy and dependent, with a smothering love just like her mother's. Consciously, Jack wanted a wife who would devote herself to him, meet his emotional needs, and always be close to him—yet unconsciously, he found someone as distant and independent as his parents had been.

Both had found the substitute parents their storehouse brains were looking for—and now both were reenacting the emotional struggles of the past. Both were fighting to achieve what had been denied them in childhood—and they didn't even realize it! The very traits that had brought them together in courtship were now pushing and pulling them in opposite directions in marriage. Jack and Shanna were left wondering how they could have been so wrong about each other when they decided to get married.

Looking for the Missing Parts of Ourselves

There's another reason Shanna and Jack were attracted to one another and now find it painful to be together. We all have a tendency to project onto our spouse or intended spouse those parts of ourselves that we have disowned and cannot accept. For example, the serious, button-down, uptight businessman in the three-piece suit learned early in life to repress his carefree, spontaneous, fun-loving side—so when a carefree, spontaneous, fun-loving woman comes into his life, she seems to supply everything he no longer has, everything he has suppressed and repressed within himself.

In the case of Jack and Shanna, Shanna recognized in Jack something that she had shut away within herself—a longing for emotional connection, affection, and dependency. Though, on one level, she might resent Jack's "clinginess," his "whining," his "mooning" over her, on another level, she would like to return to childhood, to be smothered by love, to have someone attend to her emotional needs and make a fuss over her. She long ago denied and repressed that part of herself in her rebellion against an emotionally overbearing mother, but a part of her feels incomplete without that smothering love in her life. Therefore, though she is often antagonized by Jack's dependent behavior, she unconsciously recognizes in him a part of herself that is missing and that he completes.

Thus, in courtship, we have an image of our intended spouse that is partially made up of (1) the image of our parents or primary caregivers from childhood and (2) parts of ourselves that we have denied and stored away. These images are kept in the storehouse of our right brain, along with a lot of additional symbolic information, which we will explore in chapter 6.

Are we saying, then, that the image of our intended spouse is totally distorted by the symbols in our storehouse brain? Not at all; there is usually some objective reality there, a kernel of truth, at least. But all too often there is far more image than reality in our perception of our intended spouse.

THEN WE GET MARRIED

With all of these images, needs, and continuing struggles in operation, we choose this person to be our lawfully wedded wife or husband. And suddenly, the very traits we found appealing and exciting in our spouse before, now become irritating and a source of major conflict. We find that denied parts of ourselves are being mirrored back to us by our spouse—and we don't like what we see. We also find ourselves caught in the old struggles we thought we had escaped when we emerged from childhood—only these are now adult struggles, and they are much more intense.

We look at our spouse and think, *I married you so that you could heal these wounds and meet my emotional needs. But instead of healing my wounds and meeting my needs, you are turning out to be just like the absent father who was never available to me* (or the smothering mother who threatened to overwhelm me or the critical stepparent who always belittled me). With each conflict, our focus narrows. We become less and less able to see the complex, varied personality of our spouse. Instead, our spouse becomes a caricature of our parents. We see only a few selected traits—and these traits grate on us like coarse sandpaper.

WHAT DO WE DO NOW?

OK, you may be thinking, *so now I know how my spouse and I came together. I know that my storehouse brain has been manipulating my feelings and my behavior without my conscious awareness. I know that much of the conflict I have with my spouse arises because my storehouse brain superimposes the symbolic image of my parent onto my spouse. But what now? What am I supposed to do about it? I guess my marriage is just doomed!*

Not at all! There's plenty you can do about it—now that you understand the source of the problem. Here are some practical pointers for resolving today's problems today, logically and lovingly:

Recognize That Understanding the Workings of Your Unconscious, Symbolic Mind Gives You an Edge.

You don't have to be controlled by your brain's unreasoning force. You have the power to harness your emotional energy for healthy, healing purposes. Whenever you become angry, exasperated, annoyed, or impatient with your spouse, or whenever you become fearful of being abandoned or emotionally smothered by your spouse, ask yourself, *Are these feelings proportionate to my spouse's behavior, or are they out of proportion? Are my feelings based in fact and reasonable, or am I responding with anger and fear because this is a long-standing "sore spot" in my soul?*

Take an Emotional Reality Check.

Before responding to your spouse, pause a few moments to get in touch with your feelings and to understand what has triggered those emotions. Ask yourself, *Does this situation remind me of the dynamics of my childhood? Do I feel small and powerless right now, as if I were a child again? Do I feel that my spouse is treating me like a child or making me feel like a child?* Understanding why we feel the way we do is the first step toward resolving those feelings.

Recognize That Your Spouse Has a Survival Brain and a Storehouse Brain, Too.

If he or she is responding to you in a way that seems disproportionate and unreasonable, recognize that there may be childhood pain, fear, anger, and resentment underneath it all. Realize that the surface issue ("You spent too much on that dress" or "Why did you stay so late at church?") may not be the real issue. It may just be a symptom of a much deeper emotional deficit ("I'm afraid of reliving the stress of my childhood when my father went bankrupt" or "I'm afraid of being abandoned and alone").

Accept the Fact That You and Your Partner Both Have Unresolved Feelings and Issues from Childhood.

They may be significant and traumatic (such as abandonment or incest), or they may be comparatively minor—but they are there. Unresolved, those childhood issues are destined to create distortions in your current relationship. But if you deal with them, discussing them openly with your spouse or, if need be, getting professional help, they lose their power to hurt you and your marriage relationship.

Make a Commitment to Grow in Understanding of Who Your Spouse Truly Is—Not a Mental or Symbolic Caricature, but the Authentic Reality.

Find out what motivates, excites, and saddens your husband or wife. Find out where those "land mines" of childhood pain lie. Find out what makes him or her feel afraid, angry, insecure, or anxious. Work together to replace images and symbols with truth and understanding.

Make a Commitment to Grow and Mature As a Human Being.

Instead of making childlike demands on your spouse to meet all your needs, accept the fact that you are an adult. You have some needs that you may legitimately express to your spouse, but you also have needs that you should seek to meet out of your own resources or God's resources, as accessed through prayer. "When I was a child," said the apostle Paul, "I talked like a child, I thought like a child, I reasoned like a child. When I became a man, I put childish ways behind me" (1 Cor. 13:11).

It's time to put away childish ways. It's time to put away the past and become conscious, aware, and proactive in the present. It's time to make choices about the kind of person you will be in the here and now. In the next chapter, we will explore even more deeply how to keep the marriage relationship firmly, healthfully anchored in the present.

How Did We
End Up Together, Anyway?

Go through these exercises, using your journals to record what you discover.

1. Find a quiet place and relax. Let your mind drift back to your early childhood. Picture the house you lived in, the various rooms—your bedroom, the kitchen, the living room, the backyard. Whom do you see there? What would you like to say to them? What do you wish they had given you that you never received from them?

   Write your answers down or speak them into a tape recorder. Describe your feelings and thoughts.

2. Think back to a painful episode in your childhood. What feelings did you experience at the time? What feelings do you have now as you think about that situation?

3. Recall a recent struggle or argument with your spouse. What feelings did you experience at the time? What feelings do you have now as you think about that situation?

4. What contrasts and similarities do you see between the two situations—the episode of childhood pain and the recent episode of marital conflict?

5. Relax again. Picture the house you live in today. Picture the various rooms of your married life—your bedroom, the kitchen, the living room, the backyard. Are you happy in this house? If not, why not? What do you lack that would make you happy? In other words, what emotional needs are currently going unmet?

6. Picture your spouse. What would you like to say to him or her? What do you wish your spouse had given you that you have never received?

7. Share your impressions and feelings with your spouse, then listen to your spouse's impressions and feelings. What did you learn about your partner's past history and present feelings that you never knew before? How has your image of your spouse changed as a result of this exercise?

6

Why
Do We Have
the Same Argument—
Over and Over
Again?

"It's the same stupid argument over and over," Martin complains. "It just takes different forms, that's all. For some reason, Lanie feels she has to continually attack my manhood!"

"Oh, puh-leeeeze!" Lanie rolls her eyes heavenward. "Martin, why don't you just get over it!"

Instantly, Martin comes unglued. "You see! You see! She did it again!"

"Did what?" Lanie fires back.

"You attacked my manhood!"

"Did not!"

"Yes, you did! 'Martin,'" he repeats, mocking her tone, "'why don't you just get over it!' It's sneaky and subtle, but that's what you're doing—trying to make me feel small, trying to make out that I'm some kind of wuss just because I don't like the way you're always attacking me!"

"It's all in your mind, Martin," says Lanie. "I don't attack your manhood. Just because one time, I said—Oh, forget it!"

"No. Let's get it out and deal with it, Lanie. What about that one time?" I asked.

"That was three years ago!"

Martin folds his arms and huffs, "I remember it like it was yesterday! I was at the grocery store, trying to do you a favor, doing your errand, trying to make you happy—"

"I asked you to pick up a few things at the store—some milk, some cereal, and a box of feminine pads. Three lousy items! For that, you had to spend twenty-five cents at a pay phone to ask me a lot of questions?"

"I wanted to get the stuff you wanted! I didn't know if you wanted whole milk or low-fat. I didn't know if you wanted the cereal with raisins or the cereal without raisins. I didn't know if you wanted regular pads, maxi pads, thin maxi pads, or extra-mini-thin-ultra maxi pads! I said, 'A man shouldn't have to make such decisions!' And what did you say?"

"Why do you have to drag this up?"

"You said, 'A real man doesn't have so much trouble making a decision.'"

"I said I was sorry, didn't I?"

"Two days later! After you ran me into the ground over and over. After you made a big deal about my spending a whole quarter on a phone call! After you made me feel like a failure, like I had just spent our last two bits and it was time to declare bankruptcy!"

"Well, we are on a tight budget, Martin."

"You seem to enjoy reminding me of that fact, Lanie, because that means I'm a lousy provider—and, ergo, a wuss, a wimp, and not a 'real man.'"

Lanie groans. "Stop reading something into everything I say! All I'm saying is you could be a lot more careful about how you spend your money. Like last week, ordering two magazine subscriptions when we can't even afford to get the car fixed!"

Martin throws up his hands. "Money, money, money! If you're not belittling me, you're nagging me about money!"

And so it goes. . . .

THE ISSUES THAT KEEP COMING BACK

Again and again, throughout their married life, Lanie needles Martin about money, and Martin whines about being needled. Why do Lanie and Martin get stuck on the same issues over and over again? In fact, why do most couples seem to have the same argument repeatedly, with only slight variations from fight to fight?

Here again, we are dealing with issues, motivations, and emotional symbols that operate at an unconscious level. We are dealing with unresolved feelings from childhood that come back in disguised form to haunt us in our adult relationships.

Fortunately, it is possible to bring these hidden and unconscious issues out into the open so they can be consciously examined and disarmed. The hidden engine that drives marital conflict can be shut down only when we begin to understand all the items we accumulated in our storehouse brain (see the previous chapter). Every marriage is affected by these powerful symbolic forces, and until we understand them, they will cause old issues, old hurts, and old struggles to resurface and recur again and again.

THE MENTAL MAP: YOUR PERCEPTION OF REALITY

We all have mental "maps" in our unconscious storehouse. Without consciously realizing it, we consult these maps continuously on our journey through the landscape of relationships. Our maps are our perceptions, impressions, deductions, and conclusions about reality, based on our experience. We tend to confuse the map with the actual territory, to think of our interpretation of reality as being reality itself.

Most of us draw up our mental maps on the basis of a fairly sketchy sampling of reality. If you go to a restaurant and have one bad meal, you will probably never go back; on your map of reality, you will write BAD FOOD—AVOID THIS PLACE! over your mental image of that restaurant. It may, in fact, be a bad restaurant—or it may be a very fine restaurant that happened to serve one bad meal. But the map of reality that you have drawn, based on your limited experience, identifies it as a bad restaurant, period.

A map is a useful tool. Our maps show us how to act in a given situation. But when our map is wrong, when it doesn't match the territory—watch out! If our map of reality contains some false notions about a given restaurant, there's little harm done. There are many other restaurants we can choose from. But if our map of reality contains false impressions of the person we've married, the results can be catastrophic.

How do our mental maps affect our behavior in the real world? There is a three-step process by which each of us interacts with the world around us. Those steps are as follows:

SEE ➡ INTERPRET ➡ ACT

That is, we see and sample the world through our experience. Then we interpret that experience. Then we act upon that interpretation; we chart our course and base our lives on the map that we have drawn.

Mental maps of reality are not always a bad thing. In fact, they serve a vital function, guiding us through the landscape of life and showing us how to behave in various situations. The more accurate our mental map of reality is, the more helpful a guide it will be in our lives. But if the map is inaccurate, we are much more likely to get lost in our relationships.

Unfortunately, we never seem to be aware of these maps. We go through life on automatic pilot, responding to problems and conflicts from an emotional rather than a volitional level, being controlled by the unreasoning, symbolic parts of our right brain rather than our thoughtful, analytical left (or logical) brain. If we fail to review and revise our maps periodically, we will keep doing what we've always done—and we will remain stuck.

"Reality" according to Whom?

We all tend to assume that everyone else sees the world much as we do; in truth, no two people view reality in the same way. Each person puts a unique interpretation on reality, and this interpretation prompts our behavior in every situation.

Let's say I have just walked out of a movie theater late at night. I'm walking down a darkened street, heading for my car, when I hear footsteps behind me. I turn and see a strange man silhouetted against the wall. What will my next action be? It all depends on my mental map.

If I have been mugged on a dark street before, or if the movie I just watched depicted a street mugging, or if I have been reading a lot in the newspaper lately about crime statistics, then I'm likely to have a mental map in mind regarding strangers on dark streets: DANGER! So I see the strange man, I interpret him to be a mugger, and then I act by running away as fast as my legs will take me!

Now, is the stranger really a mugger? Or is he a kindhearted man who followed me out of the theater to tell me I dropped my wallet in the aisle? Clearly, objective reality and my mental map of reality could be two very different things! The map is not the territory. *Reality* and *our interpretation of reality* are not the same thing.

SYMBOLS: SMALL THINGS THAT HAVE TREMENDOUS POWER

A major part of our mental map consists of symbols that we have accumulated in our mental storehouse. These symbols have an enormously strong meaning at an unconscious level of our minds—meanings such as "love," "security," "control," "abandonment." An incident that is comparatively trivial to one partner may be powerfully, emotionally symbolic to another.

For example, Ginny turns to Rob after dinner and says, "Can you help me with the dishes?" Rob replies, "No, not tonight." At this, Ginny explodes! Why does she explode? Not because the dishes are so important but because they symbolize something crucially important in her mental map: "He doesn't care about me."

Or consider what happens between Ginny and Rob the following Saturday: Rob grabs his keys, heads for the front door, and calls out, "Ginny, I'm going down to the hardware store to buy a shovel. I'll be back in a few minutes." Ginny responds, "Can I come, too?" She just wants companionship with him. But Rob instantly becomes annoyed. "What's the matter?" he snaps. "Don't you trust me to buy a decent shovel?" In his mental map, her request symbolizes an attack on his competency.

Our maps tend to magnify isolated actions and incidents into powerful, emotional symbols. A single word, a facial expression, a gesture can suddenly take on an intense, crushing burden of meaning.

In the following paired statements, notice that the first sentence is an observation of a comparatively common and minor behavior that occurs in all relationships, such as "You disagreed with me today." But that sentence is followed by a conclusion that supercharges the issue, giving it far more emotional energy than the situation demands, such as "You don't respect my opinions or my feelings."

- You turned your back on me while I was talking.
  You don't care for me; you are rejecting me.

- I just did something nice for you, and you didn't acknowledge it.
  You are thoughtless and insensitive, and you don't appreciate me.

- You were quiet at the dinner table tonight.
  That kind of withdrawal must mean you don't love me.

- You interrupted me just now.
  You don't respect my feelings or value my ideas.

- You want to be alone.
  You have rejected me, and you don't want me anymore.

- You don't want sex tonight.
  You must think I'm unattractive and unappealing.

- You were angry tonight.
  You hate me.

- You criticized my cooking tonight.
  You must think I'm a horrible wife.

- You criticized my driving tonight.
  You must think I'm completely incompetent.

Past events have etched certain symbols on our mental maps. Old images lurk beneath the surface of our consciousness, ready to haunt present relationships when current experiences remind us of old events.

Josh's mother, for example, was an obsessively controlling woman who continually intruded on his life, made his decisions for him, and chose his activities for him. Now married, Josh goes ballistic anytime his wife even makes a suggestion to him. Because some of his wife's traits unconsciously remind him of some of his mother's traits, his wife's mildest suggestions often symbolize his mother's control, disrespect, and disregard for Josh's feelings. The more resentment he displays, the more she suggests that he needs to change his behavior, which in turn stirs up more resentment, and so forth—a self-perpetuating cycle of conflict and distorted communication.

Another example: Elaine never felt loved and accepted by her father, an emotionally distant military officer who frequently expressed regret over having a daughter instead of a son whom he could raise in the military traditions of his family. Now married, Elaine constantly pursues her husband for affection and reassurance. Elaine's husband finds her "clingy" behavior off-putting, so he retreats from her. "You come on too strong," he tells her. The more he retreats, the more he reminds Elaine of her emotionally distant father. She becomes panicky and pursues her husband all the harder, and he retreats even more—a self-perpetuating cycle. In Elaine's mind, her husband's emotional withdrawal symbolizes her father's lack of love. Without realizing the childhood source of her fear, she is terrified that she will be unloved and unaccepted by her husband—and her own behavior is the wedge that drives her husband away.

Unresolved wounds of the past are invariably projected into the present. When there are unhealed wounds and unresolved conflicts dotting our mental maps, our storehouse brain attempts to work them out in present relationships. *If our mental maps are inaccurate, our behavior will tend to make matters worse, not better.* In order to have healthier, happier relationships, we must bring our unconscious maps out in the open, where we can consciously examine them and redraw them to better match the territory.

FILTERS AND FRAMES:
HOW WE PUT OUR INFORMATION TOGETHER

How would you punctuate the following line?

that that is is that that is not is not is that it it is

Properly punctuated, this seeming gibberish becomes a series of intelligible thoughts: "That that is, is. That that is not, is not. Is that it? It is!"

Or take this unpunctuated statement:

Woman without her man is a savage

Who is the savage in that statement? It depends on how you punctuate it. This sentence could read: "Woman, without her man, is a savage." In this case, the woman is the savage. But the sentence could also be punctuated to read: "Woman: without her, man is a savage." Now, it is the man who is the savage in this statement.

Punctuation enables us to make sense of an otherwise meaningless stream of words. Similarly, we "punctuate" our experiences in order to make sense out of life. The difference between the way we punctuate a sentence and the way we punctuate life is that in human experience, punctuation is entirely arbitrary and subjective. Here's how punctuation works in a marriage.

Wife: "My husband is withdrawn."
Husband: "My wife is a nag."

The reality is that when the wife "nags," the husband "withdraws," which causes the wife to "nag" even more, which makes him "withdraw" more. A classic case of the chicken and the egg. Both share the same experience, but they "punctuate" it differently, they interpret it differently.

This interpretive process is called "filtering" and "framing." When things happen in our lives, we don't attend to every detail of the experience, because there are simply too many details for our memory to contain. Instead, we filter. We combine bits and pieces of experience, pay attention to certain details, and ignore other details. Then, patching this filtered information together with the symbols and maps from our storehouse, we form our frame, our unique perspective on the experience.

Everyone's frame on any given situation is bound to be different. John and Jane, for example, go to a movie. They see exactly the same sights and hear exactly the same sounds. John hates the movie, while Jane loves it. John: "What a sloppy, sudsy, maudlin piece of mush!" Jane: "It was so moving and full of emotion. This movie made me feel things I never felt before!" Same experience, same stimuli, completely different frames of the experience. Why? Because each person filtered the experience differently, according to his and her own map of reality.

When the Frame Fits—and When It Doesn't

During the courtship and honeymoon phase of a relationship, we place a golden frame around everything that happens. We highlight and magnify every wonderful aspect of our partner. We dismiss and ignore the little flaws and irritations in our partner's behavior, attitude, and mannerisms.

But as the newness of the relationship wears off, as we begin to accumulate more and more grievances, and as annoyances become too large or too numerous to ignore, we remove the golden frame and replace it with a grim, black frame. Now we begin to highlight and magnify the flaws and irritations in our partner, and we dismiss and ignore the positive aspects of our partner's character and behavior. Her delightful little laugh becomes reframed as an annoying cackle. His clever gift for witty remarks becomes reframed as a lame, corny sense of humor.

"She's such a shrew." That was Eric's frame for his wife, Susan. Why did Eric view his wife as a shrew?

"Because she's always nagging me and ragging me in front of my friends!" he says.

"Oh? When does she behave this way?"

"All the time!" replies Eric.

"Well, describe an incident of this behavior that happened in, say, the last week or two."

"Well, she—you know, she always—it's kind of hard to think of a specific incident right on the spot, but—Oh, yeah, I just remembered one! The other night, we were at a Chinese restaurant with friends and she needled me about my tie right in front of everybody!"

Susan looked hurt. "I just said, 'Honey, you dropped a piece of mu shu pork on your tie.' I even offered to clean it off for you."

"Well," Eric responded sullenly, "maybe that's not a good example. But all our friends know she's a shrew. That's why they don't want to spend time with us anymore."

The fact was, many of Eric's friends were feeling uncomfortable around Eric—not Susan—because he would often explode over inconsequential or nonexistent slights. "Susan is such a shrew" is Eric's frame, and it drives his emotions and behavior; but it is not the truth. Yes, Susan used to have a bad habit of criticizing her husband in front of their friends, but she has worked hard on this habit. Even though Susan's behavior had changed, Eric's frame had not. That's the problem with frames: Once we hang a frame on a person, we rarely go back later to see if it still fits.

Frames and filters are necessary parts of our understanding of reality. However, crooked frames and clogged filters distort not only our view of reality but also our relationships. As we correct the way we punctuate our marriage experiences, we create a happier, healthier marriage relationship.

TWO PEOPLE, SHIFTING POSITIONS

As a couple's relationship develops over time, each person comes to view the other from the perspective of his or her own versions of reality—the maps, symbols, frames, and filters we've just discussed. Instead of getting to know each other better over time, there is the real danger that they will actually build up stereotypes and caricatures of one another in their minds. Each side forms assumptions and conclusions about the other that may or may not be true.

When we define our marriage partner, and that partner defines us, we take on certain positions in the relationship. The fact is, we do not assume one overall position toward our partner; our posture toward each other will change, depending on the given issue and situation.

Couples fall into two basic positions toward one another. In one position, they compete with each other; in the other position, one assumes a dominant role while the other is more passive in the relationship. In a few relationships, both partners become passive. These different postures occur in most healthy marriages; each has its own risks and benefits.

When Both Partners Compete

In a competitive marriage, both partners are engaged in continual conflict for mastery. This category of unhealthy relationships can take many forms. For example, one side may use bullying, intimidating tactics, while the other uses scheming and manipulating; but both sides are attempting to initiate, dominate, or control, and neither will follow or submit to the other.

When both partners are involved in business or professional life, the competition can center around who has the most education, who has the best job, who makes the most money, or who gets promoted fastest. Unless the equality, dignity, and feelings of both sides are respected, the relationship is doomed to be unhealthy.

The first step in resolving the problem of competition between marriage partners is a recognition that the problem exists. Christian couples should know that God did not design marriage to be a contest between competitors. He designed marriage to be an intimate, cooperative union between two partners. *Competition destroys intimacy.* A competitive attitude in marriage says, "I am the superior partner; I deserve to be on top in this relationship. You deserve second-class status." As we shall explore further in chapter 8, one of the central questions we should ask ourselves in marriage is not, "Who's the boss?" but "Who's the servant?"

Once they become aware that the competitive approach to marriage is a destructive approach, couples should consciously adjust their thinking about roles in the marriage. Instead of seeing themselves as engaged in a contest of one-upmanship, each partner should see himself or herself as a combination coach/cheerleader/player. They are not facing each other across a line of scrimmage; they are on the same team. When one rises or falls, they both rise or fall. They should replace competition with the following:

- daily prayer for each other's success
- a daily word of encouragement
- a celebration whenever one or the other experiences a triumph
- selecting pastimes or activities that involve teamwork and partnership, and which are equally co-owned by both marriage partners (planting a garden together, remodeling the house together, starting a children's ministry at church together)

With practice and persistent effort, couples can learn to support each other and rejoice in each other's successes. As 1 Corinthians 13:4-7 tells us, the love that is to exist among Christians, and especially in Christian marriage,

> does not envy, it does not boast, it is not proud. It is not rude, it is not self-seeking, it is not easily angered, it keeps no record of wrongs. Love does not delight in evil but rejoices with the truth. It always protects, always trusts, always hopes, always perseveres.

If this is the kind of love you practice in your marriage, there will be no room for competition. Instead, your married life will be a mutual, lifelong celebration of each other's joys and successes.

When One Partner Dominates

In this type of relationship, one partner consistently has the bulk of the leadership role, respect, and emotional energy, while the other side has little or none. In these relationships, the energy consistently flows from one partner to the other. For example:

Annie and Dave have been married twelve years. Living with a strong-willed wife and two strong-willed daughters, Dave has always been the odd man out in the relationship. Whenever Dave tried to discipline his daughters, Annie intervened and corrected him. Annie had veto power over all of Dave's plans and decisions. He might argue with her, but he invariably gave in when all was said and done. Annie could be harsh with Dave, but sometimes she also mothered him, coddling him and making excuses for his failures, comforting him when he became depressed.

Looking back into Dave's early history, we find a mother who dominated him and made all of his decisions for him. When Dave married, he permitted Annie to assume the role his mother once filled. Annie, who had been raised in a household with a weak, dependent father, was in familiar territory when she married weak, dependent Dave. And yet, deep down, she didn't want a man she could mother but a man she could respect—and she was continually needling and prodding Dave in the hope that he would somehow rise to the occasion and become a "real man."

Here was a couple in which all the emotional energy (support, love, affirmation, consolation, attention, encouragement) flowed in one direction—from Annie to Dave. She sensed his weakness and neediness, and she poured her energy into him—sometimes to protect and nurture him like a mother, sometimes to discipline and scold him like a mother, sometimes to prod him in the hope of seeing him become strong and mature. Annie was dominant and giving, while Dave was submissive and receiving. The unconscious dynamic in this relationship was one in which Annie was the parent and Dave was the child.

A relationship in which one partner consistently wields the majority of the control, leadership, initiative, and influence at the expense of the other is invariably unhealthy and painful for both partners. In fact, at this point in Annie and Dave's relationship, they were headed for divorce.

Whenever I encounter a couple that is so unbalanced and has such a lack of mutual respect and power sharing, I seek to intervene so that the couple can achieve greater equality and mutuality in their relationship. This is true regardless of whether it is the husband or the wife who is in the stronger position. While there are different roles and different functions for the husband and for the wife, neither side should dominate or emotionally eclipse the other.

So, if one side is always the giver in the relationship, I have the couple consciously set aside time in which the other partner is the giver. If one side is always the leader in the relationship, I have the couple set aside specific areas where the other person is given leadership responsibility. Though these situations are forced and artificial at first, couples often learn and adopt the new dynamics as part of their way of relating to each other, and the relationship becomes more whole, healthy, and mutual.

When Both Partners Are Passive

This is one of the least common postures I see in counseling. Here, each partner is waiting for the other to make the first move. There is no leadership, no initiation, and little apparent emotional energy. And while there may be little conflict in such a marriage (since there is nothing in the marriage worth fighting for), there is also little health in the marriage. No one is willing to take responsibility for the direction of the family, the emotional well-being of the family, the intellectual intimacy of the relationship, the initiating of conversation or sex, or even the decision about where to go on vacation. Both sides need to become more assertive, more passionate, more involved in life, and more involved in the marriage relationship.

In a healthy relationship, both partners take turns initiating and leading. In this way, the strengths of both partners are utilized, the gifts and abilities of both are exercised, and the weaknesses of both are compensated for. For specific, practical guidance in how both partners can become more actively involved in initiating and leading in the marriage relationship, see chapter 8.

When Positions Get Reversed

Many couples encounter a situation that causes a radical change in their positions in the relationship. This may be an illness, the loss of a job, a bout of depression, or some other circumstance.

Fred and Becca were trained professionals, both of whom had master's degrees in related fields and were working on their doctoral degrees. Over the course of their eight-year marriage, they had hammered out a relationship involving mutual respect and reciprocal roles. If there was any tilt at all in their postures, it might have been to give Fred a bit more responsibility in the leadership department, since he was earning a bit more and was acknowledged by Becca to be more savvy and more interested in the details of financial management.

But during their respective doctoral courses, problems arose. It's tough enough on a couple when one partner is pursuing an advanced degree, but it can be murder—in terms of stress load and strain on the relationship—when both are pursuing the same goal at the same time. Because of unexpected health problems and some difficulties with his doctoral research, Fred was unable to complete his thesis. While Becca was happily placing a new degree behind her name, Fred was becoming more and more depressed. Finally, he dropped out of the doctoral program altogether.

Fred's professional disaster had a profound effect on their private life together. Before, he had felt highly confident and competent. He had done a good job of responding to his wife's emotional, sexual, intellectual, and spiritual needs. In many ways and at many times, Fred had been the dominant partner, although theirs was, overall, a mutually giving relationship.

But stuck in his depression and self-pity, Fred suddenly became very needy. He expected all emotional energy to flow in his direction, while returning no support or affirmation to his wife. Becca, meanwhile, was unaccustomed and uncomfortable in a long-term dominant posture toward her husband. As time went on, she felt she could not single-handedly sustain the relationship. Without intervention, they would have ended up in divorce court.

What Does a Healthy Relationship Look Like?

In a healthy relationship, each partner's position toward the other has room to shift according to the needs of both and the demands of the given situation. Both partners willingly, eagerly, and lovingly take turns leading and following, helping and being helped, giving and receiving. There will be sharing and trading off of responsibilities and burdens. Leadership roles will be agreed upon and periodically reassessed. Duties and chores will be shared. Affirmation, encouragement, comfort, and emotional support will be freely exchanged. As a result, the relationship will change over time; it will grow in joy, maturity, and experiential depth. Both partners will experience fulfillment and a sense of adventure in a relationship where every day is something new and fresh, not merely a repeat of familiar yet unhealthy patterns.

**TURNING DISTORTED REALITIES
INTO HEALTHY RELATIONSHIPS**

When our storehouse is filled with distorted maps, distorted frames, distorted filters, and distorted postures, what else can we expect but distorted thinking, distorted communication, and distorted relationships? Instead of reacting to what actually happens in the relationship, we react to what our minds tell us is happening. We become prone to distorted thinking and responses. A few are described here:

We see with tunnel vision. We see only what fits our perspective, while ignoring the rest.

We overgeneralize. We use words like *always* ("She's always criticizing me") and *never* ("He's never on time").

We exaggerate. In our eyes, our partner's behavior and traits, whether positive or negative, become magnified.

We think in black and white. We don't leave any room for negotiation. "This way is the only way" or "Either you do things my way or we get a divorce."

We don't give each other the benefit of the doubt. We automatically assume that the other person's motives are impure. "He's only being nice to me because he wants something from me."

We use negative speech. "He's a bully." "She's a slob."

We believe we can read the other's mind. "I know what he really means by that."

We make our partner responsible for our feelings. "I feel depressed; it must be because my husband is never home."

We remember selectively. We take events out of context and arrive at an inaccurate conclusion. For example, a couple is at a dinner party. The wife relates a funny story about going to a restaurant, getting lost, and the food being bad; the husband becomes angry because all he "hears" is a criticism of himself.

We allow our mind-set to overrule the facts. For example, a wife sees her husband sweeping the porch. He is thinking, *I have some spare time, so I'll help out a little.* She thinks, *He's only doing that to criticize my work.*

We take things personally. We believe that the actions of our spouse are directed at us personally. "She's doing that to annoy me."

All of these patterns of thinking get us stuck, again and again, in the same pointless conflicts and unproductive patterns of behavior. It's no wonder our arguments repeat themselves. And it's no wonder we wear out emotionally over time and get discouraged with the relationship. Sometimes, simply understanding how these dynamics work in a marriage helps us begin to make constructive changes. Understanding gives us the power to break destructive cycles. Once we become more aware of how we are perceiving situations and reacting to them, we can

- correct our maps of reality,

- readjust our frames,

- unclog our filters,

- and improve our posture.

Sometimes we need additional, personal help in order to see our maps, frames, filters, and postures more clearly. Professional marriage and family counseling can be very helpful in this regard. A psychologist has many tools at his or her disposal that can help to bring hidden dynamics into better view. For example, the Meyers-Briggs* personality profile helps couples to see themselves and each other with greater clarity and understanding.

Once these hidden dynamics are brought out into the open, they begin to lose their power to enslave us in old, repetitive patterns of knee-jerk reactions and unproductive conflict. The sense of frustration and helplessness begins to fade, to be replaced by a new and exciting sense of growth, healing, and progress toward wholeness.

For further information on the Meyers-Briggs materials, write to: Consulting Psychologists Press, 577 College Ave., Palo Alto, CA 94306

Why Do We Have the Same Argument— Over and Over Again?

1. Think of a time in your life when you discovered that your mental map did not match reality. How did you feel when you discovered you were operating on the basis of an incorrect map? What did you learn from that experience?

2. Think of a time when someone (not necessarily your spouse) misjudged your motives, essentially saying to you, "I have you all mapped out; I know why you did what you did, and your motives were evil." How did that situation make you feel?

   Can you think of a situation in the past year when you might have done the same thing to your spouse? What do you think your spouse was feeling when you misjudged his or her motives?

3. What are some of the unhealed wounds and unresolved conflicts that may be affecting your mental map, distorting your frames, clogging your filters, and skewing the position you take toward your spouse?

4. Read the following statements that describe a husband and wife's posture toward each other. Put a check beside the statement that you feel describes your marriage. Or, write that statement in your journal. Explain your answer.

	WIFE'S RESPONSE	HUSBAND'S RESPONSE
Our marriage is a competition.	_____	_____
My spouse dominates the relationship.	_____	_____
I dominate the relationship.	_____	_____
We're both passive, and no one seems to initiate anything.	_____	_____

	WIFE'S RESPONSE	HUSBAND'S RESPONSE
Our postures have changed recently due to the following changes in our relationship:	_____	_____

5. On a scale from 1 to 10, where 1 equals "Very Dissatisfied" and 10 equals "Very Satisfied," how satisfied are you with the level of leadership and responsibility you are able to exercise in your marriage?

   On that same scale, how satisfied are you with the level of mutual sharing you experience in your marriage—the sharing of thoughts, conversation, and intimacy?

   How satisfied are you with the level of mutual expression of emotional energy, support, love, encouragement, and affirmation in your marriage?

6. If you and your spouse are doing this exercise together, compare your answers to question 5 with those of your spouse. Is there a disparity between your level of satisfaction and that of your spouse?

   Discuss your answers with your spouse. Listen carefully, openly, and nondefensively to the reasons your partner gives for his or her answers—especially if he or she indicates a lower level of satisfaction than you do. Seek to understand your spouse rather than to defend yourself. Try to set aside your preexisting maps, frames, and filters as you listen; make an effort to really hear and understand what your spouse is saying to you about his or her problems and pain in the marriage relationship.

   After you have discussed your answers, pray and covenant together to make corrective changes in your maps, frames, filters, and postures.

7

Why Can't I Say
What I Mean
without Getting into
Trouble?

Grace and Monty were just not communicating. As a result, they were on the verge of divorce. "What's wrong?" I asked.

Grace volunteered to open. "Monty withdraws. He crawls into his cave and hibernates until I go away."

"Is that how you respond when he withdraws?" I asked. "You go away? You ignore him?"

"Well," she paused, recalling past incidents, "that's what I do now. I just don't care anymore." I could hear it in her voice: She really did care. A lot.

"So," I said, "Monty withdraws, so you withdraw."

"That's about right," said Grace. "But I didn't always withdraw. I used to try to drag him out of his cave and get him to open up. Back when I cared, I mean. I used to ask him what was wrong, why he was pulling away from me, why he was going into his silent mode."

"How would Monty respond when you pursued him?" I asked.

"He withdrew even more. He'd get quieter."

I turned to Monty. "Is that true?"

"Well," he replied, hedging, "I wouldn't say I 'withdrew,' exactly." He didn't like the sound of the "withdrawal" frame; he chose his words carefully and reframed the situation in a softer and more favorable light. "I'd say I like to be quiet and contemplative at certain times. If Grace can't just give me a little peace and quiet, then I have to pull away a bit. You know." He shrugged.

Grace rolled her eyes in an exaggerated, derisive way. "The way I see it, he's just moody. I really hate that. He used to get moody like that when we were dating, but I never bothered to confront it. I didn't realize how moody he could really get. I didn't know what I was in for. It drives me up the wall when he pulls away like that."

Monty shot a glare in her direction. He obviously disapproved of the way she insisted on framing his behavior as "withdrawal," but he said nothing.

"OK," I said. "One of you, tell me about the last time this 'quietness' of Monty's caused a problem. Monty? Grace? Who wants to start?"

"I'll start," Grace said, almost eagerly. Monty bit his lip. "I remember when we had lunch at the restaurant with my sister," Grace continued. "I didn't think Monty conducted himself appropriately."

"How so?" I asked.

"He was withdrawn. Sullen, even. My sister noticed it. When she and I left the table and went to the ladies' room, she said, 'What's wrong with Monty?'"

Just then, I heard Monty mutter something.

"Pardon me?" I said. "What's that, Monty?"

"I said, I wasn't withdrawn and I wasn't sullen," he said.

"Did you tell him you disapproved of his performance at lunch?" I asked Grace.

"Oh, yes! I told him!"

"Did she ever!" Monty added like a rifle shot.

Grace returned a stare that would scorch steel.

"What happened then?" I asked.

"We had a long drive home," said Grace. "I tried to draw him out, but he wouldn't speak to me."

"You kept hammering at me," said Monty, "so I shut you out and went to Tahiti in my mind."

"Were you angry with her?" I asked.

Monty shrugged. "I didn't like the way she talked to me, the way she yelled at me. I don't have to take that. No man should have to put up with that."

"So you were angry," I said, putting my frame on his feelings to see if it fit.

"OK, yeah," said Monty. "Sure, I was mad. Who wouldn't be? She was trying to manipulate me, boss me around, control me!"

"I wasn't either," Grace retorted acidly.

"Do you feel that way very often, Monty?" I asked. "Do you feel Grace tries to boss you or control you?"

"Yeah. At times."

"Like . . . ?" I prompted.

"Like the time she wanted me to get rid of my favorite shirt."

Grace practically came out of her chair. "What?!! What shirt? I never—"

"The blue one!" countered Monty. "The one with the alligator on it."

Grace spluttered. "I didn't tell you to get rid of—"

"Monty," I interjected, "you said Grace wanted you to get rid of that shirt. That word 'wanted' implies you didn't do what she wanted you to do. You still have the shirt, don't you?"

"I love that shirt," he answered defensively, not responding directly to my question, but close enough.

"When she asks something of you," I said, "you feel controlled. To break her control over you, you refuse to comply with what she wants. Am I right?"

"But I didn't tell him to get rid of that shirt," Grace interposed. "I just said it wasn't my favorite." It was clear that she felt she was being painted as a "nag," and she didn't buy that frame.

"That's not what you said," Monty insisted. "You said, 'Monty, why do you always wear that ugly shirt?' That means you wanted me to get rid of it."

"Monty," I said, "you really feel that Grace was trying to control you."

"Exactly."

"Was there ever another time in your life," I continued, "when you felt other women were doing the same thing to you? Trying to control you? Trying to boss you around?"

The question seemed to catch him off guard. His eyebrows went up in surprise. "Well, yeah," he said. "I never thought of it that way before, but you're right. I once dated a girl who was trying to change me and control me all the time. She was always telling me to go here, to do this, to wear that."

"You dumped her?"

"You bet."

"Sounds like a part of you down inside is very sensitive to being controlled by a woman. Why do you think that is?"

"That's easy," he said. "My mother has been something of a buttinsky since Day One. I love my mother, but I always resented the way she tried to control me."

"So, Monty, it seems to me that you've developed a sore spot in your personality that is very sensitive to this issue. You very much resent any suggestion or indication that a woman is trying to control you."

"I never thought of it that way before, but yeah, I guess you're right."

"So the question is: How can the three of us craft a solution to this problem? How can we find a pattern of communication that would enable Grace to register her preferences without your feeling that she is trying to control you?"

That was the big problem the three of us needed to solve together.

FROM DIFFERENT WORLDS

The issue that brought Grace and Monty to the brink of divorce was one of communication. Grace wanted to know, "Why can't I say what I want without getting into trouble? Why, when I express my feelings, my thoughts, and my preferences, does Monty withdraw from me and punish me with his silence?"

Much of the trouble Grace and Monty experienced could be traced to simple biology: Grace was born female, and Monty was born male. There are some people today who would label that statement "sexist." Because of the rise of feminism and the political-correctness movement in the past few decades, it has become unfashionable to even acknowledge that there are genuine male-female differences—especially when it comes to the different ways men and women think.

Certainly, there is something to the argument that many of the differences between men and women are culturally ingrained. Boys are brought up to think and behave like boys; girls are brought up to think and behave like girls. But many of the differences between men and women have nothing to do with training and environment. They have to do with the fact that men are born men, women are born women, and these two sexes are fundamentally different. Men and women don't just have different plumbing; they have different wiring as well. The brains of men and women actually function differently.

For example, there is a structure in the brain called the *corpus callosum.* This small bundle of nerve fibers connects the right hemisphere of the cerebral cortex with the left hemisphere and allows the two halves of the brain to interact with each other. As we discussed in chapter 5, these two halves of the brain—which I have labeled "the storehouse brain" (right) and "the logical brain" (left)—have specific and differentiated functions. Neurological researchers have found that the corpus callosum tends to be thicker in women than in men, which means that women have more nerve pathways connecting the two brain hemispheres. This may account for the fact that women tend to be more "whole brained" in their thinking and emotional expression, while men tend to be "left-brain dominant" in their thinking.

Language researchers have found that there are communication characteristics that are gender related, some of them predominantly male, others predominantly female. Women tend to focus on feelings and relationships, while men tend to focus on information and tasks. Take a simple component of communication, such as a question, and you will find that men and women use that component for fundamentally different purposes. Women tend to ask questions as a means of maintaining a conversation, eliciting feelings, and furthering a relationship. Men tend to ask questions in order to obtain information and complete a task.

In a marriage, these fundamentally different styles of communication will inevitably come into conflict, resulting in misunderstanding and suspicion. In a very real sense, men and women come from different worlds, leading marriage counselor John Gray to observe that "men are from Mars, women are from Venus" in his best-selling book by the same title. We are alien beings to each other, trying to communicate across a deep gulf of biological and psychological difference. Yet, in a marriage, we are forced to coexist in the same living space and find some way to get along and to love each other.

We enter marriage with little awareness about male-female communication. We think that because men and women use the same words, they must mean the same things by those words. We think that men and women use those words for the same purposes and in the same way. In fact, men and women use the same words to achieve very different purposes.

We also tend to project our own needs, feelings, and thought patterns onto our partner. *You need what I need,* we think. *Therefore I will give you what I would like to receive.* We fail to understand that what we want may not be what our partner wants.

We ascribe magical power to this thing called "love"—including the power of mental telepathy! *If you really loved me,* we think, *you'd know what I mean.*

These faulty assumptions are at the root of an enormous amount of marital strife and pain. Somehow, we must find a way, as men and women, husbands and wives, to bridge the gender communication gap. In order for a marriage to be healthy, both partners must learn how to communicate with each other's world.

A MAN'S WORLD

How does a man view and define himself?

What follows is a generalization. Men are individuals, and not all men fit this generalization; but you will find that most men tend to see themselves in the following terms.

Status: A man sees himself as an individual in a hierarchical social order. Telling others what to do is high status; being told what to do is low status. The respect of his peers is very important to a man's self-esteem.

Communication: Men process information more readily than they share feelings. They discuss problems in order to arrive at solutions. A man's sense of self is defined through his ability to get results.

Empowerment: A man prides himself on autonomy, efficiency, power, and competence. Men are empowered when they feel needed (for example, as providers or problem solvers).

Fear: His greatest fear is that he is not good enough, that he will fail. He will project an attitude of total self-sufficiency even though he is almost obsessively concerned that he is not sufficient at all. In order to maintain an image of adequacy and to keep others from finding out that he is inadequate, he will often lock up his emotions, refusing to share himself and possibly appearing to be uncaring. The fact is, he may care a great deal—but his fear prevents him from showing it.

Relationships: He tends to be more interested in objects and structures than in people. He would rather talk about sports, politics, business, computers, or movies than about feelings and relationships. In the realm of intimacy, men may periodically pull away, retreat, and even hide—then seem to move closer when they need reassurance, support, admiration, or "strokes."

A WOMAN'S WORLD

How does a woman view and define herself?

Again, what follows is a generalization—but a very useful and highly accurate generalization.

Status: A woman sees herself as part of a network of connections and relationships. Consensus and intimacy are key: Differences are minimized; superiority is avoided. Her sense of self is defined by her feelings and the quality of her relationships.

Communication: Women discuss problems in order to get close, not necessarily to arrive at solutions. Whereas men may feel affronted by the advice of others (especially a wife or another woman), a woman sees an offer of help and advice as a sign of caring.

Empowerment: Women are empowered when they feel cherished and valued.

Fear: Since the great desire of a woman is for relationships, the great fear of a woman is abandonment.

Relationships: In the realm of intimacy, women are like ocean waves: As they feel loved, their self-esteem rises. But this can suddenly change as the wave crashes.

WHEN WORLDS COLLIDE

When the female and male worlds collide, both sides are wounded—and both sides are often left bewildered about exactly what happened. Why did we have that argument? Why did communication break down? Why doesn't he/she understand me? Why can't I understand my spouse? Why is our marriage falling apart? The confusion lies in our strangeness to each other. And healing lies in learning to understand each other.

One common scenario involving this collision is a wife trying to help her husband by giving him advice. According to the rules of her world, when someone offers help or advice, it means that person cares about you. She doesn't understand that according to the rules of his world, advice is an indication that someone thinks he is incompetent. Advice is an insult to a man's sense of status and self-esteem. He doesn't feel helped or cared for. He feels controlled, even humiliated. A husband is especially likely to overreact to his wife's advice if he has experienced critical, controlling parenting in childhood or if he saw his father being bossed by an overbearing mother.

A man, too, often gets into trouble by trying to be helpful. For example, Larry's wife, Sabrina, comes home frustrated and angry about her job. "Boy!" she fumes. "When I took that promotion to vice principal, I had no idea what I was getting into! We've got 150 ESL kids and only one teacher to handle them. The health aide they sent us from the downtown office is clueless when it comes to first aid. Thirteen kids took wrong buses and had to be rounded up and brought back to school. And to top it all off, I had to call in a caseworker on a child-protection case today! I just don't know if I'm going to make it!"

"Maybe you should go back to teaching," Larry offers helpfully.

"What!" Sabrina retorts. "How can you say that! I love this job!"

"Well," Larry responds, trying to undo the damage he unwittingly did with his first suggestion, "maybe you should hire somebody to handle the overflow."

"There's no budget for more personnel!" Sabrina counters, her anger mounting.

"I was just trying to offer some helpful suggestions!"

"It might be helpful if you would just listen to me once in a while!"

"I *was* listening to you! What do you think I was doing?"

"You weren't listening," she answers, fuming. "You were talking."

"I was trying to help you solve your problems!"

"You always think you have the answer for everything, but you don't know diddly-squat about my problems!"

And so on and so forth.

It all began when Sabrina poured out her troubles and Larry tried to solve them for her. Sabrina just wanted someone to listen to her tale of woe, someone to be a supportive friend and a sounding board. Information-oriented, task-oriented Larry thought she wanted someone to fix her problems for her. The result: frustration on both sides. Larry was trying to be helpful; but the entire conversation blew up in his face, and he didn't have any idea where he went wrong.

When a woman is upset, tired, sad, or confused, she is usually not in the market for someone to come in and solve her problems for her. She just wants to be heard and understood. She wants emotional support. She wants to have her feelings validated, not discounted. To sum it all up, she really just wants a friend. When her husband takes the time to listen, to offer his empathy and his time, she feels loved and valued—and she is able to put her problems into a better perspective.

Another place where male and female worlds collide is in the way words are used. Women tend to use words to express emotion, and they will often amplify the expression of their feelings by using higher-wattage words. When a woman says, "We never go out" or "Why do you always forget to take out the garbage?" her message is actually, "I feel very strongly about the fact that we don't go out often enough" or "I really want you to understand how upsetting it is that you often forget the garbage." She is not using "never" and "always" in a literal sense.

But men, being information oriented rather than feelings oriented, tend to jump on the fact that their wives have not accurately stated the facts. Eager to cancel out the criticism they hear in their wives' message, they seize upon the literal inaccuracy of the words "never" and "always." They counter with, "How can you say that? I took you out to dinner just three months ago!" or "I don't always forget! I remembered the garbage all by myself the Sunday before St. Swithins Day, remember?" And because she doesn't feel she's being heard, because her feelings are being ignored, the woman is likely to respond by cranking up the emotional wattage (and from the male point of view, the inaccuracy) of her words even more.

Now we have a full-blown argument—and neither side has even agreed on the terms of the discussion! She is arguing her feelings. He is arguing the content of words. She feels that her feelings are being disregarded and invalidated. He is simply trying to win the argument on debating points. No one wins this kind of argument.

A DEAFENING SILENCE

The "silent treatment" is one of the oldest tricks in the book. It is one of the biggest challenges to marital communication. Both men and women use the silent treatment, but they tend to use silence in different ways and for different purposes.

Men sometimes withdraw from a conversation. They just stop responding. Sometimes they are mulling it over, processing information, and trying to come up with a response that will swat their wives' arguments right out of the ballpark. At other times, they use silence as a way to assert their control over a situation: "You want to have a conversation; I don't. So I'm going to just sit here and read the paper as if you don't exist. Ha-ha, I win."

Whatever a man's reasons for using the "silent treatment," a woman is likely to interpret it as his lack of caring for her. Women value understanding, connection, empathy, and being cherished. Above all, they want to be heard, and they want their feelings validated. Silence says, "I don't want to understand you or be connected to you. I have no empathy for your problems. I don't value you as a person. I couldn't care less about your stupid feelings. Go away and leave me alone."

There could hardly be a more destructive and insulting message than that! For many women, silence triggers their worst fear—the fear of abandonment. This is why so many women become desperate, almost panic-stricken, in their pursuit of a withdrawn husband.

Often, a woman who has lapsed into silence and apparent withdrawal is not withdrawing at all. In fact, she may actually be trying to protect the relationship rather than inflict hurt on her husband. There are things she could say, things she wants to say—but she's afraid that if she says what's on her mind, it might be too damaging to her husband or to the relationship. So she bites her tongue.

Women also tend to go silent when they feel insecure in a situation. If a woman feels that she can't compete with her husband's debating skills, she may go silent rather than be made to look foolish. In any case, women are more likely to use silence as a matter of defense rather than offense. They stop talking to protect the relationship, to protect themselves, and even to protect their husbands from their own anger!

When we know there is a desperate need for communication in the marriage, silence can be deafening! Now that we understand some of the reasons a partner may lapse into silence from time to time, it is important to develop a strategy for responding to the silence.

The instinctive response is to charge right in and try to force a response. The first attempt may be sweet, kind, and patient: "Come on, honey. Talk about it. Tell me what's wrong. You know you'll feel better."

The second attempt seeks to probe for clues: "Is it something I said? Something I didn't say? Something I did?"

With the third attempt, patience begins to wear thin: "Look, I'm trying to help. I really want to know what's going on, but you're not giving me anything to work with. I'm beginning to feel, well, a little frustrated."

By the fourth attempt, the gloves come off, and we're at it, bare knuckles: "All right, you stupid jerk! That's the way you want it? Just sit there like petrified wood and see if I care!" *Slam!*

The above procedure is not recommended. Here's a more productive way to respond to your partner's silence.

- Give your partner some space. As much as possible, avoid registering disapproval; be patient and accepting.

- Avoid questioning your spouse or trying to draw him or her out.

- Avoid trying to solve his or her problem by offering advice.

- Get on with your life. It's difficult not to think about the situation. One person's gloom has a tendency to settle over the whole family. That can't be avoided altogether, but as much as possible, try to carry on a normal routine. Do something to take your mind off your spouse's emotions: Pray or read your Bible. Take a walk, or take the kids to the zoo. Call a friend. Put on your favorite music. Do some gardening. Read a good book.

While you should feel a sense of connection with your spouse, you should not let his or her moods control your feelings. Your emotions shouldn't rise or set with your spouse's emotions. If that's a major problem for you, see a counselor for insight and help into establishing healthier emotional boundaries between you and your spouse.

HOT TALK

When communication heats up, we call it an argument. On the surface, there are all kinds of things we argue about: money (that's a big one), major decisions, minor decisions, discipline and child rearing, schedules and appointments, chores and responsibilities, in-laws, friends, and incredibly minor trivialities. Beneath the surface, however, there are usually only a few issues: fear of being controlled, fear of being abandoned, perceived lack of respect, perceived lack of understanding. Many couples actually have only one argument—the same one over and over—but it is repackaged in a different surface issue each time. The surface packaging is just camouflage for the big emotional symbol at the heart of it all: the sense that we are not being adequately loved and valued. Some examples:

He argues: "Why do you keep getting mad at me for such picky little things?" What he really feels (even though he may not realize it or be able to articulate it): *Why can't you accept me and love me just the way I am?*

She argues: "Sure, yell at me! Pound the table! Why don't you just haul off and let me have it! You're just itching to pop me one, aren't you?" What she really feels: *Your yelling and fist pounding scare me and make me feel insecure. I don't feel loved, valued, and cherished right now.*

He argues: "Can't you stop telling me what to do and treating me like a kid?" What he really feels: *I need to be loved and respected as a competent man.*

She argues: "How stupid can you be, forgetting our anniversary? What did you think that big red circle on the calendar was for?" What she really feels: *If our anniversary is unimportant to you, then you must not love me.*

He argues: "Quit trying to run my life!" What he really feels: *Please love me and respect my own decision-making ability.*

She argues: "Don't tell me I shouldn't feel this way! These are my feelings, not yours, and I can feel any way I want to feel!" What she really feels: *Please don't tell me my emotions are not valid. Please love me and support me where I am right now.*

Once we begin to see beneath the surface issue, the packaging of the argument, we find a throbbing human heart, yearning to be loved. When we focus on the needs of that human heart rather than on the surface issue, the argument begins to unravel. In order to communicate across the gulf that separates the world of men from the world of women, we must look beneath the surface, and we must feed the heart of our marriage partner with the thing it hungers for:

Love.

Why Can't I Say What I Mean without Getting into Trouble?

Discuss the following questions with your spouse. It may be helpful to write your individual responses in your journals to help each of you think through them. Then you can discuss your responses.

1. **Complete these statements:**

   In our marriage, I/my spouse is more likely to withdraw and go silent.

   I think I/he/she chooses silence rather than communication at these times because

   _____

2. In this chapter, we discuss the fact that men and women use language in fundamentally different ways. Discuss a recent event in your marriage that may have resulted from the different ways you and your spouse use language. Is there an insight (or are there several insights) from this chapter that help you put that event into perspective?

   How could that situation have been handled differently with an understanding of basic differences between male and female communication patterns?

3. Do you agree or disagree with the statement in this chapter that husbands and wives are "alien beings to each other, trying to communicate across a deep gulf . . . [yet] forced to coexist in the same living space"? Explain your answer.

4. What are some of the specific issues over which your world and your spouse's world collide?

   After reading this chapter, are you able to see deeper symbolic and emotional issues that underlie the surface "packaging" of your marital conflict? If so, what are some of those deeper issues?

How can understanding those deeper issues enable you to manage your conflict more effectively in the future?

5. Which of these statements is true for you?

My spouse's mood affects or controls my own emotions.
I am able to separate my feelings from those of my spouse.

Complete this statement:

When my spouse is angry or unhappy for reasons that have nothing to do with me, I have some favorite activities that can keep me from getting overshadowed by his/her storm clouds. Those activities are

_____

6. In what ways do you see the desire for love (your desire and your spouse's) as being at the heart of most or all of your marital arguments?

Discuss how the two of you can demonstrate love (or make each other feel loved) in such a way that these arguments will become less frequent and less intense.

7. Read 1 Corinthians chapter 13, then pray together, asking God for a loving heart and a deeper understanding of each other's need for love. Ask God to remind you both, when you get into conflict, of your mutual need to give and receive love. Remember that it is in the situations in which love is most urgently needed that it is often the most difficult to express love.

8

Who's the Leader,

and

How Do We Know?

Clark and Brandy came into my office for counseling. Clark was quiet and sullen. Brandy was frustrated to the point of fury. "Ever since we've been married," she said, "almost fifteen years now, I've had to take the leadership role in this family. He never initiates anything. He's never spontaneous. He never takes the lead. He never has any ideas. He's a wimp!"

Clark sent a hostile glare in her direction but said nothing.

"Clark," I said, turning in his direction, "do you agree or disagree with Brandy's assessment?"

"Well, I guess I don't really initiate very much around our house. I don't get a chance! She's always telling me what to do before I get a chance to do it on my own. Like, she's always saying, 'Be spontaneous! Be spontaneous!' Well, doesn't she see that the moment she tells me to be spontaneous, she makes it *impossible* for me to be spontaneous? Anything I do after that point will seem to be nothing more than my responding to her dictatorial command that I be spontaneous!"

Clark had just articulated a common leadership problem in marriage—The "Be Spontaneous" Paradox: How can anyone be spontaneous on command? The moment Brandy demanded that Clark lead, she, in fact, became the leader! The more she told him to lead, the more she paralyzed him as a leader.

But Brandy was also caught in a paradox of her own: If she didn't lead or tell Clark to lead, *no one* would lead! Clark really was too passive in the relationship. Her problem was: How do I get Clark to lead without telling him to lead? Up to the moment they came into my office for counseling, she couldn't. She was checkmated. If she waited for him to lead, she might well wait forever. But if she led in the relationship, she was accused of mentally and emotionally castrating her husband!

My task as a counselor was twofold: (1) I had to help Brandy learn new patterns of relating to Clark so that she could moderate her impulses to initiate and berate her husband for not initiating, and (2) I had to encourage Clark to initiate action and demonstrate leadership at home.

I had to be careful because Clark's first response when I encouraged him to initiate and lead was to ask me, "What should I do?" In other words, he turned to me for leadership! I turned it right back on him: "Oh, no, Clark! If I told you what to do, I'd just be replacing Brandy as the leader in your home. You have to assume that role. You have to do your own thinking, your own planning, your own initiating. You must be the leader now—and Brandy has agreed that she's going to make an effort to step back and let you lead. She pledges to give you the space you need to carve out a new leadership role in your family. Take this opportunity to choose what needs to be done in your family, then initiate whatever action it takes to accomplish it."

Over the next few weeks, the three of us continued to meet together. It was a classic case of two steps forward, one step back. Old patterns died hard, and Clark found it difficult to become creative, confident, and assertive in his new role as leader. Brandy frequently had to be reminded to allow her husband to find his way in the new role.

During our sessions, I shared with Clark and Brandy the principles contained in this chapter.

The leadership issue is a *big* one in most marriages. Who leads? Who follows? And when?

AN ISSUE OF ROLES, NOT CONTROL

Most leadership problems arise when couples misunderstand what leadership is all about. Leadership is *not* a "power" issue. It's not about who "controls" or who is the "boss." It is an issue of *roles*. In some family matters, the husband may be more gifted to take the leadership role. In other matters, the wife may have a greater natural aptitude for leadership.

Authentic leadership does not come from a strong will or a loud voice. Rather, it consists of the ability to initiate, direct, influence, and inspire others to follow. In a healthy marriage, leadership is reciprocal and shared. Sometimes one leads, and the other follows; then they switch. The reins of leadership are passed from hand to hand. In less healthy marriages, one *always* leads, and the other *always* follows; both struggle for power, or both withdraw.

Healthy couples have come to terms with the power issue. They do not feel threatened when they find themselves in a following role from time to time, and they can make the adjustments necessary to either lead or follow at the appropriate times, depending on the circumstances.

Leadership can take the form of initiating sex, planning meals, earning money, budgeting the family finances, planning vacations, and so forth. In many areas of the marriage and family life, each partner can lead according to the strengths of his or her personality. This way, the partners complement one another instead of competing with each other.

Our tendency is to look at the role of leadership as one of status—of being exalted over other people. That's the way the world looks at leadership, but that's not the way the Bible views it. The beautiful leadership paradox presented in the Scriptures tells us that the one with the greatest leadership responsibility must be the servant of all (see Luke 22:26; John 12:26; and Phil. 2:7).

Whether in the office, church, or home, leadership is a quality with many facets. A good leader must be a good manager, responsible for everything that goes on under his or her stewardship. Nothing should take place without the manager's awareness and approval. A good leader is also a good delegator, utilizing the abilities of others and developing their skills rather than doing everything himself or herself. A good leader is a visionary who can inspire others to catch and implement his or her vision. A good leader doesn't have to intimidate people into following. People's natural response to a good leader is to want to follow him or her.

Both the husband and the wife are called to be leaders in the home. They have equal status and equal worth. Both are worthy of honor and respect. The husband and wife have different roles, but both are leadership roles—and both are also roles of Christian servanthood.

THE LEADERSHIP ROLE OF THE HUSBAND

The Scriptures describe the husband's role in a marriage as being one of headship. In Ephesians 5:23, the apostle Paul writes that "the husband is the head of the wife as Christ is the head of the church, his body, of which he is the Savior." Very pointedly, Paul compares the leadership role of the husband to the leadership role of Christ. And what kind of a leader was Christ? He was the one who, when his twelve followers were arguing about who was the greatest, took out a basin of water and a towel and began washing their feet. He was the kind of leader who, as Paul says in Philippians 2:5-7, set aside his exalted position as God and "made himself nothing, taking the very nature of a servant."

True leadership is servanthood. Even the leader whose job it is to exercise authority and "call the shots" in a given situation must do so lovingly, humbly, and with the attitude of a servant, not a boss.

The husband's leadership role is one of self-sacrificing love, as Ephesians 5:25 tells us: "Husbands, love your wives, just as Christ loved the church and gave himself up for her." Whenever a husband makes decisions for the family, he should be careful to base those decisions on authentic love for his wife and family. He should consider their needs ahead of his own needs for prestige, honor, fulfillment, pleasure, or material goods.

"He who loves his wife loves himself," Paul adds in Ephesians 5:28-29. "After all, no one ever hated his own body, but he feeds and cares for it, just as Christ does the church." Husbands have a duty (and it should be a joyful duty!) to nourish their wives emotionally and spiritually. A husband should exercise leadership in the home by cherishing, honoring, protecting, and building up his wife. He should make her feel emotionally and physically secure. He should welcome her feelings and her thoughts. Any husband who exercises his leadership role in the home without adequately cherishing and caring for his wife has missed the essence of what Christlike, husbandly leadership really means.

THE LEADERSHIP ROLE OF THE WIFE

Many people (both men and women) mistake the biblical role of women in Christian marriage as being a perpetually passive follower. Nothing could be further from the truth. In the Old Testament book of Proverbs, chapter 31, we find some statements about the role of a wife that sound as if they could have been taken straight from one of today's popular women's magazines. And why not? Proverbs chapter 31 was written out of the advice King Lemuel received from his mother—and this woman knows whereof she speaks!

In verse 10, she makes a great self-esteem-boosting statement about the value of a good wife: "She is worth far more than rubies." The wife described in Proverbs 31 is a businesswoman, a real estate investor, a merchant, and the manager of a busy household:

> She selects wool and flax
> and works with eager hands. . . .
> She considers a field and buys it;
> out of her earnings she plants a vineyard.
> She sets about her work vigorously;
> her arms are strong for her tasks.
> She sees that her trading is profitable,
> and her lamp does not go out at night. . . .
> She makes linen garments and sells them,
> and supplies the merchants with sashes. . . .
> She watches over the affairs of her household
> and does not eat the bread of idleness.
> Proverbs 31:13, 16-18, 24, 27

This good wife is also involved in reaching out to her community with compassion. "She opens her arms to the poor," says verse 20, "and extends her hands to the needy." As a result of all she accomplishes in her busy, responsibility-laden life, her husband praises her (verse 29): "Many women do noble things, but you surpass them all." Like so many women of our own time, she is gifted, capable, and resourceful. She is a leader.

COMPLEMENTARY ROLES

Together, a godly husband and a godly wife make an unbeatable team. The responsibilities of a household can be divided in many ways to maximize the gifts and strengths of both partners. In many marriages, the wife is handier with a checkbook and a calculator, so she handles the bill paying and the family ledger. In some cases, the husband enjoys cooking, and the wife hates it—so he regularly carries out what was once considered a "wifely" chore.

One partner may be an emotion-based decision maker, while the other is more methodical, pragmatic, and fact-based; by taking both approaches into account when making major decisions, the couple is able to make more balanced choices. One partner may be overly optimistic, while the other is extremely realistic and can help to rein in the tendency of the first to take on too large a challenge. One may be impulsive, the other a careful planner. One may be a risk taker, the other overly cautious. Whatever their character traits, two people who share their leadership roles according to their strengths and deficiencies tend to balance each other and to steady what might otherwise be a very rocky boat.

But what about this idea that the husband is the head of the wife and of the family? We have to understand that headship does not imply a master-servant relationship. In fact, it is the head who is, in the truest sense, the servant. The important thing to remember is that leadership responsibilities are to be shared and delegated according to each partner's strengths and deficiencies. A wife supplies in those areas the husband lacks and vice versa.

Clearly, the fact that the Bible confers headship on the husband does not mean that he simply makes decisions and issues edicts to his wife. In a biblically sound marriage, the wife is intimately involved in the decision-making process. Channels of communication between both partners must be wide open continually, including not only information and opinions, but also feelings, fellowship, prayer together, and even laughter.

Both partners should be fully supportive of each other in front of the children. Mom should make it clear to the children that Dad wears the headship hat in the family and they should never undermine the respect that is due him. Dad should continually praise and support Mom, verbally and in other ways, so that children see her competence and her leadership role valued.

A husband can delegate many responsibilities to his wife. It is important to note, however, that there are some areas of leadership which a man should never abdicate in the home. The husband should be the spiritual leader in his family, guiding them in regular devotions and discussions of spiritual issues. Major long-term problems can arise when the father is passive and gives his wife total responsibility for shaping his children's behavior and character. Dad should be sure to maintain an active role in disciplining the children and making child-rearing decisions.

LEADERSHIP PROBLEMS AND SOLUTIONS

Initiative is the ability to define a situation, set a direction, and move oneself and one's team in that direction. Initiative is a prime ingredient of leadership. Many of the problems that surround the issue of leadership have to do with either too much initiative, which makes no allowance for the initiative of others, or not enough initiative.

Dominating Relationships

It is not healthy for a relationship when one partner does all the initiating and leading while the other partner always follows. Each partner should lead in the areas of his or her strengths, and in some areas they should trade off from time to time.

Competitive Relationships and Passive Relationships

If both partners continually try to initiate all the time, the result is a constant head-butting contest between the husband and the wife. If both sides withdraw and wait for the other to act, little or nothing is achieved. Neither of these patterns is healthy. In either case, both partners need to learn to share the responsibility. Those who are consistently passive and withdrawn need to learn how to initiate and be assertive; those who are consistently barging through with little thought of the other person need to learn to share, delegate, and trust the abilities and judgment of their partner.

The passive noninitiator tends to be a person who lacks self-confidence, who doesn't trust his or her own abilities and instincts. "I can't lead," this person says. "I can't initiate. The leadership role just doesn't work for me." Afraid that their partners will not follow, passive individuals choose the role of chronic follower. Often, they have learned to get what they want through passivity—by acting as if they are helpless or incompetent so that others will initiate and do the work for them.

"But," you might say, "what if I'm ready to lead in a certain area of our relationship but my spouse won't follow?" When followers won't follow, there is usually a reason—and frequently that reason is related to a lack of trust. In order to follow, a follower must believe that the leader is trustworthy and is working in the follower's best interests. Whether the issue is sex or finances or a major life move, the follower has to be able to say, "If I follow you, things will turn out all right. You will not lead me into a hurtful situation."

When a leader leads and the follower doesn't follow, there is a natural tendency for the leader to choose one of three unhealthy responses:

- The leader withdraws and refuses to initiate.

- The leader becomes belligerent and angry and attempts to force the follower to comply (male leaders often turn to this response when frustrated, thereby confirming a wife's worst fears about bullying, tyrannical men).

- The leader turns to manipulation and hidden agendas, trying to trick the follower into following.

All of these responses tend to undermine trust in a relationship. A much healthier response is for the leader to communicate openly with the follower about the situation, not only talking and trying to persuade the follower to follow, but listening attentively to the follower's reasons for holding back. Communication builds trust, and trust enables followers to follow so that leaders can lead. After all, a leader is empowered by the followers and is powerless if no one follows.

A leader can inspire individuals or groups to move together toward a common goal; the leader's job is to channel the power of the group in a productive direction. In the context of a family, that means that a leader is able to inspire the rest of the family to carry out their roles and fulfill their functions. When this happens, the family becomes satisfied, well organized, emotionally strong, spiritually strong, successful, loving, and mutually cooperative.

HOW HUSBAND AND WIFE CAN HELP EACH OTHER BECOME STRONGER LEADERS

Here are some ways you and your spouse can encourage and support each other to become more effective in your respective leadership roles:

Be observant; affirm areas of strength and ability that you observe in your spouse, and encourage him or her to exercise leadership in those areas.

Take time out at least once a year (perhaps around your wedding anniversary) to discuss your respective roles, and make any adjustments in expectations, duties, and areas of leadership. Also, keep the lines of communication open throughout the year, and readjust roles as needed.

In apportioning roles and responsibilities, make sure one partner doesn't get all the "glamour" jobs while the other gets all the "grunt work." Make sure the feelings and dignity of both partners are respected.

Encourage each other to take on new challenges, to try out new roles, to stretch yourselves, and to move out of your respective comfort zones. Leadership should be a growing experience, not a static role.

If you have agreed to let your partner lead in a given area, step back and let him or her lead. When it's your turn to follow, follow. Even if he or she does not do the job the way you would, resist the temptation to jump in and say, "You're not doing it right! Here, let me show you. . . ."

Pray for your spouse. Ask God to give him or her strength, wisdom, and confidence in the leadership role in the marriage.

The key to a successful balance of leadership roles is love—both partners continually seeking the best for each other and for the family unit as a whole. In a healthy marriage, both partners trade and share. Both lead and follow. Sometimes the husband leads, sometimes the wife. But at all times, in all ways, whether leading or following, both sides serve and both sides love. Our example is Jesus, who came, not to be the boss, not to be served, but to serve. There is no higher, purer form of leadership in marriage than the form Jesus showed us—that of service.

Who's the Leader, and How Do We Know?

1. List several areas in which you lead on a consistent basis:

_____

_____

List several areas in which your spouse leads on a consistent basis:

_____

_____

List several areas in which you and your spouse take turns leading:

_____

_____

2. Decide together which statement describes the leadership relationship between the two of you:

We compete with each other.
We complement each other.

Other _____

To what factors in your marriage do you attribute the leadership relationship between you and your spouse?

3. Place a check beside the statement that is true, or write it in your journal. Then discuss your individual responses.

	WIFE'S RESPONSE	HUSBAND'S RESPONSE
My self-esteem and sense of being valued are diminished by the ways leadership is demonstrated in our marriage.	_____	_____
My self-esteem and sense of being valued are increased by the ways leadership is demonstrated in our marriage.	_____	_____
My self-esteem and sense of being valued are not affected by the ways leadership is demonstrated in our marriage.	_____	_____

Explain with specific incidents why you answered as you did.

4. Read Philippians 2:1-11. How does this passage affect your view of leadership and servanthood in your marriage relationship?

5. How could you and your spouse renegotiate and reapportion your leadership roles so that you would each maximize your gifts and strengths? Name some specific changes you and your spouse could make in your leadership roles in such areas as spirituality, child rearing, finances, sex, meal planning, chores, home maintenance, vacation planning, and so forth.

6. Here's a useful exercise for you and your spouse to do in order to help you both share leadership roles more equitably. First, divide up the days of the week, with one partner taking odd days, the other taking even days. On your day, think of one small action that you can initiate (for example, selecting a restaurant for dinner, a movie to see, a game to play at home).

Second, practice changing the way you communicate with your spouse about decisions and needs. Communicate in a direct, decisive, first-person way. Instead of asking "Would you like to do X tonight?" state what you want: "I would like for us to do X tonight." Become aware of the difference between these two statements: The first is a question, stated in the second-person voice from a passive point of view, putting all the responsibility for a decision on the other person. The second is a first-person statement from an active point of view, taking personal responsibility for one's own wants.

I have used these exercises with good results in counseling couples who needed to better balance their leadership roles and communication patterns.

9

How Can We Disagree without Tearing Each Other Apart?

Darlene heard the crash and clatter from three rooms away. She heard the *stamp-stamp* of Gary's heavy, angry tread, and she quickened her own steps, hoping to intercept him. Too late. Just as she reached the entryway to the living room, she heard her husband's hard voice, lashing like a whip. "Kevin! Look what you did! Look at that lamp! What did I just tell you about throwing that ball in the living room? Huh? Answer me! What did I tell you?!"

Darlene rounded the corner in time to see her 220-pound former college-football-player husband towering over their seven-year-old son. Little Kevin seemed to have shrunk to half his size. His eyes were wide with fear, and his mouth formed a silent *O* that seemed to want to scream but couldn't. "Gary!" Darlene said sharply, trying to find just the right note to get her husband's attention without angering him any further. "Gary, you're scaring him!"

"He *should* be scared," said Gary. "Look what he did!"

Darlene glanced at the lamp, one of a pair of table lamps. It lay on the floor; the light bulb had shattered and sliced through the papery lamp shade like a sword. And there were tiny slivers of light bulb all over the carpet.

"I'm—I'm sorry!" Kevin stammered.

"Not half as sorry as you're gonna be!" Gary growled.

Just the sound of her husband's voice sent a horrible thrill of fear through Darlene's body, from the back of her neck, down her spine, to the pit of her stomach. Gary was not a violent man, and he had never beaten her or her son, but his anger and the force of his voice could be intimidating beyond belief. "Gary," she said, placing a hand on her husband's shoulder, "let's just take a moment to think about this—"

Gary shook her hand off. "Stay out of this, Dar!"

That did it! Like a mother bear defending her cub, Darlene sprang into action. She latched onto her husband's shoulder with both hands and spun all 220 pounds of him around like he was made of straw. She had a brief moment to savor the stunned look on his face before she launched into him. "Kevin is my son, and no one tells me to 'stay out of this, Dar,' when it concerns my baby! Now let's go in the bedroom and talk this over!"

Gary was about to speak, but Darlene turned to her son and added, "Kevin, you sit down in that chair by the fireplace until Daddy and I come back out to talk to you. Just stay away from the broken glass. Everything's going to be OK. Come on, Gary."

Without waiting for Gary to respond, Darlene turned and headed for the hallway to the bedroom. It was a daring gambit—but it worked. With a quick backward glance, she saw that Gary was fuming, but he was following.

Once in the bedroom, Gary roared, "That's it, Dar! You have really crossed the line! You undercut my authority and made me out to be the heavy when I was doing my job as a father! He deliberately disobeyed me by throwing that football around after I told him—"

"You don't have a clue what Kevin did or didn't do!" Darlene countered. "You weren't in the room when that lamp got broken, and you didn't ask Kevin what happened. You just started screaming at him and scaring him to death!"

"I didn't need to ask him what happened!" Gary snarled. "That lamp didn't jump off the end table all by itself! He was throwing that football—"

"Where *was* his football?" Darlene interrupted. "Did you see it?"

"It was on the floor someplace," Gary said, shrugging. "Who cares where—"

"It was not! I looked in Kevin's bedroom when we came down the hall, and his football was sitting right on his bed! Face it, Gary, you were wrong! You heard a crash, and you went into that living room, romping and stomping and scaring the living daylights out of a little boy who idolizes you so much he wants to be a college football star like his Daddy!"

"Oh, puh-leeze, Dar!" said Gary, his voice dripping with sarcasm. "Stop it with the hearts and flowers! The fact is, that lamp got busted, and Kevin was the only one within twenty feet of it when it happened. The kid's got some explaining to do!"

"So let him explain!" shouted Darlene. "The problem with you is, you never listen! You just launch!"

"Oh, here we go again! I'm getting sick and tired of—"

"You know, Gary, I really couldn't care less what you're sick and tired of! You need to hear this, and you're gonna hear it!"

And so on and so forth, for the next half hour. Meanwhile, little Kevin, sitting and sniffling in a chair half a house away, could hear every bitter, angry, hurtful word—and he took all the blame and guilt for this incident onto himself. If he hadn't tried to be helpful by crawling under the end table to retrieve the TV remote control his father had accidentally dropped there, this whole mess never would have happened.

CONFLICT—HEALTHY OR DESTRUCTIVE?

One of the most destructive and pervasive forces in any human relationship is conflict. It divides marriage partners, and it bruises the souls and emotions of both children and adults. It creates painful memories and distorts the way people relate to each other. When conflict arises in a marriage, devastating things are said by both sides, momentary anger sours into long-term grudges, and the cycle of conflict tends to spiral out of control. As in the case of Gary, Darlene, and Kevin, conflict usually results from a lack of understanding, even from a series of misunderstandings. Many marriages and families have been completely broken apart by conflict.

Paradoxically, however, a family in which there is no conflict is often as unhealthy (or more so) as the war-torn husband and wife who are battling their way toward divorce court. Every once in a while, I encounter a couple who proudly announce to me, "We haven't had an argument in thirty years of marriage!" I think, *This couple is being dishonest—either with me or with themselves.* In a marriage that shows no sign of conflict, there's a strong likelihood that issues are being buried.

Conflict is inevitable in every living, breathing relationship—even in the best of relationships. Couples will always have differing tastes, personalities, and ideas, all of which will produce tension and friction from time to time. In fact, I believe a certain level of conflict is actually healthy for a relationship. There should be dynamic, creative tension in a marriage. There should be differences of opinion that challenge both partners to learn, change, and grow.

The goal of a marriage relationship should not be the elimination of conflict but the healthy management of conflict. Handled in a healthy and mutually loving way, conflict leads to resolution, understanding, and a strengthened relationship. Handled poorly, unresolved issues continue to lurk below the surface like the bulk of the iceberg that sank the *Titanic.*

In a healthy relationship, both partners learn to articulate their own points of view. They disagree, they negotiate, and they achieve resolution. Each partner stays in the present while discussing the issues and avoids the temptation to dredge up old issues or wounds to use as ammunition. Ideally, both partners should attempt to keep the lines of communication wide open, even when conflict tempts one or both of them to close down and withdraw. By monitoring and resolving problems while they are small, couples are able to keep emotional pressures from building to explosive levels.

Normal everyday conflicts that are faced squarely, discussed frankly, and resolved promptly are like minor earthquakes. Geologists and seismologists tell us that little 3.0 earthquakes serve a valuable function, relieving pressure and stress along fault lines in the earth. There are places in California where the land along fault lines is actually bulging upward with unrelieved pressure. When there are no small quakes for long periods of time to reduce the pressure, scientists get nervous. That is why they are predicting that the Big One—an 8.0 or higher on the Richter scale—is just waiting to happen.

Marriages are like that. Some people—and in some marriages, both people—have never learned to express their needs or to negotiate their expectations. They go along with their spouses, never disagreeing, rebelling, or engaging in open conflict, but they are profoundly unhappy in the relationship. Pressures are building. There are no little 3.0 conflicts in the relationship, and everything looks oh-so-civilized and oh-so-serene; but the Big One is coming! An 8.0 catastrophe is on the horizon for such couples—and neither partner realizes it.

These buried-beneath-the-surface conflicts and hidden pressures are often picked up and absorbed by the children in the family. Sometimes, even though the parents never fight, the children end up doing the fighting for them. In one case I saw, a young teenage boy was continually fighting with his mother, screaming at her and insulting her in the most vile terms imaginable. The boy was brought in for counseling because the parents considered his behavior a problem that was out of their control. They both said that their relationship was very close and conflict free.

After talking to the boy, a very different picture emerged. He was not the source of the family's problem—he was simply acting out the hidden conflict that the parents refused to acknowledge. The mother was an extremely demanding woman, and the father was very passive and always buckled to his wife's demands. The son, who couldn't stand to see his father treated like a doormat, responded by jumping into the situation and attacking his mother. The father never moved to stop him. He let his son fight his battles for him.

In order for conflicts to be managed in a healthy way so that both marriage partners and the children can grow through conflict instead of being crushed by it, we must look at conflict for what it is: a dynamic force for change in the relationship. Conflict can hurt us or help us, depending entirely on how we respond to it. The goal of healthy conflict management is to devise solutions that enable both sides to win.

THE GOAL OF CONFLICT: BOTH SIDES WIN

In *The Seven Habits of Highly Effective People,* author Stephen Covey gives six patterns that people commonly adopt in responding to conflict (and which I have adapted below).* Four of these patterns are unhealthy and destructive to people and relationships; the fifth and sixth patterns are healthy and cooperative. They produce better solutions, happier people, and stronger relationships.

Win/Lose. An unhealthy approach. The prevailing attitude is: "I intend to win, and I intend to make you lose. I get my way; you get nothing." This is a competitive approach and in some situations, authoritarian as well: "What I say, goes." The Win/Lose approach does not respect the feelings and needs of others, and it closes down intimacy. To keep intimacy working in a marriage, through the stress of conflict, you need an approach to conflict that places a premium on cooperation, not competition.

Lose/Win. Another unhealthy approach. This might also be called the "Doormat Approach" to conflict. There's no competition, but there's no cooperation either. The attitude: "Go ahead, have your way. I'm a loser. I'll do anything and sacrifice anything just to keep the peace." People who use the Lose/Win approach are the pleasers and appeasers who bury their feelings and deny their own needs.

Lose/Lose. This is the vindictive approach and is also unhealthy. When two Win/Lose competitors go head-to-head and one of them loses, the loser adopts the Lose/Lose position: "OK, I lost—but I'm going to see to it that you lose, too." This person's focus is no longer on winning but on doing whatever it takes to even the score.

Win. This unhealthy approach is subtly different from Win/Lose. The Win/Lose person is competitive and seeks to come out on top at the

Stephen R. Covey, *The Seven Habits of Highly Effective People* (New York: Simon & Schuster, 1989), pp. 204-234.

other person's expense. But the person with the Win approach doesn't necessarily want the other person to lose. The Win person is not competitive, just selfish. He/she says, "All I care about is that I get what I want. I'll secure my own needs. It's up to you to secure your own."

Win/Win or No Deal. This approach, while not fully satisfying, is often the best compromise possible in a situation of conflict. The Win/Win or No Deal option says, "If we can't come up with a solution we both agree on, we can at least agree to disagree agreeably. Maybe we can get together on this issue some other time, but for now—no deal, and that's OK." With this approach in mind, we don't feel a need to manipulate, coax, or cajole our way to an agreement. We recognize that if we insist on getting our own way, it will make the other person feel bad about it, and ultimately it will erode the relationship. "No Deal" is better than a bad deal.

Win/Win. This is the goal of all good, smart negotiators. This is the goal of Christian relationships. This is the goal of Christian marriage. We continually seek our spouse's benefit while avoiding the doormat role. There will be times when consensus is not possible, but if Win/Win is always our goal, we can frequently come up with creative solutions that make everybody a winner. In the long run, everyone maintains his or her dignity and integrity while discussing the issue.

COMMON CONFLICT STRATEGIES

Most people adopt certain strategies when they are in the midst of conflict. Like the father who allowed his son do his fighting for him, people fall back on a position that has become, if not comfortable, at least familiar.

- *Accommodation.* One partner instantly yields to the other's desires or demands.

- *Avoidance.* One or both partners respond to conflict by withdrawing or avoiding the other.

- *Smoothing.* One partner tries to conciliate and "make nice." This could be done by backing down or by patronizing the other person.

- *Forcing.* A very unhealthy posture that works against intimacy, this strategy uses intimidation and threats in order to win.

- *Persuasion.* One partner tries to convince the other to change his or her position. Persuasion usually involves both partners' adopting postures of equality, both being willing to listen and reconsider their views.

- *Bargaining.* This posture can be a healthy way of reaching agreement. It involves exchanging concessions until both sides are satisfied with the agreement.

Bargaining and persuasion are healthy Win/Win postures to adopt in dealing with conflict. Accommodation, avoidance, smoothing, and forcing discount the legitimate feelings and desires of either oneself or one's spouse.

Healthy couples know how to disagree without being disagreeable. They continually think "Win/Win." They understand that conflict can serve a positive role in a healthy marriage. The purpose of conflict is not to establish a winner but to create understanding between the partners regarding issues and emotions. When couples focus on listening to each other, understanding each other, and managing and resolving their conflicts instead of winning arguments, they create a strong foundation for healthy, satisfying marital intimacy.

ANGER, THE EMOTION OF CONFLICT

Conflict always comes packaged with anger. Anger is a difficult emotion for most of us to deal with, but we can learn about how it works and how we can manage and work with it. Here are some essential facts to remember about anger:

Anger Is a Feeling, Not a Behavior.

It's not wrong to feel angry. Emotions are universal and unavoidable. You can't help it that a certain circumstance provokes you to feel angry—but you *can* control your behavior. That's why Ephesians 4:26 tells us, "In your anger do not sin." God knows it is normal for human beings to experience feelings of anger, but we are responsible not to respond to those feelings with sinful, destructive behavior.

Anger Is Usually a Secondary Emotion, a Response to a Primary Emotion.

For example, I get embarrassed; then I get angry. Or I feel powerless; then I get angry. We commonly experience anger in response to such conditions as a major loss, grief, danger (feeling threatened by competition at work or by crime or by financial reversal), and frustration (such as not being able to achieve life goals or not being able to have expectations met in a relationship). The normal anger that these experiences provoke in us can be magnified many times over when we are already experiencing negative feelings such as helplessness, hopelessness, guilt, regret, or worry. Deeper, overriding issues feed our anger. Some of these core issues: *I am not accepted and loved. I am not in control of my life. I am not respected. I am not competent.*

When a negative experience happens to tap one of these core issues, the message that goes to the brain (completely distorted and magnified out of proportion) is: "You have been massively disrespected" or "You have been seriously threatened" or "You will be abandoned." When this is the message we receive, our anger can become massively supercharged, detonating like a bomb!

We have a choice as to how we will behave after we become angry. It is not easy to make the right choice during the anger because anger triggers emotional and physiological activations such as increased levels of adrenaline. Our ability to think rationally and choose righteously is clouded by feelings of anger. Some people have a serious deficiency in their ability to control their behavior when angry; for them and the people around them, anger can be a very dangerous feeling.

Some people respond poorly to anger because of poor role models from their family of origin. Perhaps one or both parents were "rageaholics," anger addicts who continually expressed anger with threats or violent behavior. If that was your model all through your childhood, then that is going to be the style you tend to adopt in your own relationships—until you get help for your anger through counseling or an anger-management support group.

The issue of anger management and behavior control is critical to conflict management in relationships. If I can be angry and maintain control and if the other person can do the same, then we can both resolve our issues in relative safety. Anger can be expressed—that is, verbalized—and we know we're going to be OK when it's over. When we don't trust ourselves or the other person to maintain control through the conflict, we do not feel safe, and the resolution of the conflict is thrown into doubt.

Anger That Is Intense, Extreme, and out of Control Is Called Rage.

A person in the grip of rage is not only scary but also potentially violent and dangerous. Anger that settles in for the long term is called bitterness; bitterness is displayed in the form of grudges, malice, and revenge. Both rage and bitterness are sinful and destructive responses to anger.

Ephesians 4:31 warns us, "Get rid of all bitterness, rage and anger, brawling and slander, along with every form of malice." And Hebrews 12:15 describes bitterness as a "root" that causes long-term trouble and defiles people from within. Anger that is not quickly resolved but is allowed to fester and settle in the soul becomes a poison that damages us, the marriage relationship, and the lives of the children who grow up under our care. There is nothing sinful or harmful about experiencing temporary feelings of anger, which we manage and deal with quickly and honestly. But there is something very sinful and very harmful about inviting anger to take root in our souls and poison us from within.

Anger Is Often Triggered by Hidden Issues and Symbols That Hide from Our Conscious Awareness.

We can sometimes identify these issues and symbols by monitoring our anger and looking for patterns. For example, we may observe, "I tend to get angry with this person, in these situations, and these are the factors that lead up to it."

You may find, for example, that you fly off the handle if someone happens to make even a totally harmless comment about what you eat or what you wear. After some reflection, you realize that you are very sensitive about the issue of weight and eating, not because you are tremendously overweight, but because one of your parents was, and as a child, you felt shamed by that. Now, having identified that issue, you know to head off those kinds of discussions—and if a comment happens to arise and you begin to feel angry, you now know the source of that anger, and you can put it in its proper perspective. As a result, you learn to respond appropriately even when your feelings are totally inappropriate. The best way to manage anger is to head it off before it gets out of control.

Unfortunately, many people, in a misguided attempt to relieve their anger and tension, turn to a third party for help. This third party might be a person (a child, an in-law, or a lover outside the marriage), but it is sometimes a hobby or a job. Human or not, this third party offers a temporary sense of relief from anger and tension because the focus is now on the third party instead of on the conflict between the husband and wife.

Bringing in a third party, however, can cause damage to the child, the illicit lover, or other person chosen to ease the tension. This person is being used, perhaps even abused, as a substitute for anger resolution. His or her needs and personhood are not being respected. It can be especially harmful to place a child in this role since that child is likely to find himself or herself in the middle of the conflict, which is an emotionally scarring experience.

The marriage relationship is also damaged when a third party is used in this way, because the conflict never gets resolved. Issues and anger don't just go away. They must be dealt with or they will reappear—usually with greater force—somewhere down the road.

RULES FOR FIGHTING FAIR

Fights happen. But fights don't have to be verbal slugfests from which both sides come out emotionally bruised and bloodied. Some years ago, counselor John Bradshaw devised a ten-point list of principles for "fighting fair" in marriage. These are rules for clear and productive communication. If a couple will agree to these rules in advance, then commit to sticking to them when tempers begin to flare, they will find their conflicts to be much more manageable and easier to untangle than before.

Rule No. 1: Be assertive, not aggressive. Instead of blowing off your anger, verbalize it. State the fact that you are angry in a way that respects your spouse's dignity, feelings, and personhood. (For a more complete discussion of assertive versus aggressive anger, see chapter 10.)

Rule No. 2: Stay in the "now." Resist the temptation to dredge up old wounds or to focus on what might or might not happen in the future. Focus on what is.

Rule No. 3: Avoid lecturing. Give specific, concrete examples. Many people, when they fight, get bogged down in generalities: "You're always so selfish." Generalities make the other person feel personally criticized and attacked, while giving him or her little specific guidance to work with. Instead, be pinpoint specific: "I felt hurt today when you left me out of the conversation. I wish you would remember to include me when we're visiting with your family." When you deal in specifics, the other person is more likely to feel you are asking for a change in behavior rather than condemning his or her personality.

Rule No. 4: Avoid judgment. State your needs, your expectations, and your requests, but avoid condemning the other person.

Rule No. 5: Be rigorously honest. Honesty is not only right, it's smart. Your spouse can see right through you, so why hide? Use times of conflict as opportunities for honest self-revelation, because honesty leads to intimacy.

Rule No. 6: Don't argue details. Many couples could get to agreement much more quickly if they stayed in the realm of broad principles (especially the principle of loving one another) and agree to let go of the niggling little details.

Rule No. 7: Don't assign blame. When you assign blame, you are thinking Win/Lose, not Win/Win. You love your spouse. Why would you want your spouse to be a "loser"?

Rule No. 8: Use active listening. Repeat what you hear the other person say. Don't just parrot back the same words—restate your partner's meaning in your own words to see if you are grasping the full import of his or her message. If you aren't hearing it correctly, patiently listen for a reexplanation. Active, engaged listening is one of the most beautiful gifts you can give your spouse.

Rule No. 9: Fight about one thing at a time. Nothing is more confusing, frustrating, or self-defeating than an argument that whizzes from subject to subject like Ping-Pong balls. Stay focused. Resolve one issue before proceeding to the next.

Rule No. 10: Unless you are abused, hang in there. You may recall that in chapter 7, I advised you to give your partner "space" if he or she withdraws. Now I'm telling you to "hang in there." Isn't this a contradiction? No. Withdrawal is never a good strategy for resolving conflict, but if that's the way your spouse chooses to deal with conflict, then don't pursue—just get on with your life and give your spouse time to sort things out. Romans 12:18 says, "If it is possible, as far as it depends on you, live at peace with everyone." This verse acknowledges the fact that peace is a two-way street—and sometimes there's a roadblock in the other lane. It takes two to resolve a conflict. As long as your lane is open and clear, your conscience should be clear as well.

If at all possible, however, both partners would do well to make a rule (call it a covenant) not to withdraw but to lovingly hang in there until resolution can be reached. If resolution can't be achieved, then either treat it as a "No Deal" situation or agree to talk about it later after you've both had time to calm down and reflect.

I would hasten to add that "hang in there" does not necessarily mean "resolve it right now." Sometimes, one partner needs a little more time to gather his or her thoughts and reflect on the problem. That's OK; the other side should grant him or her that time without framing it as withdrawal. It's just a time-out.

I once counseled a couple in which the man always insisted on immediate resolution of all disagreements. He couldn't stand to let any problem, no matter how small, go unresolved for as long as a few minutes. "Let's talk this thing out," was his standard line—and that line drove his wife up the wall! He would push her for resolution, and she would back off—not a full-scale withdrawal—just seeking a few minutes to collect her thoughts. But her miniretreat would cause him to make a major push for resolution. She would pull back further; he would advance like General Sherman marching through Georgia. Finally, feeling backed into a corner, she would withdraw—fully, finally, and with a door slammed in her husband's face! At that point, he'd feel vindicated: "You see? She just wants to run away from the problem!"

This couple would have ended up in divorce court if the husband hadn't finally agreed to test-drive a new approach to conflict. He agreed to abide by the rule that he would always give his wife up to half an hour to collect her thoughts. She agreed that half an hour would be more than enough time to get her thoughts together. When he began to "take five" during conflicts and give his wife some breathing room, they started to deal much more constructively with their conflicts. He learned that he could "hang in there" without pushing his wife into a corner.

Important note: If the argument escalates to actual violence or abuse, then withdraw—pronto! Get out of the situation. Get your children out of the situation. Don't hesitate, don't stop to pack your bags, just leave! Contact a pastor, a trusted relative, a friend from church, a shelter for abuse victims, the county mental health agency, or the police. There is help available just a phone call away. If nothing else is available, dial 911 or the emergency number is your area. But never, ever submit yourself or your children to your spouse's physical violence or sexual abuse.

How do you know whether you are being abused? You are being abused by your spouse if any one of these conditions describes your situation:

- You feel that your spouse's anger is out of control, and you fear for your life or your safety.

- Your spouse has inflicted physical pain or injury on you.

- Your spouse has threatened to kill you or injure you.

- Your spouse has attempted to kill you or injure you.

- Your spouse has wielded a weapon against you.

- Your spouse has locked you in a room, degraded your body in any way, or has attempted or threatened to do any of these things.

- Your spouse has forced you to do something you didn't want to do or that made you feel humiliated, ashamed, or degraded.

- You have had to call the police to settle a domestic dispute.

> ### POINTS TO REMEMBER ABOUT CONFLICT

With insight and understanding, we can make conflict work *for* the marriage instead of against it. Here are some insights that many couples have found helpful.

Conflict Is Painful, but Some Pain Is Good.

Disagreement is unpleasant. Arguments make our stomachs hurt. But not all pain is destructive pain. Like the pain of surgery or dentistry or strenuous exercise, some things that hurt are good for us. Conflict brings pain, but it can also bring about meaningful dialogue and exchange of feelings and ideas. When conflict is viewed as an opportunity for creating deeper understanding, it becomes a tool for intimacy instead of a weapon of division.

Conflict Is Risky, but with Risk Comes Growth.

Anger can get out of hand—which is why so many people avoid conflict at all cost! But the most important aspects of life are the most risky. If we dare to manage our conflicts with understanding and love, those conflicts can actually lead us deeper into our most important relationships.

Conflict Doesn't Always Lead to Consensus.

For example, my wife, Marcy, and I disagree on several issues, and we know that we will never agree on them. Fortunately, these are not disagreements over basic values; they are in the realm of secondary issues such as: At what age should a child be allowed to see a PG-13 movie? Every once in a while, we drag out one of these issues, hash it out for a while until we remember that this is an issue we will never agree on—then we put it back on the shelf until next time.

You might think, *Well, isn't that just avoiding conflict?* No, because we do not avoid conflict per se—only a few specific conflicts over relatively minor issues. As a general rule, we work to resolve all our conflicts constructively and honestly. If there were a major issue in our marriage that we just could not resolve between us, we would obtain help from a counselor so that we could lay the issue to rest. In those few secondary areas where we just happen to see things differently, we have made a decision to accept our differences, to set the issue aside, and to get on with the business of living together and loving each other.

Conflicts Are Made Up of Gradations.

It's important to recognize low-level disagreements and petty annoyances for what they are. Some people seem to have only an ON/OFF switch when it comes to conflict—no channel selector, no volume control. For them, irritation over panty hose hanging in the bathroom rates the same level of anger and conflict as inviting a ne'er-do-well brother-in-law to come stay as long as he wants when he gets out of prison. It's important to recognize that there are levels of conflict and to develop a capacity for disagreeing without going ballistic on every issue.

In Any Conflict, There Is Usually As Much (or More) Going On beneath the Surface As There Is above the Surface.

What you think you are arguing about is usually not what you are really arguing about. There are often deep symbolic issues lurking in the shadows. You may think you are arguing about the socks on the floor or the missed appointment or the offensive remark, but in most cases you are really struggling over such questions as, Am I loved? Am I respected? Will I be abandoned? Am I being controlled? Am I being emotionally smothered?

Many of the arguments we have today are simply extensions and resurfacings of conflicts we had with our spouse over the past years—or even conflicts that go back all the way to childhood. It is always helpful, when conflict arises, to step back emotionally from the situation and ask ourselves, "What am I really angry about? What is my partner really angry about? How can we both get our real wants and needs met so that this cycle of conflict can be broken?"

Many of the Conflicts We Experience Are due to Inadequate Boundaries and Insufficient Emotional Distance between Both Partners.

It is more difficult for couples to see issues clearly and resolve them when the partners are in the "Stuck" stage of marriage. Issues and symbols are jumbled and confused. Both partners are simultaneously hostile and dependent. They can't live with each other, and they can't live without each other; so they fight constantly about everything. Each fight is like World War XXVIII, and each making-up is as intensely passionate as a scene from a steamy romance novel.

A certain amount of emotional distance is useful in resolving conflict. Only when a couple is able to move from the Stuck to the Unstuck stage can both partners see each other and their issues clearly enough to find resolution. (For insight on how to move from Stuck to Unstuck in your marriage relationship, see chapter 12.)

In Times of Conflict, Seek Practical Solutions; Avoid Taking Emotional Stands.

Some people approach marriage as if it were the Alamo: "I'd rather die than surrender!" Such an approach dooms the relationship to an unending cycle of conflict—and quite possibly divorce. There are many simple, practical steps couples can take to reduce the level of conflict in a marriage without sacrificing core beliefs and selfhood.

Anticipate danger. You shouldn't have to walk on eggshells around your spouse—both partners have a right to feel safe in the relationship. However, you both know that there are certain issues, behaviors, and remarks that tend to produce conflict, so why venture unnecessarily into those areas? Avoid provoking each other needlessly. Watch for warning signs that conflict and tension may be building, and take action to defuse them.

Move in promptly. When you see the early warning signs of conflict, act immediately to intercept the situation before it grows into all-out war. If appropriate, apologize. And remember, you don't have to be "in the wrong" to apologize. You can say, "I didn't mean any harm, but I know you were hurt by what I did or said; so I want you to know I'm sorry. I never meant to hurt you."

Look for alternatives. In Genesis 13:1-12, Abram and his nephew Lot had a disagreement over some real estate, so they worked out an agreement whereby they divided the land between them. They avoided an argument by finding a creative alternative. In our marriages, that should be our goal as well. So many of the conflicts that couples bring into the counseling room are over issues about which no one is willing to give an inch or be creative. Just a little bit of flexibility and a willingness to think and act in new ways is often all it takes to turn a knock-down-drag-out marital war into a peace treaty or at least a truce.

Be willing to give up the lesser in order to gain the greater. Couples seem to spend most of their fighting energy over lesser things: purchases and possessions, offhand remarks, curfews and which TV shows the children should be allowed to watch, household chores, who's to blame for making the family late to church. Very few of the conflicts couples bring into my office are of the life-altering variety.

What are the greater, more important issues in a marriage? Trust. Love. Mutual support. Feelings. Needs. Intimacy. If we could learn to give a little on the lesser things, we could focus more emotional energy on the greater things. We could live happier lives. We could have stronger marriages.

As we focus our energy on the marriage relationship and on all it takes to make intimacy work, all the side issues, irritations, and disagreements will lose their power to hurt us. Conflict is inevitable, but conflict doesn't have to drive a wedge into the relationship. Properly managed, conflict can actually become an opportunity for two people to bond more closely and intimately than ever. Our goal is a workable and doable goal: to continually find ways to turn conflict into understanding.

How Can We Disagree
without Tearing Each Other Apart?

1. What is your usual response to conflict? Check the
   appropriate statements here, or write them in your journals.

	WIFE'S RESPONSE	HUSBAND'S RESPONSE
I avoid conflict at all costs.	_____	_____
I think a little conflict is healthy in a relationship.	_____	_____
What conflict?	_____	_____
I believe in getting things out in the open and talking them through to resolution.	_____	_____
When disagreements arise, I need a little time to settle down and collect my thoughts.	_____	_____
I thrive on conflict.	_____	_____
Other _____	_____	_____

2. How do you and your spouse usually deal with conflict?

	WIFE'S RESPONSE	HUSBAND'S RESPONSE
Declaration of war and all-out hostilities.	_____	_____
We both try the best we can, but conflict is still very difficult for us to resolve.	_____	_____
I try, but my spouse doesn't seem to care about how I feel.	_____	_____
We do a pretty decent job of managing conflict and caring for each other's feelings.	_____	_____
We bury feelings and deny issues.	_____	_____
We never have conflict.	_____	_____
Other _____	_____	_____

3. **Talk together about your most painful episode of conflict during the past week or two.**

   Why was it so painful?

   What was the surface issue that you argued about?

   Now that you think about it, was there a deeper issue involved on your side? What was it?

   Do you think there was a deeper issue on your spouse's side? What do you think it was?

   How could that episode have been handled better by your spouse?

   How could you have better managed your own behavior?

   Suggest some covenants between you and your spouse that could help keep conflict from getting out of hand.

4. **Which of the six approaches to conflict, identified by Stephen R. Covey, is your usual approach?**

	WIFE'S RESPONSE	HUSBAND'S RESPONSE
Win/Lose. "I win, you lose."	_____	_____
Lose/Win. "I'm a doormat."	_____	_____
Lose/Lose. "OK, I lost—but I'll get even."	_____	_____
Win. "I'll get what I need. It's up to you to get yours."	_____	_____
Win/Win or No Deal. "Let's agree to disagree agreeably."	_____	_____
Win/Win. "Let's find a solution so that we both win."	_____	_____

   What positive steps would you be willing to take to become more of a "Win/Win" negotiator when conflicts arise?

5. **What is your biggest problem in dealing with your own feelings of anger?**

   What is your biggest problem in dealing with your spouse's anger?

What steps can the two of you can take to enable you both to better manage anger in your times of conflict?

You may want to covenant together to observe Bradshaw's "rules for fighting fair," below. Consider making a written covenant between you to help cement the agreement.

Rule No. 1: Be assertive, not aggressive.
Rule No. 2: Stay in the "now."
Rule No. 3: Avoid lecturing.
Rule No. 4: Avoid judgment.
Rule No. 5: Be rigorously honest.
Rule No. 6: Don't argue details.
Rule No. 7: Don't assign blame.
Rule No. 8: Use active listening.
Rule No. 9: Fight about one thing at a time.
Rule No. 10: Unless you are abused, hang in there.

Also, if either you or your spouse has a major problem with anger that is out of control, you should seriously consider obtaining counseling to enable you to better manage your anger.

10

What Is
Real Intimacy—
and How Can We
Develop It?

"I don't get it," says Alan. "I just don't get it! She keeps telling me she wants intimacy. I try to give her what she wants!"

"No, you don't," Jennie retorts. "You try to get me into the sack! You just want sex!"

"But that's what you want!" Alan responds, authentic astonishment in his voice.

"No! I don't want sex!" Jennie fires back, her voice a plea to be heard and understood. "I mean, I want sex *sometimes,* but when I want *intimacy,* I don't want sex!"

"It's the same thing!" says Alan, spreading his hands.

"It's not the same thing!" Jennie wails, shaking her fists.

Alan's face looks stricken. He hesitates, then ventures, "So . . . like, are you telling me you want more foreplay, or what?"

Jennie slumps in her chair, and her eyes roll heavenward, an eloquent "Why me?" expression etched on her face. She moans softly, and the words sound vaguely like, "Clueless . . . totally clueless!"

Alan's confusion is understandable. In our culture, we sometimes use the word *intimacy* as a synonym for *sex.* But as we use the word *intimacy* in this book, it refers to a dimension of the marriage relationship that is much deeper and more fundamental to marriage than sex. In its truest sense, intimacy is the emotional/intellectual component of the relationship.

Intimacy is the intersection at which two human souls connect. Intimacy is the fulfillment of the words of Genesis 2:24: "For this reason a man will leave his father and mother and be united to his wife, and they will become one flesh." While they become physically and symbolically "one flesh" in the act of sex, a husband and wife become experientially "one flesh" throughout their lives as they grow in genuine intimacy with each other. Intimacy has many facets, including:

- emotional intimacy (the level of deep feelings)
- intellectual intimacy (the sharing of ideas)
- aesthetic intimacy (the sharing of experiences of beauty and pleasure)
- creative intimacy (the sharing of creativity, imagination, and enterprise)
- spiritual intimacy (the sharing of spiritual meaning and nurture)

A couple must learn to nurture a sense of togetherness in each of these areas. We come to this intimacy through a process, and it doesn't happen by itself or without complications.

SAFETY + HONESTY = INTIMACY

Until we feel safe and are able to be honest with our spouse, intimacy won't develop as we would like it to. Some of the most common barriers to intimacy are represented by the following statements:

- What will he/she think of me if I reveal this part of myself?
- Will he/she accept me or reject me?
- Is it safe for me to reveal who I really am?

Creating Safety in a Relationship

Safety is created by promises that are made and kept (see chapter 3). Ideally, our sense of safety and security begins in childhood. We develop our sense of self in a safe environment created by parents who make and keep promises. Our sense of self continues to unfold with our marriage partner, who (again, ideally) is also expected to make and keep promises. If we have difficulty experiencing intimacy in marriage, it may be due to a lack of safety and security, because either a parent or our marriage partner (or both) has broken important promises in a significant way.

Making Honesty Your Policy

When two people feel safe and secure in a relationship, they are free to be honest and open with one another. If you feel you cannot share your true self—your real thoughts and feelings—then true intimacy is not possible. Another person cannot know you intimately unless you are willing to pry the lid off the deep recesses of your life and reveal who you really are.

To be honest with another person, you must first be honest with yourself. You must know yourself—and that's not as easy as it sounds. Most of us, to some degree, are distanced from our emotions. We are in denial about some of our bad habits and traits. We have blocked out painful memories. We reject the knowledge of some of our worst sins and try to pretend we have no dark side.

As we become more honest with ourselves (and such honesty often requires involvement in counseling, accountability groups, recovery groups, or support groups), we become more capable of sharing our true selves with our marriage partner. Over time, we move through ever deepening levels of knowing one another.

THE INTIMACY GAP

Tom considers himself a "sensitive '90s guy." He shares with Nicole about his ambitions in life, his frustrations, and his past. He confided to her that embarrassing incident with his first girlfriend, Ellie What's-

Her-Name. He never lets a day go by without telling Nicole that he loves her. Whenever Nicole has something to tell him, he hangs on every word. He figures he's operating at about a 100 percent intimacy level. How much more intimacy could she want?

But that's not the way Nicole sees it. She's hurt. She wonders what's wrong with their relationship and why Tom always holds back. Why isn't he more honest and open with his feelings? Why doesn't he tell her how he really feels about her? Why doesn't he open up with her about his past as she has done about hers? Why doesn't he ever talk about the things that make him happy, the things that make him cry, the dreams he has of their life together? Maybe he doesn't have any dreams! Maybe he doesn't love her anymore! Otherwise, why would he stop at 40 percent instead of giving her 100 percent of his thoughts, his emotions, his story?

There's a big disparity here. Tom's 100 percent equals Nicole's 40 percent. He frames himself as wide-open, honest, sensitive, maxed out in the intimacy department, nothing left to say. Nicole, however, frames him as closed, hiding something, insensitive, guarded, and possibly losing his love for her! Poor Tom—he's not hiding anything; he's just clueless! He simply can't imagine a deeper level of sharing than what he's already doing. There's a big gap between Tom's perception and Nicole's, as you can see in the chart below. I call it "the intimacy gap."

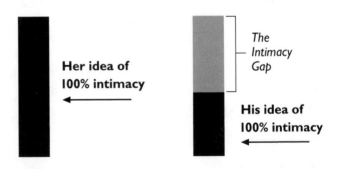

Her idea of 100% intimacy

The Intimacy Gap

His idea of 100% intimacy

Men and women tend to be very different in their need for intimacy. They have different definitions of what it means to be together. They differ on what constitutes a satisfying, intimate relationship. They differ in the intensity of intimacy they require. A woman tends to expect a very deep level of feeling, emotional vulnerability, sharing of experience, and disclosure. Many men consider themselves to be sharing at a deep level if they are talking about sports or politics!

So while Nicole sees Tom as holding back, he says, "Huh? Me? I'm an open book!" There's a level of intimacy that's completely off his graph and outside his scope—and it's right there in the intimacy gap.

OTHER FACTORS THAT AFFECT INTIMACY

Our attitudes and postures toward each other also play an important part in our ability to share intimacy with one another. We must see our spouse as an equal in order to be intimate. We are not inclined to open up and become intimate with those we feel are beneath us in the relationship. Nor are we inclined to be intimate if we, ourselves, feel inferior. So self-esteem—both our own and our spouse's—plays a large part in intimacy.

If you sense a major inequality in postures and self-esteem levels in your marriage, consider the following steps to bring the relationship into balance so that intimacy can more easily take place:

If you feel superior to your spouse, work on readjusting your attitude. Remember that 1 Corinthians 13:4 says that authentic love "does not envy, it does not boast, it is not proud." Ask yourself why you feel superior to your spouse. Why do you feel your accomplishments in the world outweigh his or hers? Have you recognized the supportive role your spouse has played in enabling you to achieve those accomplishments? Did your spouse help you get through school? Did he or she encourage and motivate you through the tough times?

Is it really correct to say that success in the business world or a ministry is worth more than managing the household or having a less prestigious job? Is it Christlike and biblical to view some people as worth more than others because of outward status? Is that the way Christ viewed and treated people? Once you honestly view yourself and your partner in light of these questions, it becomes much more difficult to think of yourself as superior to anyone else, especially your spouse.

Affirm your partner's self-esteem and sense of self-worth. I'm not advocating empty or patronizing praise. Instead, look for one thing your spouse does or one quality he or she has that you can genuinely affirm. Focus on character and accomplishments rather than physical appearance when you affirm your spouse. Also, reassure him or her that your love is unfailing and unconditional. Build your spouse's sense of security and worth by being supportive and loving even when he or she fails or makes a mistake. As you intentionally look for ways to affirm your partner's self-worth, you will see your own attitude toward your partner change. He or she will rise in your esteem as well as in his or her own esteem.

Include your spouse in your own accomplishments. Make statements such as "I couldn't do it without you" or "It wouldn't mean anything without you here to share it with." Be sure to make these statements in the presence of other people sometimes.

If you suffer from broken self-esteem, take positive steps to rebuild it. People with low self-esteem feel alienated, isolated, and unworthy to experience a relationship with another person; these feelings form major barriers to intimacy. Get into counseling to uncover and heal the emotional sources of your low sense of self-worth. (Because the majority of a person's adult personality is formed by age six, childhood experiences and emotional wounds tend to play a large part in low self-esteem; in counseling, these issues can be resolved and healed.) Recognize that you are created in God's image, and though you are (like all human beings) fallen and prone to sin, you have enormous value to God.

Additional self-esteem boosters. Practice accepting praise from others without discounting it or rejecting it with some self-deprecating remark. Avoid putting yourself down; forgive yourself for mistakes. Practice thinking positively; instead of saying, "I can't" or "I have to," say, "I can" and "I will."

No one should be "up" or "down" in the relationship; practice meeting each other in the middle. As you and your spouse see your relationship and your attitudes coming into balance, you will almost certainly experience a growth in intimacy and togetherness.

Dealing with Anger—and the Fear That Results

Marriage must be a place where all of our feelings, including anger, can be safely expressed. But anger should be expressed in a way that respects the feelings of the other person.

There is a difference between *aggressive* anger and *assertive* anger. Aggressive anger includes ranting, screaming, throwing things, putting your fist through the wall, and committing other acts of physical violence. These kinds of expression generate fear and shut down intimacy—fast.

Assertive anger involves verbalizing your feelings in a way that is meant to communicate, not intimidate. Assertive anger says, "When you do such and such, I feel angry." Assertive anger owns the emotion rather than blaming the emotion on someone else; it says, "This is what I feel," not "You make me feel this way."

If there is anger to be expressed, that anger should be listened to and understood. Allow your spouse to express those feelings, and decide whether or not you are in any way responsible for them. If you are not responsible for his or her anger, you can still listen, hear, and understand. When you do that, intimacy is enhanced, not shut down.

Many of the problems between men and women are related to fear. Sometimes it is the woman's fear of aggressive anger in her husband. But much of the time the man is the one experiencing the fear; he panics in the face of his wife's anger. It is common for men to worry about keeping their wives happy, protecting their wives from getting angry, and feeling responsible (rightly or wrongly) for their wives' emotional states. Men tend to shy away from their wives' emotional expression, especially their expression of anger. That is why so many men struggle to keep things upbeat, to stay away from problem areas in the relationship, and to "walk on eggshells" around their wives.

For some reason, few men think to ask themselves, *Why am I so afraid of her? Is it really my responsibility to keep her from getting mad? Shouldn't she be allowed to be angry if that's how she feels? Can I deal with her anger?* There are also questions of responsibility: *Maybe it really is my fault that she's angry. She may be angry because I've been a jerk—and if that's the case, then I need to take responsibility. I need to apologize and try to reconcile.*

Women are sometimes angry for reasons that have nothing to do with their husbands. Unfortunately, many men feel responsible anyway. They swing into action and try to fix their wives' emotions even though they had nothing to do with the problem and are unable to fix it. In fact, by trying to fix it, they only make things worse. Husbands—and wives—need to allow their partners to feel and express even those emotions that cause some discomfort at the time. When one person is angry, it is time for the other person to listen as attentively as possible. When we try to squelch the emotions of our spouse or simply "fix" him or her, we slap yet another barrier in the way of intimacy.

When both partners in the marriage learn to express anger in an assertive, respectful way rather than by means of naked aggression, the reasons to be fearful dissipate, and the marriage becomes a safe place. And when they learn to discuss why they are angry and *discern together* what can be done about it, the building of intimacy can continue.

Chronological Stages of Life

The dynamics of intimacy have a tendency to change over time, varying with the different chronological stages of life. During the courtship phase of the relationship, the drive for intimacy will be intense. The couple will want to be together constantly, unfolding and exploring each other's mysteries with an almost obsessive fascination. When they are newlyweds, the intense drive for intimacy increases steadily, then levels off and submerges as both partners become more comfortable and familiar with each other. Soon, distractions such as work schedules and, eventually, the arrival of children, begin to creep into the relationship.

In midlife, distractions accumulate. One or both partners become immersed in a career, the drive for success, church activities, community activities, or leisure activities that may exclude the other partner. It is easy for couples to let intimacy wither and die during this phase. The empty-nest stage of marriage can be the best time of a couple's married life, when they have more freedom to reconnect, to travel together, to do things as a couple instead of as a family, and to talk together without interruptions and distractions. Or it can be a time when two people face each other and the fact that they have been neglecting intimacy for decades. Intimacy is as important in the retirement years as it ever was, but by this time, many people have settled into familiar (but not always healthy and intimate) ways of relating.

There are many things two people can do together to build intimacy, to deepen the friendship of a lifetime; they don't have to simply rattle around in an empty old house together! It can be as simple as watching favorite old movies together or as exciting as taking a honeymoon vacation to Europe. Whatever they do, they should share their feelings and their thoughts with each other. No matter how many years two people have lived together, there are still mysteries to be explored and hidden facets of the soul to be revealed.

HOW TO BUILD THE INTIMACY IN YOUR MARRIAGE

What can you and your spouse do about the intimacy gap? about the fears and cover-ups that so easily thwart togetherness? Here are a few suggestions:

Create a zone of safety in the marriage. There are two continuums in the marriage relationship—you could call them "Intimacy Indicators"—and by rating your marriage on these indicators, you can get a very accurate sense of the level of intimacy in your marriage. The first of these indicators is The Safety Indicator. On a scale of 1 to 10, how do you feel around your partner?

1	2	3	4	5	6	7	8	9	10

Fearful and Anxious   Safe and Secure
(I walk on eggshells   (I can safely share any
and watch what I say.)   thought or feeling.)

The second of these indicators is The Honesty Indicator. On a scale of 1 to 10, do you feel that communication between you and your partner is characterized more by anger and defensiveness or honesty and openness?

1	2	3	4	5	6	7	8	9	10

Anger and Defensiveness   Honesty and Openness

If you and your spouse both rate your relationship on these two scales and you find a significant disparity between your respective ratings, that indicates a crucial difference between your perception and your spouse's perception. Often, the person who rates the marriage lower in these areas feels intimidated by the anger of the other partner. The person who rates the marriage significantly higher in these areas is often not clued in to the emotional needs and feelings of the other partner.

The level of intimacy in a marriage cannot rise above the level of anger or fear in the marriage. Anger generates fear, and fear shuts down intimacy. A marriage that rates only a 5 on these two scales rates only a 5 on the intimacy scale. We create a zone of safety in the marriage by

- managing anger and disagreement in a healthy, appropriate way,

- learning to accept and respect each other's feelings, and

- learning to accept each other's differences as a positive rather than a threatening force in the relationship.

Over the next few pages, we'll examine ways to make both partners feel safe to express and reveal themselves honestly in the marriage relationship.

Accept the natural gender differences between yourself and your partner—but also try to bridge those differences. Women filter people and experiences differently than men do; the fact that one partner in a marriage is female and the other is male is a massive, crucial factor in communication and intimacy. *As a rule* (meaning, there are exceptions), men tend to initiate sex, and women tend to initiate conversation. We don't want to erase the differences between men and women. But as we accept those differences, we should also make an effort to move toward each other and to create a more balanced, mutual, and reciprocal arrangement. Sometimes the wife should be sexually aggressive; sometimes the husband should take the initiative in sparking emotional and intellectual togetherness. If one side initiates all the time, the relationship is out of balance.

Recognize that being together means more than just "being together." Couples often spend time together without being truly engaged and open with one another. Two people can hold hands, look deeply into each other's eyes, and carry on a conversation that is completely meaningless. Yet some of the most mundane marital experiences can take on a sense of excitement, wonder, and depth of soul when approached in the right way.

For instance, if you are doing a remodeling project together, don't work in opposite ends of the house; work room by room together, and use the time that would otherwise be spent just slapping paint on the wall as an opportunity for conversation about thoughts, dreams, fears, feelings, and histories. Find creative ways to turn mundane chores—a long drive, a wait at the doctor's office, a shopping trip—into an opportunity to become better acquainted. When you go out to dinner or a movie, treat it as a date, and use the occasion as an opportunity to explore each other's mysteries, just as you did when you were courting.

Learn to accept each other's feelings. Intimacy has to do with sharing feelings—emotions such as fear, sadness, pain, regret, joy, and anger. When women express their feelings—particularly unpleasant feelings such as anger—their husbands tend to want to "fix the problem." Men are not, by nature, comfortable with their wives' emotions. Instead of allowing their wives to simply express and work through their emotions, most men try to turn off the spigot and solve the problem so that everyone can be OK again. This, unfortunately, closes the door on intimacy.

True intimacy requires that we allow each other to acknowledge our emotions and share them with each other. When men learn to be comfortable around their wives' emotions, intimacy is enhanced, husband and wife are drawn closer through understanding and being able to share themselves authentically and feel accepted. When you try to shut down another person's emotions, you are saying to that person, "I don't accept your feelings." At that point, intimacy grinds to a halt.

Learn about, and adjust to, the differences in your personalities and perceptions. A person who grew up loved and affirmed in a secure home filters people and experiences differently from a person who grew up abused in an insecure environment. A person who is open and optimistic by nature filters people and experiences differently from a person who is wary and negative. Couples are continually filtering each other throughout their life together.

I can illustrate this principle with an example from my own marriage. My wife, Marcy, and I once took the Meyers-Briggs Personality Inventory, and we discovered that we are opposites in virtually every personality indicator! One of the significant ways in which we are different is that I am an "E" (External Thinker) and Marcy is an "I" (Internal Thinker). An External Thinker does his or her thinking out loud, verbalizing half-baked ideas and letting them bounce around like Ping-Pong balls, watching them collide with other ideas, waiting to see which ones fly and which ones collapse on the ground. This is sometimes called "brainstorming" or "spitballing."

An Internal Thinker, by contrast, works through an idea silently, mentally testing it, working out all the angles and calculations and possibilities before ever verbalizing it. Only when the idea is very well-formed is the Internal Thinker ready to voice it.

Once an Internal Thinker voices an idea, he or she is frequently ready to go to the wall to defend it. After all, it has been carefully thought out and now has the force of a conviction. An External Thinker, however, frequently voices ideas or opinions without feeling any great allegiance to or ownership of them.

Being an External Thinker, I would often be discussing an issue with Marcy, and I'd make a statement, thinking, in effect, *Here's a possibility; let's run it up the flagpole and see if anyone salutes.* Well,

Marcy, being an Internal Thinker, would hear my nutty, off-the-wall, half-baked idea and think, *He's stating a core conviction—and it's the craziest doggone thing I ever heard of!* She would look aghast, an anguished look would come over her, and she would say, "Do you really believe what you're saying?" Meanwhile, the core conviction that she had just stated with such feeling and intensity was, I thought, just an opening gambit, a spitball, just like most of my ideas.

We were filtering each other's communication through the storehouse of our own experiences, our personality traits, and our gender. Until we began to understand each other's thinking styles, these differences often caused some very tangled communication patterns. If we are not aware of how these factors influence marriage communication, they can seriously distort our relationships and diminish our intimacy.

Teach yourself to be more aware of the filters that get in the way of your seeing things as they really are. Help one another clarify what you mean when you make a statement or react to a situation in a certain way. Be thoughtful about the interaction that can so easily thwart healthy communication.

Beware of the cycle of pursuit and withdrawal. This cycle is a common cause of the breakdown of marital intimacy. Usually, the wife is the one who pursues intimacy and togetherness, while the husband tends to withdraw from intimacy. Men often tend to withdraw because they have been conditioned by social expectations of the male role to be cool, nonemotional, and unexpressive.

A woman will pursue intimacy with her husband for a while, but eventually she tires of the chase. She can't get her husband to enter into her idea of intimacy and togetherness, so—frustrated and helpless—she finally gives up.

When intimacy fails, divorce results. It might be a legal divorce, with attorneys, a judge, and a written decree. Or it could be an emotional divorce—a hollow shell of a marriage in which two people live separate lives and direct their emotional energies away from the marriage relationship. The partners find alternatives to intimacy. He turns to work, hobbies, church activities, drinking, golf, or another woman. She turns to work, female friends, church activities, children, compulsive overeating, compulsive overspending, or another man.

Maintain a continual and vigilant emphasis on relationship building.
Intimacy is developed through confessions, explanations, and soul-searching. Couples must periodically ask themselves, "Where are we as a couple right now? Where have we been successful? When were we most successful at practicing intimacy, and what did we do right back then that we have since neglected? Where are we emotionally—Stuck, Unstuck, I-ness, or We-ness?" The marriage relationship must continually be diagnosed and its vital signs checked.

It's a good idea to set goals for intimacy and check your progress toward those goals on an annual basis—say the night before each anniversary. (Why the night before your anniversary? So you can spend your anniversary celebrating!) Sit down together and have a serious talk about the state of your relationship.

Reevaluate and readjust your goals for the marriage. Set plans for vacations, minihoneymoons, days out, evenings out, and sabbaths (rest days). Put your heads together to come up with ideas for spending quality time together. Think of favorite old places and brand-new places for togetherness getaways.

The soul of a relationship is intimacy—the sharing of your lives together. Make time for intimacy, and the reward will be a marriage that lasts a lifetime!

What Is Real Intimacy—
and How Can We Develop It?

1. Make a list of your "exits"—alternatives you use to avoid spending time with your spouse. Do you overeat, stay at work late, play golf, or even something as seemingly positive as spending a lot of time with your kids?

   You may have never thought of these activities as "exits." You may be thinking, "Sure, I do things like that—but not because I'm avoiding intimacy!" You may be right—or you may not be fully aware of all the reasons you do these things. Before you decide to skip this question, pray and ask God to search your heart and reveal any hidden resistance to intimacy that may lurk within you. Ask for insight and awareness to recognize any "exits" you may be using to avoid intimacy in your marriage.

2. Make a list of your spouse's "exits." Share your lists with each other. Place a check beside "exits" you want to eliminate. Place an X by those you feel will be difficult to eliminate. Pray together for wisdom and power to make constructive changes in the way you use your time in the marriage. Covenant to be accountable to each other and to check in with each other at least once a week as you close your "exits" and move closer together in your relationship.

3. Tonight, write a covenant statement: "During the coming year, we agree to work on (area of intimacy) in the following way:"

   _____

   Sign the statement and check in with each other on a weekly basis to see that you are making progress in this area of your marriage.

4. Evaluate the various facets of the intimacy dimension of your marriage on a scale from 1 to 10. Each partner should fill out this evaluation separately, perhaps by listing each area in your

journals and writing down the numbers that seem most accurate to you.

Afterward, compare your responses and discuss them, both the responses on which you agree and those on which you disagree. In areas where there is divergence of opinion, seek specific instances that led you and your spouse to respond as you did. As you discuss, try to lower your defenses and listen carefully, and try to see the relationship from your spouse's point of view.

(Most negative) 1 2 3 4 5 6 7 8 9 10 *(Most positive)*

Communication

1	2	3	4	5	6	7	8	9	10
The lines have been cut.							The lines are open.		

Listening

1	2	3	4	5	6	7	8	9	10
All right, I admit it. I'm a lousy listener.							I listen attentively to my spouse.		

Being Heard

1	2	3	4	5	6	7	8	9	10
My spouse is a lousy listener.							He/She is a terrific listener.		

Feelings

1	2	3	4	5	6	7	8	9	10
I don't accept or understand my spouse's feelings.							I welcome and understand my spouse's feelings.		

Affection

1	2	3	4	5	6	7	8	9	10
We never touch.							We're as cuddly as teddy bears.		

Sex—Frequency

1	2	3	4	5	6	7	8	9	10
What sex?							We can't keep our hands off each other.		

Sex—Satisfaction

1	2	3	4	5	6	7	8	9	10
I'd rather watch paint dry.							Pure ecstacy!!!		

Growth Together

1	2	3	4	5	6	7	8	9	10
Intimacy is stagnant.							We grow closer daily.		

Spiritual Togetherness (as my spouse and I relate to God)

1	2	3	4	5	6	7	8	9	10
We have nothing in common.							We worship/believe as one.		

My Goals

1	2	3	4	5	6	7	8	9	10
I feel my spouse doesn't understand what I want out of life.							My spouse is in perfect sync with me about my life goals.		

My Spouse's Goals

1	2	3	4	5	6	7	8	9	10
I don't understand what my partner wants out of life.							I fully understand my partner's life goals.		

Encouragement

1	2	3	4	5	6	7	8	9	10
I discourage my spouse.							I encourage my spouse.		

Time

1	2	3	4	5	6	7	8	9	10
I avoid my spouse.							I spend quality time with my spouse.		

Self-Esteem

1	2	3	4	5	6	7	8	9	10
I hate myself.							I like myself.		

Optimism/Pessimism

1	2	3	4	5	6	7	8	9	10
The glass is half empty.							The glass is half full.		

Responsibility for Feelings

1	2	3	4	5	6	7	8	9	10
It's my spouse's fault I feel the way I do.							I take personal responsibility for my own feelings.		

Fairness

1	2	3	4	5	6	7	8	9	10
One partner carries the whole load.							We share marriage responsibilities fairly.		

Conflict, Part 1

1	2	3	4	5	6	7	8	9	10
I fight to win. I have to be right.							I resolve conflict because I love my spouse.		

Conflict, Part 2

1	2	3	4	5	6	7	8	9	10
My spouse fights to win. He/she has to be right.							My spouse resolves conflict because he/she loves me.		

Crises: When problems, pain, or tragedy strikes, what happens to your marriage relationship?

1	2	3	4	5	6	7	8	9	10
We fall apart.							We pull together.		

Leisure

1	2	3	4	5	6	7	8	9	10
Separate vacations, please.							Leisure time with my spouse is an adventure!		

Fun

1	2	3	4	5	6	7	8	9	10
My marriage is as dull as dirt.							My marriage is more fun than human beings should be allowed to have.		

The higher the numbers you accumulate on this evaluation, the richer your experience of marital intimacy is likely to be.

Don't forget to examine closely—and openly—any significant disparities between your answers and your spouse's.

Place an *X* before any areas in which you and your spouse need to make constructive changes. Covenant together to make those changes and be accountable to each other on a regular basis to work for improvement.

Take time to study and discuss with your spouse the following Scripture passages:

1 Corinthians 7:3-4
Ephesians 5:21-33
Colossians 3:12-21

11

How
Important Should
Sex Be?

Franci closes her eyes and waits for it to be over.

Kyle feels her stiffen. Her skin is like ice to his touch—hard and cold. Like so many times before, he senses no desire in her. Only anxiety. No, more than anxiety. Fear. He tenses, all passion draining out of him.

"What's wrong?" he whispers into the darkness. The darkness makes no reply. "Franci? . . . Franci?" Kyle waits a long time, then he rolls away from her. He thinks he feels the trembling of her sobbing, transmitted through the bed, but he's not sure. Should he be angry? Hurt? Should he talk to her? Leave her alone? Go out to the couch and fall asleep in front of the TV?

And there is a larger question that gnaws at his insides: Can he stay married to a woman who doesn't even want him in her bed?

HOW IMPORTANT IS SEX?

Studies show that roughly one out of five married Americans has no sex life at all. Through their behavior (or lack of it), they are saying that sex is completely unimportant. Another 10 percent of Americans suffer from uncontrollable sexual urges—that is, sexual addictions. To them, sex overshadows everything else in their lives. For those who want to have a healthy marriage, the issue is striking the right balance and making an appropriate place for passion in their relationship.

The good news, according to a Family Research Council study released in 1994, is that 72 percent of those who see sex as belonging exclusively within marriage report a high degree of sexual satisfaction— a much higher degree, in fact, than those who admit engaging in promiscuous or extramarital sex. The act of sex is not the be-all and end-all of marriage, but it is important—and 72 percent of faithfully married, sexually active Americans will tell you it's well worth the effort!

Sex in the Bible

As described in the Bible, the act of sex is designed by God as a powerful, dynamic symbol of the sacred covenant-love relationship between a man and a woman. The physical act of sex demonstrates how God has planned to move us from isolation and aloneness into true, intimate connection with one another in the marriage relationship. In Genesis 2:18, God looks at man and says, "It is not good for the man to be alone," and then he creates a woman to be his companion and partner. This woman is paradoxically like man and unlike man; she is enough like him that they can share thoughts, feelings, and drives, yet it is her differences that make her alluring, attractive, and desirable to him—and vice versa. She complements him, completing what he lacks, and he does the same for her.

The sex act physically seals the covenant between the husband and wife, symbolizing the mutuality, intimacy, and exclusivity of their love. It bonds their committed relationship and demonstrates to them their need to live in dependence upon each other.

A Mutual Agreement

Both partners have to want sex. They don't have to want it at the same time or with equal intensity, but each, in his or her own way, must send the other the message, "I want you." In fact, wanting to be sexual, sensual, and affectionate may not always have a lot to do with intercourse. Men tend to be very "goal-oriented" in their lovemaking—with the goal, of course, being orgasm. Women have a lot to teach men about the other pleasurable and intimacy-building behaviors of sex—talking, holding, caressing, and exchanging nonverbal signals of affection.

When one partner initiates sexual signals, the other must respond appropriately. It must be clear who is asking for what. Many people—particularly women—don't want to have intercourse all the time but would like to be close, to be held and fondled. I've heard many women say in counseling, "I'd like to have him close, but every time I try to convey that to him, he takes it as an invitation to 'go all the way.' That's not what I was asking for."

In the early stages of a marriage, temporary problems with sex are common and usually involve inexperience, inhibitions, or communication problems. But for many couples, sexual problems are a symptom of deeper distortions in the relationship. If left unresolved, sexual problems tend to crystallize. The sexual dimension is a crucial dimension of a marriage. Properly understood, approached with love and practical insight, sex can be an important tool for building long-lasting intimacy, satisfaction, and harmony in a marriage relationship.

More than Pleasure

The sex act produces the most intense, concentrated pleasure in all of human experience, yet—amazingly!—pleasure is probably the most superficial benefit we derive from sex.

In the sex act, the husband and wife express to each other the fact that they have truly forsaken all others and that they unreservedly open themselves to each other. Expressed within the safe and private boundaries of marriage, the sex act is more than just a pleasurable biological drive. It is an emotional statement that a husband and wife make to each other: "I commit to you an aspect of my emotions, my soul, and my physical being that I share with no other human being on earth." In sex, we uncover the deepest, innermost self and offer that to our partner as a precious gift.

Sex has a way of gathering up and focusing many of the other emotionally charged issues in a relationship. In the physical act of sex, a husband and wife are completely vulnerable to each other. Their boundaries disappear, and they enter each other. Trust is an essential aspect of a satisfying sexual relationship because both partners must trust each other in order to accept each other in a physical way. A satisfying sexual relationship is built on the foundation of a promise, a binding covenant. Covenant relationships are safe places where intimacy, vulnerability, and trust can grow.

YOUR SEXUAL EQUIPMENT

Most of us tend to think of sexual pleasure as something we experience in a few selected "erogenous zones" at strategically located points of our anatomy. Sometimes we forget that our most important sex organ is located right between our ears. All the sensory input that generates sexual arousal and pleasure—the sights, the sounds, the fragrances, the sensation of skin on skin, the feelings of warmth, wetness, and undulation—are all transmitted from the distant sensory points of the body to a single location: the brain.

And it's right here, in the brain, where all of our sexual problems begin as well. Worries, anger, distractions, fears, memories, misconceptions—these are the obstructions that can jump up and block the door to sexual pleasure and satisfaction for both husbands and wives. As we noted in chapter 7, the brains of men and women are wired differently. As a result, men and women not only communicate differently but they also experience sexual desire in very different ways.

Men and Sex

Men experience arousal primarily through imagery. A man can easily be stimulated to sexual arousal by visual imagery, but imagery doesn't have to be visual. A sexually laden image can be formed in his mind by word pictures, by something he hears or reads that creates a sexual image in his mind, or by his own memories and imagination. A man "turns on" quickly, and he can generally achieve sexual release more quickly than a woman. Just as a man is physically constructed to thrust and penetrate, he is also emotionally designed with a drive to fuse with a woman in an active, throbbing, aggressive, and penetrating way.

Men begin their sex life without a partner, through adolescent wet dreams and masturbation. Their first sexual experience tells them, "You can be aroused and experience orgasm all by yourself." A man must learn to be with a partner, to care for her needs, and to allow her to be involved in his arousal and pleasure. Men need to learn that sex is interactive, not just a selfish grab for pleasure.

Unlike women, men are able to personally disengage themselves from their sex partner and see a woman as a object, even as a possession. As a result, men sometimes get involved in very unhealthy sexual patterns, becoming observers of a woman as an object (say, through pornography or strip shows) rather than caring for her needs in a committed relationship. Men are also prone to reducing sex to a set of techniques instead of the uninhibited opening of oneself in a relationship as God intended it to be.

Women and Sex

Women experience arousal primarily through communication. When a woman experiences a sense of security, intimacy, and emotional connection with her man, she is warmed and moved to open up the recesses of her being to him. Words of tenderness and caring are more important than images in arousing a woman.

Just as a woman is physically constructed to be joined with and penetrated, she also is emotionally designed with a desire to reveal her inner secrets to a man in an act of total vulnerability, openness, and reception. When she feels safe, loved, and accepted, her boundaries relax, and she is not only willing but actively desires to be physically, mentally, emotionally, and spiritually penetrated, because penetration represents connection, the ultimate means of being joined in relation-ship to another human being.

An Example of Our Differences

Mick had an unusual complaint about his wife, Darcy: "She's always after me for sex! Always, she's got these slinky, filmy things on, putting her hands all over me, trying to coax me into bed!"

Darcy looked away as Mick spoke. She looked sullen, angry, and embarrassed. "Most men would be happy to have a wife who's affectionate," she muttered. "It's not like I'm unattractive or anything." Darcy had a point—she was very attractive.

Mick grimaced. "There's a difference between being affectionate and being oversexed!" he responded.

"There's such a thing as being undersexed, you know!" Darcy shot back.

With a little probing, I determined that Mick was not "undersexed"; he and Darcy had sexual relations about four to six times a week. But sometimes Mick just said no when Darcy pursued him. His libido simply wasn't up to Darcy's demands.

"How do you feel about your relationship with Mick?" I asked Darcy, "apart from the issue of sex?"

"I feel . . . underappreciated," she said. "Mick doesn't, well, cherish me like I want him to."

"What do you mean?"

"He takes me for granted. There's no romance in our lives. He doesn't treat me special."

"When Mick agrees to have sex with you, do you feel special then? Does the sex satisfy your need to be cherished?"

She thought about it for several seconds, then, "No, it really doesn't."

I then gave Mick an assignment: He was to initiate various acts of treating Darcy special—not with sex but with kindness. Mick worked hard on his assignment for the next couple of weeks. He called her from work just to chat. He sent her notes and cards. He surprised her with a night out. Within days, the level of Darcy's sexual pursuits dropped to a level that matched Mick's own sex drive. Darcy didn't realize it, but sex had never been the real issue in her pursuit of Mick. She just wanted to know that she was loved and accepted, and sex became a metaphor for the emotional satisfaction she was lacking. Once Mick began to treat her as someone who was special to him, Darcy ceased to be "oversexed."

THE SEQUENCE OF SEX

It is the responsibility of both partners to make sex comfortable and enjoyable for each other. They need to take mutual responsibility for knowing each other's preferences and arousal patterns. The sex act takes place in a four-step sequence: Arousal, Passion, Climax, and Resolution.

Arousal

Arousal begins in the emotions of one or both partners. The man may experience arousal quickly, almost instantaneously, with a single image or sight or a single kiss and embrace. The woman's experience of arousal may emerge slowly, almost imperceptibly, beginning as early as a morning hug in bed or a compliment over the breakfast table. The slow building of desire may continue with a caring phone call from work or an offer to help clear the table after dinner—an offer that symbolizes caring and connectedness. For a woman, the act of sex does not take place during a brief time in bed together; it is the culmination of a network of acts, words, thoughts, and feelings that have taken place throughout the day.

When a couple experiences sexual dysfunction at this point in the process of sexual intimacy—for example, if one partner consistently fails to experience arousal so that sex rarely or never takes place—the sexual problem is usually the result, not of a physical problem, but of emotional problems or conflicts embedded in the relationship.

Passion

In the second step of the sequence, we move from the emotional phase to the physical phase of the sex act. Both the man and the woman experience a pink flush as the pulse quickens and blood pressure rises. And that's not all that rises: The man experiences an erection of the penis, and the woman experiences an erection of her nipples and clitoris, accompanied by the release of a lubricant from her vagina. The man is ready to move into her, and she is ready to be entered. But satisfying lovemaking is patient and slow; the couple need not progress immediately to intercourse at this time.

Sometimes a man does not fully understand the important role his wife's breasts and clitoris play in her sexual pleasure. His lack of attention to her need for physical stimulation—especially if she hesitates to communicate directly with him about her needs—often produces sexual dysfunction in marriage. Couples should use the passion stage as a time for exploring each other, caressing and enjoying each other, and communicating—slowly, pleasantly moving toward the moment of climax. Most women need some manual stroking of the clitoris in order to achieve orgasm.

The man, whose passion tends to build more quickly than the woman's, may need to pace himself and match himself to her rhythms so that the experience can be more mutually satisfying. The longer he delays his climax, the more intense it is likely to be. Men who speed to intercourse and early climax often do so because of anxiety about their performance. He may not experience as high a degree of arousal as he feels he needs to sustain his passion. He fears losing his erection, so he rushes toward orgasm. Counseling can often help reduce the anxiety level so that sex can be more mutually satisfying.

Climax

The third step of the sequence is the climax (or orgasm), where the man and the woman experience in an overpowering and profound sense what the Bible means when it says that the husband and wife "become one flesh." Here, the sexual experience reaches its peak. The man experiences the release of semen in an explosive wallop of pleasure. The woman's orgasm is subtly different, usually longer lasting, involving powerful throbs of pleasure, like ocean waves. Even after the last wave has subsided, her body is sensitively atingle for some time.

Despite the popular romantic mythology of books and films, most couples find simultaneous orgasm to be an elusive goal most (if not all) of the time—and, from the standpoint of sexual satisfaction, it's hardly a necessary goal. In fact, it is not necessary that every sexual encounter result in orgasm for both partners; sometimes just holding and caressing can be enough, especially if one or both partners are just too tired to achieve climax. If couples feel the pressure to perform heroic feats of sexual prowess, the results can be "fake orgasms," which lead to sexual unhappiness and dishonesty on both sides.

Physical problems that may interfere with the enjoyment of sex during the passion and climax stages include painful intercourse for the woman, and for the man, premature ejaculation or loss of erection. Sources of physical sexual dysfunction include fatigue, stress, drug or alcohol use, certain blood pressure medications (such as beta-blockers), being overweight, hormone imbalances, or disease. A medical doctor should be consulted about such problems. Emotional problems that interfere with the sexual experience—anxiety, distractions, guilt, and so forth—can usually be resolved through counseling.

Whether sexual dysfunction is physical or emotional in nature, clear communication between the marital partners is crucial. Sometimes problems clear up when both partners convey to each other what kinds of sexual technique produce the greatest arousal and pleasure. If communication between partners does not solve the problems, a couple should not hesitate or be embarrassed to take those problems to a medical or psychological professional for treatment.

Resolution

The fourth and final step of the sequence is the resolution phase. Men and women experience this phase differently. Once a man reaches orgasm, you can (as the saying goes) "stick a fork in him—he's done." His sexual energy has been spent. But the woman is not done yet. She comes down from her climax more slowly and can achieve multiple orgasms, particularly if a state of emotional connection is maintained. During the resolution phase, both the man and the woman experience a warm sense of well-being, which is conducive to hugging, tender words, and intimacy building.

SEXUAL PROBLEMS—AND HOW TO SOLVE THEM

God designed the gift of sex to be enjoyed, explored, and experimented with by two partners in a committed, community-recognized enclosure called marriage. The Bible describes married sex as a clean, beautiful thing before God (see Song of Sol.; 1 Cor. 7; and Heb. 13:4). Within marriage, both partners should feel free to engage in a wide variety of sexual techniques and behavior, so long as both partners agree and find it pleasurable. Sex should be experienced without guilt or undue inhibition between these two interconnected, interdependent human beings, the husband and wife.

Within marriage, the expression of physical and emotional passion is a beautiful thing before God and a healthy thing in our human experience. An active, regular sex life is conducive to good emotional health and to genuine intimacy. The joy and well-being that a good sex life produces in a marriage are essential to the emotional health of a family. However, a sex life that is frustrating or imbalanced in some way is sure to affect other aspects of the relationship, as well as general family life.

Unhealthy Views of Sex

Sexual dysfunction often occurs when one or both partners in a marriage do not have a healthy, biblical attitude toward sex. Many people, particularly those raised in legalistic homes, enter marriage with a set of unhealthy attitudes toward sex as a result of sexual taboos acquired in childhood. Some people, thinking that sex is sinful, become sexually dysfunctional in marriage because their conscience doesn't allow them to enjoy sex. People who are brought up viewing sex as sinful sometimes develop an attitude that the more sinful an act is, the sexier and more exciting it is; these people often develop sexual addictions; that is, they get caught up in forms of sexual behavior that are clearly not healthy and not an expression of Christian married love (such as group sex, spouse swapping, or sadomasochism). The results are broken relationships, sin, guilt, shame, diminished self-esteem, and sexually transmitted disease.

History of Sexual Abuse

Both men and woman who have experienced sexual abuse in childhood tend to experience some form of sexual dysfunction as adults. This is not surprising since the sexual abuse of a child violates that child's boundaries and innermost being at a time when basic personality, emotional boundaries, and lifelong attitudes are being shaped. Abuse victims have endured the ultimate betrayal and are unable to feel safe so that they can relax their boundaries and become vulnerable in the sex act. There is no aspect of our being that is more intimate and personal than our sexuality, and the invasion of this dimension of ourselves produces scars and distortions that rarely heal without intervention through professional counseling.

Guilt

Many issues that are rooted in guilt interfere with sexual enjoyment and sexual functioning: sexual secrets, old sins or illicit affairs, abortion, or childhood abuse (even though victims of abuse are innocent, they often feel tremendously guilty, even decades later). In order for a couple to experience a healthy sex life, old memories must be purged, old sins must be forgiven, old losses must be grieved—and it is often necessary for a couple to undergo professional counseling in order to achieve these goals.

Ordinary Problems

Not every sexual problem a couple experiences is a true dysfunction. Many problems are temporary and work themselves out. Some problems are related to cycles and seasons in a couple's relationship and their level of intimacy. Sometimes one or both partners may get tired of a sexual routine that no longer seems new and exciting. Then, within a few weeks, they may bounce back with a desire to try new techniques or new forms of sexual expression. There is nothing abnormal or alarming about this; it's just one of those rhythms that couples go through over the course of their life together.

Sometimes periods of fatigue or stress in other areas of life will interfere with sexual activity for a time. Illness, grief, even medication, can cause a glitch in the normal schedule of sexual play and intercourse. During such times, it is important for husband and wife to discuss frankly what the underlying problem may be. Seek the help that seems most appropriate—such as a visit to your physician or the readjustment of a killer schedule in order for one or both partners to get more rest and relaxation.

KEEP THE FOCUS ON INTIMACY

Finally, the key to a satisfying sexual relationship is to focus, not on sex, but on intimacy (for a complete discussion of intimacy, see chapter 10). Sex and intimacy are mutually reinforcing components of a healthy marriage. A satisfying sex life helps to deepen the intellectual, emotional, and spiritual intimacy of a marriage. And genuine intimacy serves to heighten the passion in the marriage.

Many people, unfortunately, place such a high premium on the physical pleasures of marital sex that they forget about the emotional and spiritual pleasures of intimacy. Some, reaching a point where sex with the same partner no longer seems as exciting as before, decide that the romance is gone from the marriage. They become bored and they stray. They have missed the whole point of marriage.

Couples who make intimacy their aim discover that marital sex is an ever changing, ever deepening experience. The fact that two people have sex doesn't mean they are truly intimate with each other. In the Bible, we find two terms which are used to describe the act of sex: *to lie with* and *to know*. In the Bible, if a man "lies with" a woman, it is usually an act of casual sex with a prostitute or (as in 2 Sam. 13:14, KJV, where Amnon "lay with" his half sister Tamar) an act of rape. To use the popular vulgarism, it is just "screwing." But when the Bible says, for example, that Abraham "knew" his wife Sarah, it speaks of an act that took place within the safe, satisfying enclosure of promise, intimacy, and genuine love. To "know" one's spouse in an intimate way, in every sense of the word, is a beautiful, satisfying thing.

The pleasures of sex don't diminish for a truly loving couple because both partners are continually reaching for deeper levels of intimacy, connection, discovery, and understanding. Sexual desire finds its most profound and meaningful release in the context of a loving, mutual relationship with someone who is not merely a sex partner, but a soul mate for life.

How Important Should Sex Be?

1. Do you feel that you truly want to experience a satisfying sex life in your marriage? Why or why not?

2. Check any of the following statements that express a belief or attitude you have been holding about sex:

	WIFE'S RESPONSE	HUSBAND'S RESPONSE
The subject of S-E-X is too personal and embarrassing for me to talk about with my spouse.	_____	_____
The goal of sex is for both partners to experience simultaneous orgasm.	_____	_____
Good sex must be a graceful, almost dancelike performance, like in the movies and romance novels.	_____	_____
Each sexual episode in our marriage must lead to orgasm for both partners or it is a failure.	_____	_____
A wife should do whatever her husband wants—even if she hates it and it makes her feel bad.	_____	_____
A Christian wife is sexually passive; it is not right for a woman to initiate sex.	_____	_____
Men need sex more than women do; women can do without sex.	_____	_____
Men must be manipulated so that women can get what they want.	_____	_____
A woman must use sex to control a man.	_____	_____
No man can be trusted.	_____	_____
Sex is for procreation, not for pleasure.	_____	_____
It's my partner's fault I don't reach climax. I shouldn't have to talk about it. He/she should just know what I need and do it.	_____	_____
Sometimes you have to use sex as a threat or a reward to get what you want.	_____	_____

	WIFE'S RESPONSE	HUSBAND'S RESPONSE
I don't see anything wrong with having sex outside of marriage.	_____	_____

Based on the information in this chapter, what marital or emotional problems do you think result from the attitude or attitudes that you checked?

3. **Complete these statements by circling or checking the correct response (each partner using a different color ink) or by writing it in your journals:**

   When I experience a problem with sex, it usually occurs at the arousal/passion/climax/resolution stage.

   When a problem gets in the way of my sexual satisfaction, the source of the problem is usually

   ―――――――――――――――――――――――――――

   Examples: my partner; my thoughts or emotions (such as guilt, anger, or worry); my attitudes about sex (such as "sex is sinful"); a physical problem (fatigue, stress, medication, etc.)

4. **Do you feel you have unhealthy or unbiblical attitudes toward sex? If so, where do you believe those attitudes came from?**

5. **Many unhealthy attitudes toward sex arise in childhood, either because of what we were taught or because no one took the time to teach us the truth about sex. The following checklist may give you a clue as to the source of some of your misconceptions about sex. Check any statements that apply to you.**

	WIFE'S RESPONSE	HUSBAND'S RESPONSE
My parents' behavior toward each other was completely nonsexual and unaffectionate; I never saw them kiss, hug, or speak affectionately to each other.	_____	_____
Sex was a taboo subject in our family—never discussed.	_____	_____

	WIFE'S RESPONSE	HUSBAND'S RESPONSE
I received no sexual information from my parents.	_____	_____
I was taught in the home or in church that sex is a sin.	_____	_____
My mother told me that sex is a wife's duty.	_____	_____
My parents slept in separate beds or separate rooms.	_____	_____
One of my parents had an extramarital affair or a series of affairs and brought great hurt to our family.	_____	_____
I was sexually abused by a parent or other adult when I was a child.	_____	_____

If you checked any of the above boxes—and especially if you checked the last box—you should consider seeking the help of a professional counselor.

6. **Consider making a "Romantic Covenant" with your spouse, including any lovemaking wants, needs, or issues that are important to you and your spouse. You may want to include the following issues:**

   We mutually agree to respect each other's desires and feelings in our sexual relationship.

   We agree to be frank and honest in discussing our needs and our sexual relationship.

   We agree to take the pressure off our lovemaking—no more "sexual goals" like simultaneous climax.

   We agree that sex is not to be used to get what we want from each other.

   We agree to ask for what we want but not to criticize or belittle the other's wants or sexuality.

   We mutually pledge our caring, patience, and understanding, and we promise not to make unreasonable demands or to inflict guilt upon our romantic relationship.

We mutually promise to be faithful and exclusive to each other in our sexual relationship; we will not violate the boundaries of our relationship by taking our sexuality outside of marriage or even discussing our sexuality with others (except, if necessary, a professional counselor).

We agree to replace misguided inhibitions or worldly excesses with God's teaching about the beauty, goodness, and exclusiveness of our sexual relationship in marriage.

7. **This week read a chapter a day from the Song of Solomon. (There are only eight chapters; so read two on Sunday, and you'll get through the whole book in a week.) Notice how frankly erotic this book is in its description of marital love. Notice also that the bride who speaks in this "song" is very comfortable with her anatomy and her sexuality, that she dresses seductively for her husband and is quite forward and playful in a sexual way in the privacy of their lovemaking.**

8. **Read 1 Corinthians 7 and Hebrews 13:4. What do these passages tell you about how God views sex in marriage?**

12

What Do We Do
When Our Relationship
Changes?

Her name is Glee—how ironic! Her mood is anything but gleeful.

"Karl tells everyone we have the perfect marriage," she says, her eyes red rimmed, moist, and puffy. "I look around at our lives and think, *What marriage?*

She falls silent for several long seconds, gathering her thoughts and her emotions. Then she explains. "Here we are in our early fifties with all this time on our hands—time we could be spending together. After all, Karl sold the hardware business and retired early, and I'm not working outside the home. We could be doing things together. We could be going places. We could just sit and talk like we used to. We used to dream about this time in our lives. He always planned to build up the business to a point where he could sell it at a big profit—then he'd retire and we could do all the things we dreamed of. Well, the dream has come true, and I've never been more miserable.

"It's not like we live separate lives, exactly. We eat together, we sleep together, we take trips and vacations together, we have sex—two, three times a week, in fact. His lovemaking technique is good, always has been; so physically, I'm satisfied. But I feel that our sex life has become mechanical—he does what has always worked. It's not an act of intimacy; it's just one of those things that has to be taken care of, like going to the bathroom or brushing your teeth.

"We never really talk anymore. Not like we used to. Not about feelings. Not about hopes and fears. Not about dreams and the things we want out of life. If I try to engage him in conversation, he answers in monosyllables and finds some excuse to cut off the conversation. We don't fight. We don't argue. He just has his life—his friends, the golf course, his church board meetings—and I have my life, such as it is.

"Every day I wonder, *What happened to us?* I don't understand it. Why does a relationship change so much over the years? Why are things so different from when we first got married?"

Glee asks a question that many people ask. And it can be a very painful question.

You are not the same person you were yesterday or ten years ago. Neither is your spouse. We sometimes assume that two people who find each other and love each other ought to be able to come together as husband and wife and everything should click into place, if not automatically, at least with the passage of time. Many people assume that after an initial settling-in period, conflicts should smooth out, intimacy should deepen, the friendship should strengthen, and things should get better and better with time. The fact is that the marriage relationship is a very complicated transaction at the beginning, and it remains a complicated transaction throughout its various stages.

THE CHRONOLOGICAL STAGES OF A MARRIAGE

Every marriage is as individual as the two people who make up that marriage. Yet there are also certain features and stages that are common to virtually all marriages. These stages can be mapped out to make a useful time line of a marriage. Because couples are constantly growing and changing—both as individuals and as a marital unit—it is important for every couple to consider where they are in life's journey. By understanding the pressures and stresses that are common to each of these stages, a couple will be better equipped to cope—and less inclined to panic or give up—when these natural pressures and stresses arise. The seven stages of marriage are:

Stage 1: Courtship

Stage 2: Getting married

Stage 3: Two become three

Stage 4: The children start school

Stage 5: Midlife

Stage 6: The empty nest

Stage 7: The (alleged) "golden" years

Not every marriage will follow this sequence; these stages are sometimes skipped or reshuffled, especially in remarriages, blended families, couples without children, or couples where one partner is significantly older than the other. But most couples will recognize the general outline of the chronological development of their relationship in these seven stages.

Stage 1: Courtship

Marriage begins with separation.

A young man and a young woman have grown up in their respective families. Ideally, as they have matured, their parents have turned more and more responsibility and freedom over to them, helping them to separate from their families of origin so that they can now form and fully enter into a new family system. If their upbringing was healthy and successful, this man and this woman come together with a sense of security, confidence, and a capacity for trust. They feel that relationships with others can be safe. Upon leaving their families of origin, these two people have established a strong sense of self, a sense of boundaries, a sense of "this is who I am." Now each is ready to develop a deep intimacy with another human being—an intimacy designed by God to last a lifetime.

As these two young people go out into the world, they begin to find each other. Strong attractions—largely sexual and unconscious in nature—propel them toward each other. Unfortunately, the powerful forces that drive them into each other's arms have little to do with sustaining a relationship over the long haul. To lay the foundation for a lasting marriage relationship, each partner in the courtship must quickly learn to *make* promises and must be able to trust the other to *keep* promises. Both partners must develop emotional and intellectual intimacy during this initial phase of the relationship. And both partners must form healthy boundaries—that is, they must learn to separate physically and emotionally from their families of origin.

Eventually, the journey of courtship reaches its destination—the wedding day. And now the *real* adventure begins!

Stage 2: Getting Married

Rex is a youth pastor; Donna is a preschool teacher. They met at the Christian college they attended in southern California. They became best friends in school; then they fell in love, got married, and moved to Rex's hometown, where he was offered a job in his home church. Rex has many friends, an active life (he frequently takes the kids in his youth groups skiing, hiking, or on other outdoor outings). Donna hardly knows anyone and doesn't have any close friends to talk to.

At the end of each day, Donna waits for Rex to get home from church. As soon as he arrives, Donna pounces on him, starved for adult companionship and conversation. Rex, however, withdraws into his newspaper, walling himself off from her.

The problem: These newlyweds, Donna and Rex, had not yet made the transition from two "I's" to a single "we." Rex was an independent young man who enjoyed the freedom of the outdoors, the freedom to run his youth ministry, the freedom to be himself—and after the wedding, he was suddenly afraid of losing himself in the marriage. So, to maintain his individual self, he kept a shield—the newspaper—between himself and Donna. This only made her more desperate to connect with him, causing her to come on stronger, which in turn caused him to barricade himself against her even more.

When they came to me for counseling, I told them they would need to begin talking openly with each other about their feelings and their struggles. This open communication would help reduce Donna's fear of rejection and abandonment. But I also suggested that they construct a boundary around their discussion times, initially limiting those times to a firm twenty minutes a night. This boundary reduced Rex's fear of losing himself in the marriage.

Rex and Donna's experience illustrates the delicate balance that must be struck when a marriage begins. Each partner must remain an "I" at the same time both partners are becoming a "we." It is all too easy to stray to one extreme or the other as that balance is being sought.

The marriage ceremony symbolizes the bonding and binding together of two people. It is a vital line of demarcation in a couple's relationship. The commitment of these two people to each other has become clear in the eyes of society. Once the ceremony has taken place, each partner's family of origin must relate to the couple in different ways. Loyalties have shifted from the old family unit to a new family unit.

Even so, these two people have not just married each other; they have married into each other's extended families—and into all the emotional issues that go along with those families. So it is crucially important that each partner's family of origin understand that these two people have fused together into a separate entity.

The couple now begins writing a new family history. One chapter in this family history could be titled "Conflict." While disagreements have probably arisen in the courtship phase, most of them were probably papered over or resolved with a heaping helping of sugary courtship affection. Now the couple is in the crucible of marriage, from which there is no escape (except divorce, which for most people—at least at first—is The Unthinkable). Whenever two people are in a relationship—and especially when those two people must share the same living space—there will be disagreement. It's important for the couple to understand that a good relationship is not the absence of disagreement but the proper monitoring of disagreement. Whenever a couple tells me, "We never argue," I get nervous. A lack of conflict usually means a lack of resolution.

Recent studies have found that almost half of new couples have significant marital problems. This statistic is not surprising when you realize what two people have to accomplish when they come together in marriage. They must

- construct healthy boundaries around their relationship,

- learn to love in a committed, covenant way that is focused on the other person's welfare rather than on one's own needs and wants,

- learn how to be both passionate (sexually bonded) and intimate (intellectually and emotionally bonded) with each other,

- develop mutuality in giving and taking, in leading and following,

- negotiate closeness and distance, especially in regard to sex, and

- learn how to manage conflict.

During this stage, each partner must learn to see the other as the "primary resource person" in his or her life—friend, lover, confidant, counselor, cheerleader, business partner, protector, and emotional support. When this takes place, a couple experiences the amazing reality that God designed for this stage of marriage, as described by Genesis 2:24: "For this reason a man will leave his father and mother and be united to his wife, and they will become one flesh."

Stage 3: Two Become Three

Ashley came into counseling completely distraught. "My husband says he wants to date other women!" she said. "He says he wants to stay married to me, but he wants to have what he calls an 'open marriage'! I don't want my marriage to be 'open'!"

Ashley thought she had adequately met her husband's needs, and she certainly felt he had met hers. This declaration of his intention to date around came as a complete shock.

"A complete shock?" I asked. "You didn't have any clue?"

"Well," she hesitated. "He has been kind of standoffish lately. Like, for the past two years or so—maybe more. I remember one time, a couple years ago, he said the strangest thing to me—right out of the blue."

"What's that?"

"He said, 'Ashley, I don't know why you stay married to me.' I was floored. I've always wanted to be married to him. I love him."

It was a clue. I thought I had an insight into the problem. I pursued my hunch with another question. "Can you think of anything that has changed in your marriage in the last two or three years?"

She thought for a moment. "Well," she ventured, "our daughter was born about three years ago. You don't think that has anything to do with the fact that he wants to date other women, do you?"

"Why don't you have him come in with you next time?"

A week later, Ashley was back, along with her husband, Rob. I learned that my hunch was correct: Rob had lost a sense that he was "special" to Ashley when their daughter was born. He saw Ashley devote all of her attention to their child, and he felt not only ignored and unwanted, but unneeded. It seemed to him that Ashley received all the emotional nurturing she needed from their daughter, and it made him feel inadequate to meet his wife's needs.

"So," I said, "you have been feeling like you are not enough of a husband for your wife. And that's why you want to date other women."

He nodded. And with this issue out in the open, Ashley and Rob were able to communicate, to rebuild understanding, and to repair the damage done to their relationship by neglect and misunderstanding.

When children come, the challenge becomes one of maintaining a strong marriage relationship within a well-managed family relationship. Often, the addition of children to a marriage causes the parents to forget that they are still a couple. But it is so important that the couple's relationship continue to be nourished even as the family expands.

When a couple neglects the marriage relationship during the child-bearing and child-rearing years, the results range from increased tension and conflict to sexual dysfunction to major communication breakdowns. Unless a couple maintains a focus on each other as their primary love relationship, and unless both partners work on maintaining their intimacy and passion, they will tend to drift into separate parental and career roles. They may even drift apart—permanently.

When a couple becomes three, new pressures are added. The child becomes the focus of both parents' attention, especially the mother's. Husbands often feel left out of their wife's love; they sense competition from the new infant. Many men take the birth of a child as a signal to become more involved at work.

The child takes up so much of the mother's energy and time that intimacy and passion get squeezed out. Sex may take on new dimensions as the wife's body changes and is used in feeding and nurturing the child. Both partners must be aware of these issues and focus on them intentionally so that adjustments can be made and feelings can be monitored by both sides.

This can be a time of greatly increased conflict as both partners need to renegotiate their expectations of each other. If Mom works outside the home, she is likely to feel overwhelmed by assuming the heavy obligations of parenting on top of the obligations of her job. In these times of "equal parenting opportunity," in which some men are spending more time with their children and taking on a more equal share of parenting and household responsibility, the juggling of schedules and the exhaustion affect both partners.

At this stage of the marriage, the woman often finds herself in a needy position, particularly if she suffers from postpartum depression or other postbirth complications. Her body, her emotions, and her schedule have gone through extensive shifts. She feels a special need for more attention and nurturing from her husband. Can the husband adjust to all of this? Is he listening to her needs, to her spoken and unspoken expectations? Are both sides monitoring and readjusting their expectations? (For a more complete discussion of expectations, see chapter 4.)

Even though a precious new person has come into the life of this couple, they need to maintain the crucial elements of a marriage: boundaries, romance, intimacy, and passion.

Stage 4: The Children Start School

This stage is a rehearsal for the separation to come, when children grow up and leave home for good. As children start school, they make friends and encounter outside influences. These influences are brought into the home by the child and sometimes create conflict—a clash of values or ideas. Especially in a very closed family, children going off to school and returning with new ideas can be a great threat.

Disagreements between spouses over child rearing tend to intensify, especially as children become old enough and sophisticated enough to play one parent against the other. There is a tendency for one parent to be a hard-liner in discipline issues and the other to be a soft-liner. Each parent reacts to the other's parenting style extremes, and conflicts often arise as one parent attempts to rescue the child from the other parent (who is either "too lenient" or "too mean"). The tendency is for one parent to compensate by becoming more hard while the other becomes more soft.

During this stage, the conflicting demands of family and career can make intimacy harder to maintain. Children are becoming more active and heavily scheduled (music lessons, dance class, soccer practice, Little League), and all of these activities soak up marital time and energy. The more kids in the family, the harder it becomes for parents to create privacy for resolving their conflicts and for expressing their sexual passion.

Both partners must learn to focus special attention on the needs of their marriage relationship, or the marriage can begin to deteriorate due to stress and neglect.

Stage 5: Midlife

As the children reach toward independence, both parents must negotiate new ways of dealing with them. At this stage, couples often make the teenager the focus of their drama while avoiding the task of resolving their own conflicts. As long as we keep focusing on our teenager's horrid music videos, nose rings, strange attire, sullenness, plummeting grades, and what have you, we don't have to face the fact that, as a couple, we are drifting apart, we are losing intimacy, we are neglecting passion, we are foregoing romance.

At the same time, just when the teenagers start cranking up the wattage of family stress and tension, the couple's parents often become more needy. If infirm, Grandma and Grandpa may move in with the family, upsetting household routines, making demands, and hindering the honest resolution of conflict. Grandparents sometimes side with the teens against the parents, creating disciplinary havoc.

It's also the time of life when both partners in the marriage begin to face questions of adequacy, fulfillment, and direction in their lives.

Both partners are asking themselves, "Who am I?" Perhaps some dreams have died, some aspirations have been delayed and appear to be going unfulfilled. The husband may make a radical career change ("this may be my last chance to fulfill my dream of being a hog farmer in Iowa") while the wife may wish to enter or reenter the work force after years of parenting and homemaking. As a result, she may place new expectations on him: "I can't do as many of the household chores; you need to pick up some of the slack."

Midlife is a crucial passage for the marriage, and both partners should make a conscious effort to monitor expectations and renegotiate roles as needed. Issues of intimacy and passion are as important in this stage as in every previous stage, and both partners need to allow time and energy to make the relationship work.

Stage 6: The Empty Nest

Ben and Lisa's youngest daughter just left home for college. Now they can do all the things they planned to do together once the kids all "flew the coop," right? Wrong! As Ben and Lisa begin discussing their plans for the next few years of their lives, they discover they have very different agendas. Ben plans to pursue more hunting and fishing, the kinds of activities he likes to pursue—alone. Lisa figured they were going to spend more time traveling—together.

The problem Ben and Lisa have is a common one for couples in this stage of marriage: Can we let our children go and still deal with each other as marriage partners? Or, having raised our kids, have we discovered we no longer have anything in common? What do we do with each other now that our kids are no longer our focus?

This problem is particularly acute among couples who have neglected their marriage relationship during the child-rearing years. Some couples find that they have nothing to share together, nothing to talk about. As a result, this stage often catches couples off guard. They don't realize until it's nearly too late how perilous this stage of marriage can be.

The pain and peril of this stage is magnified if one or both parents maintain an unhealthy attachment to the children. As children approach maturity, they must be allowed to "leave by the front door"— that is, with the full blessing and support of the parents. There is an old saying: "Back doors are revolving doors." In other words, if the child does not leave via the "front door" of parental support and blessing, that child will not be able to make a healthy transition to adulthood. Instead, that child will be back again and again, triggering the return of old, unresolved conflicts.

In a healthy family, children are encouraged and able to leave home at the proper time, but they remain positively involved with their family of origin. They maintain healthy contact even after moving into a career and establishing their own families.

Stage 7: The (Alleged) "Golden" Years

Hal is driving June nuts. He's only been retired for a month, and already June can't stand to have him around. He follows her around all day, asking what she's doing. When she's ironing, he stands over her shoulder, observing the back-and-forth motion of June's Sunbeam steam iron as if it were an exciting instant replay on ESPN. Clearly, Hal has not made a very good adjustment to retirement. He needs to take responsibility for finding satisfying activities of his own before June runs screaming out of the house.

The last stage of marriage can be a golden stage—but there are also stresses and adjustments to be made in the culminating years of a relationship. Both partners have to adjust to financial changes, to the physical challenges of aging, to the loss of friends and family members, and to being home together more. Leadership issues may re-emerge: The primary leader-provider in the relationship may become incapacitated and become a follower-receiver. Expectations may need to be reassessed and readjusted.

And one partner must cope with the biggest change of all: the death of a spouse. When this loss occurs, the survivor often feels that life has become empty and meaningless. Somehow, the surviving spouse must learn to make a new life and find new meaning in it.

THE FOUR EMOTIONAL STAGES OF A MARRIAGE

Not only are there chronological stages of marriage but there are also four distinct emotional stages. Although these stages are more subtle and difficult to recognize, they are also more predictable. And every marriage must learn to negotiate them if it is to endure.

Stage 1: Stuck

Stage 2: Unstuck

Stage 3: I-ness

Stage 4: We-ness

Here are four truths to keep in mind as we examine these stages:

Truth 1: The order of the stages never varies.

Truth 2: You can't skip any stage.

Truth 3: Each succeeding stage is more complex than the stage before it.

Truth 4: Each stage grows from the preceding stage and prepares for the stages to follow.

Stage 1: Stuck

Occurring early in marriage, this stage involves intense bonding between two people. The purpose of this stage is attachment, and it entails a great deal of passion, giving/receiving, and nurturing. Neither partner makes many demands for the other partner to change; both people accommodate each other. Conflict is avoided and minimized. Both people sacrifice individuality in order to perpetuate the sense that "we are one." Anxiety emerges when one side glimpses the other as a different self.

Counseling couples in the Stuck stage can be very difficult—especially those couples who are in the courtship phase of being stuck! I once did premarital counseling with a couple in their upper forties, who were referred to me by their pastor. It was to be his second marriage and her third. Both were competent, intelligent, successful professionals. Yet, around each other, they behaved like giddy thirteen-year-olds! They refused to see any problems in their relationship, and they were certain that everything would be coming up roses for the rest of their lives. These two were stuck like superglue! I never got through to them. For all I know, they may both be married today—but I doubt they're married to each other.

When both partners are stuck on each other and the relationship is agreeable to both, I call it a Stuck/Stuck stage. It is not unhealthy for a couple to be stuck during the courtship and newlywed phases of the marriage. But if a couple remains stuck for years or decades, you have a picture of two people who are not progressing and growing in their relationship.

The Stuck stage can take an alternate form. This is the Stuck/Fighting stage. The partners are hostile and dependent at the same time. Each says, "I can't live with you; I can't live without you." Conflict and aggression are used to maintain both distance and contact—simultaneously. One partner fails to see the impact of his/her behavior on the other. There are strong projections of feelings and assumptions from one partner to the other: "I know what you're thinking!" They are like two boxers in a clinch: The referee tries to separate them, but they are locked together in a struggle, their gloved hands flailing and punching ineffectually, hurting each other but unable to disengage from each other. (For a complete discussion of anger and conflict, see chapter 9.)

In most marriages, the Stuck stage eventually runs its course, and a new stage emerges. What else could we call the post-Stuck stage but . . .

Stage 2: Unstuck

The couple now enters a stage of becoming unique individuals again. In a healthy relationship, partners develop the capacity to tolerate differences and to define clear areas of responsibility and authority. During this stage, both partners reestablish their own boundaries, their sense of identity. They shift from an obsession with the other partner to a process of internally defining themselves and their own independent thoughts, feelings, goals, and needs.

In relationships between emotionally immature or insecure people—people who have never understood or applied promise keeping, clear boundaries, clear expectations, and covenant-love and who have never learned to manage conflict well—the Unstuck stage is perilous. It is at this point that many marriage partners mistakenly assume, "We've fallen out of love" or "We were just incompatible." In fact, the two people in the relationship are simply passing through a normal process and rebalancing after the emotionally intense Stuck phase.

Sometimes one partner will enter the Unstuck stage, leaving the other partner Stuck. The Stuck partner, having no one to stick to, begins to panic. This situation creates the crisis that often brings people into counseling. In counseling, the Stuck partner learns to grieve the loss of the intense Stuck relationship. Once the loss is grieved and the reality of this new phase of the relationship sinks in, the Stuck partner is usually able to make the transition to Unstuck.

The task of the person moving into the Unstuck stage of marriage is fourfold:

1. Identify one's own thoughts, feelings, and desires.

2. Express those thoughts, feelings, and desires to the other partner.

3. Understand and accept the other partner as separate, distinct, and different.

4. Learn to respond effectively to those differences.

Stage 3: I-ness

Dan had spent the last few years trying to help his wife, Alice, deal with her anger, self-pity, and depression. She had been sexually abused as a child—something Dan found out only a couple years earlier. Until Alice revealed the abuse, Dan had been baffled and hurt by years of sexual dysfunction and teary episodes over issues he couldn't understand. Ever since he learned of Alice's childhood pain, Dan tried to do everything possible to make Alice happy. But instead of getting better, she seemed to grow progressively more depressed. Worst of all, she refused to seek counseling for her emotional issues. She shut herself in the house, cried, stared, or sometimes just slept through the day.

In desperation, Dan came to counseling alone. "I'm not really the one who should be here," he said. "Alice is the one who was molested as a child, but she just won't deal with it. I've tried to make her happy, but nothing works. What should I do?"

"You know something, Dan?" I said. "It's not your job to make Alice happy. It's Alice's job to make Alice happy. She has to take responsibility for herself. And as hard as it may be, you need to take responsibility for yourself and quit trying to carry Alice's burden for her."

As this idea sank in, it was as if a light came on in Dan's eyes. At that moment, Dan began the transition into the I-ness stage. From then on, he communicated to Alice, "I love you, but I can't be responsible for your feelings. You have to take that responsibility on yourself. If you really love me and care about this relationship, you'll get out of this gloomy house and get yourself into counseling so that you can get these issues out of your way and get on with your life."

In time, Alice did just that—and she experienced the I-ness stage as well.

I-ness is a healthy stage of development in the life of a couple. In this stage, each partner experiences a time of intense individuality, exploring activities and friendships outside of the marriage. The attention of each partner is directed to the external world as both seek to consolidate their self-esteem and individual power while learning to express themselves creatively in the world.

Once both partners have securely established their own identities, they can look to each other once again for intimacy and emotional support. As they begin to reconnect, there is a reemergence of vulnerability, the tender balance between "I" and "we" is cemented into place, and both partners begin to respond to each other more consistently and comfortably. Now we have reached the final stage. . . .

Stage 4: We-ness

This stage is the goal of marriage: Mutual interdependence.

This is a comfortable, peaceful, and productive stage of marriage. At this stage, two individuals in a healthy relationship can know that they have arrived at the We-ness stage because they have found satisfaction in their own lives. They have developed a deep, mutually satisfying bond, which is demonstrated in the way they share thoughts, dreams, feelings, and goals together. Two people, comfortable and secure as individuals, have arrived at a place where they can satisfy each other's needs yet without losing a sense of self. They have balanced independence and interdependence. They communicate

What Do We Do
When Our Relationship Changes?

1. On a scale from 1 to 10, where 1 equals "Very Dissatisfied" and 10 equals "Very Satisfied," how satisfied are you with the current level of intellectual and emotional sharing in your marriage?

2. Think back to a time when you were at the previous stage of marriage. Remember how you related to your spouse. How satisfied were you with the level of intellectual and emotional sharing in your marriage at that time?

   Has your level of satisfaction increased or decreased over the past few years? To what do you attribute the change?

   Discuss together what specific, practical steps you can take to improve the intellectual and emotional dimension of your marriage.

3. On a scale from 1 to 10, how satisfied are you with the level of passion and romance in your marriage?

4. Think back to the previous stage in your marriage. Remember how you related to your spouse, sexually and romantically. How satisfied were you with the level of passion and romance in your marriage at that time?

   Has your level of satisfaction increased or decreased over the past few years? To what do you attribute the change?

   What specific, practical steps can you take to enhance the passion and romance in your marriage?

5. On what issue or issues in your marriage do you feel a need to focus more attention? Check the appropriate responses or note them in your journals.

	WIFE'S RESPONSE	HUSBAND'S RESPONSE
Communication	_____	_____
Intimacy	_____	_____
Passion (Sex)	_____	_____
Boundaries	_____	_____
Time Alone	_____	_____
Time Together	_____	_____
Trust	_____	_____
Expectations	_____	_____
Keeping Promises	_____	_____
Managing Conflict	_____	_____
Mutuality in Giving and Taking	_____	_____
Negotiating Closeness and Distance	_____	_____
Mutuality in Leading and Following	_____	_____
Balancing Parenting Roles and Marriage Roles	_____	_____
Practical Duties, Chores, Maintenance, etc.	_____	_____
Doing Things Together (Exercise, Travel, Vacations, etc.)	_____	_____

6. **On which of these issues do you feel your spouse needs to focus more attention?**

7. **Share your answers with each other and listen carefully. Note the differences between your perceptions of your marriage. Avoid arguing with those perceptions; instead, try to see the relationship from each other's point of view.**

   Pray together, then negotiate changes in roles, expectations, boundaries, intimacy requirements, sexual expectations, and so forth. Work together to make the marriage more mutually satisfying. Make genuine love—seeking the welfare of the other person—your goal.

8. **Which emotional stage of marriage are you in right now?**

   Stage 1: Stuck (or Stuck/Fighting)
   Stage 2: Unstuck

Stage 3: I-ness
Stage 4: We-ness

9. Are you and your partner in the same emotional stage? Why or why not? Explain your answer.

10. Do you sense progress and growth in your marriage relationship over the past few years? Why or why not?

11. You and your partner are two very different people. Is that fact hard for you to accept? What is it about your partner's differences that makes you uneasy?

   Take a piece of paper and divide it into two sections labeled ALIKE and DIFFERENT. Then take a few minutes and write down at least ten ways you and your spouse are alike and ten ways you and your spouse are different.

   What does this exercise tell you about the stage of emotional development you and your spouse are in?

12. What interests, activities, and friendships do you enjoy outside of the marriage relationship?

13. Have you ever stepped back, taken a look at your marriage, and said to yourself, "We've fallen out of love," or "We're just incompatible"?

   Have you ever verbalized such thoughts to your spouse, or has your spouse verbalized them to you?

   Could it be that you and your spouse are simply going through the Unstuck stage of emotional development? Are there other signs that your marriage is entering the Unstuck stage? Does it help you and put you at ease to know that this is simply a passage your marriage goes through?

   Take time to pray that God will continue to guide you and your spouse toward the goal of marriage—that beautiful interdependent state of individuality balanced with the bonds of love and mutual caring.

13

What about

My Needs?

Matt and Deena had been married twelve years and had two pre-schoolers. "We're not communicating," Deena said when they came in for counseling. "In fact, Matt isn't even trying. He spends all his time at the office, leaving me at home with two little kids and no one to talk to. He's totally closed emotionally. I feel like I'm 75 percent divorced."

Matt, slumped in his chair, just shrugged.

"Matt?" I said. "Any response?"

He frowned. "I don't even want to be here."

"You see!" said Deena. "Like a clam! Totally closed!"

"How do you usually try to get through to him, Deena?"

"I just keep talking to him! I keep trying to drag him out of his shell!"

"You increase your demands on him."

Deena looked stunned. "I wouldn't put it like that."

"How would you put it?"

She thought for several moments. "I guess you're right. I guess I do increase my demands. I keep turning up the heat, trying to get a response out of him."

"It seems to me," I said, "that you've both lost your place with each other. You are no longer important to each other."

I was trying to frame the situation to see if I understood it and if they would buy it. They both bought the frame. Matt nodded. So did Deena. "I think that's it," Matt agreed aloud. "We're not important to each other."

"Is that the way you want to leave it?" I asked. "Or would you like to do something about this situation?"

There was a long silence. I noticed a tear glide down Deena's cheek. She brushed it away. "I want to do something. I don't want our marriage to end. Honey?" She turned to him.

"Can it be saved?" asked Matt.

"If you both want it to be," I answered. It was true. It was up to them.

The next time we talked, I gathered data. I learned that Deena was a perfectionist, that she liked an orderly world, and that she liked to "keep the car on the road." Matt, by contrast, was impulsive and adventurous. "I'm a four-wheel-drive kinda guy," he said. "I like to take the car off the road." Deena and Matt were two opposite personalities, and they had kept each other in balance until their first child was born.

When the baby came, all of the order and predictability went out of Deena's world. She was once very involved in meeting Matt's needs, and he had always counted on that—but suddenly, with the arrival of the baby, that was all over. Deena lacked the time and the energy to meet Matt's needs, so he withdrew to the office. He could always get his strokes at work since he got none at home.

Deena, meanwhile, became bitter and demanding. At first, Matt tried to meet her demands. He felt guilty over the rupture in their relationship, and he said yes to her demands; but his yes was empty. She asked him to supply various emotional and practical needs for her, and he agreed to her requests; but he broke most of those promises.

I gave them an assignment: When Deena made demands on Matt, Matt was to consider her request and answer honestly. Instead of saying yes and not meaning it, he would say no and stick to it. If he answered yes, he would consider it a promise, and he would keep his promise.

The next time I saw them, they both said that they felt closer, and they believed they were on the right track. Still, Deena felt Matt spent too much time away from her, "hiding" at the office. She framed his behavior as the trait of a child of alcoholics (Matt's mother had died of alcoholism). Matt rejected Deena's frame, arguing strenuously. The more Matt argued, the more Deena tweaked him about being "in denial."

Finally, I stepped in and said, "Deena, instead of arguing with him about why he stays at the office, just tell him, 'I need you.' Why don't you just avoid mentioning his mother's alcoholism anymore."

"I should just say, *'I need you'*?"

"I'd like to hear that," said Matt. "If I knew that you wanted me home because you needed me, I think I'd be home a lot more."

Deena agreed not to mention the subject of alcoholism anymore. Instead, she would express her need for Matt.

The next visit, they both reported that things were still better. But Matt had a problem. Now that he was spending more time at home, he wanted Deena to be with him, to spend time talking, doing things together, and sharing affection. But Deena was often unavailable. She was washing or ironing or cleaning the kitchen when Matt just wanted to be near her. This made him feel rejected.

At first, this made no sense. Deena had wanted, even demanded that Matt come home. Now that he was home, she kept him waiting while she ran the vacuum cleaner! It was very difficult to get to the bottom of this issue, but finally we were able to make sense of it: Deena wanted to spend time with her husband, but she wanted everything just so. All of this cleaning was an effort to bring order to her world so that everything would be perfect for her time with Matt.

Why was it so difficult to get to the bottom of this issue? Because Deena had chronic trouble expressing her needs. "My female friends can read me like a book," she said finally. "They always know what I need, and they supply it without me saying a word. If they know me that well, then I surely shouldn't have to explain everything to my own husband! He should be able to read me, too, and adjust to my needs."

"I can't do that!" Matt protested. "I'm not a mind reader!"

So I gave them another exercise to do. They were to alternate expressing needs. On odd days, Matt would express a need to Deena; on even days, vice versa.

I also gave them a written exercise to do. I had each of them take several sheets of paper and write out specific things they wanted the other person to do for them. After they completed this exercise, I had them exchange papers. Each partner was permitted to place a check mark in front of any item on the list he or she was unwilling to do at that time. Then, for the next month, they were to attempt to meet one of the remaining needs on the list every day. Each spouse could add more items to the list of his or her own needs and was encouraged to do something extra for the other as a gift, expecting nothing in return.

After doing this exercise at home for a few weeks, Deena and Matt came back full of excitement and enthusiasm about their relationship. "Remember when we said we were no longer important to each other?" Deena said, her eyes sparkling. "Remember when we said we had lost our place with each other? Well, we've found each other again!"

Many of us have been taught since childhood that it is wrong and selfish to express our needs, to say, "I want . . ." or "I need. . . ." But as human beings, we need healthy give-and-take. God did not design us to take care of our own needs, nor did he design us to demand that everyone else meet our needs. Some needs are met through people, some through our relationship with God and with ourselves.

All our lives we work toward a balance between independence and interdependence. We maintain our boundaries as individuals, yet we need each other and are deeply involved in each other's lives. As Galatians 6:2, 4-5 tells us, we fulfill the law of Christ when we meet each other's needs by carrying one another's burdens; yet we are also commanded to test our own actions and carry our own load—a careful balance between self-reliance and reliance upon each other. God designed marriage to be a safe, nurturing place where each partner remains a distinct individual yet both partners look to each other for support, companionship, consolation, affection, sex, love, affirmation, encouragement, and protection.

According to God's prescription for a healthy marriage, those needs can and should be met in a reciprocal way: One partner asks, the other provides; then they switch. Our goal, as we become more aware of our own needs and the needs of our spouse, is to learn how to express those needs to our partner, how to negotiate, how to give, and how to receive.

THE SEQUENCE FOR GETTING NEEDS MET

We must follow a certain sequence in order to have our needs met effectively within marriage. If the sequence is derailed at any point, a need will go unmet, and one or both partners will be frustrated.

1. You Must Know What Your Need Is and Be Able to Articulate It.

Many of us have a vague sense that we need something from the relationship that we are not getting, but we don't stop and think through what that something is. If you try to ask your partner to meet a need before you fully understand what it is yourself, trouble and misunderstanding will surely result.

You should be able to state your need very specifically. For example, "I need more support from you now that we have a new baby. It would help me tremendously if you could do the dishes every evening and clean the bathrooms once a week."

Often, after you have thought it through and can articulate your need to your spouse, you feel inhibited about expressing it. You think, *That sounds so selfish.* But remember: You and your spouse are a team, and clear communication and mutual support are essential to any team effort. And you can make it clear that you are ready to reciprocate in meeting your partner's needs when the occasion arises. It's your turn now; soon it will be the other person's turn.

2. You Must Ask Your Spouse to Meet That Need in a Specific Way.

Don't hint around. Don't be subtle or cute. *Ask.* Often, one or both partners takes the stance, *If he/she really loved me, I wouldn't have to ask.* Nonsense. A wedding ring does not impart supernatural abilities to read the other person's mind. In real life, to make your needs and feelings known you have to open your mouth and communicate. This can be difficult if you are talking about sensitive, personal needs—in the area of sex, for example—but if you don't ask directly, your partner is left to guesswork.

3. You Must Be Willing to Make Yourself Understood.

That means you may have to state your needs more than once, sometimes in several different ways. What you think you said may not be what your partner thought you said. A person's mind can wander; he or she may have filtered your message through a personal or emotional bias, or you may have been ambiguous in your choice of words. There are literally hundreds of things that can go wrong when one person communicates with another, and the message, as a result, can easily become distorted.

So, once you have communicated your need, it may be helpful to ask your spouse to repeat what you have just said, in his or her own words. This way you will understand what your spouse heard, and you can clarify yourself if he or she heard incorrectly. Go through this same process when your partner communicates a need to you, repeating the message so that you can be certain you have heard correctly. This kind of mirrored and monitored communication is called "reflective listening," because as you listen, you reflect the message back to make sure that the communication is taking place without distortion.

Again and again I counsel couples who are locked in an argument based on a complete misunderstanding of what is being asked or said on both sides. As soon as both partners are able to truly hear each other and agree on what they are actually fighting about, the fight often disappears and peace unexpectedly breaks out! That is why communication is so crucial in the marriage relationship. Clarity and understanding are key to the process.

4. Your Spouse Must Be Willing and Able to Meet Your Need.

He or she may respond, "I can't meet your need; it's beyond my power to meet." Or "I don't want to meet your need."

5. You Must Be Willing to Receive from Your Spouse.

Oddly, many people will follow this sequence and make it all the way from step 1 to step 4 and then find that they are unable to receive from their spouse. Because of low self-esteem, they say, "I don't want to bother you" or "I'm not worthy of having this need met."

When both partners give and receive, meeting needs and having needs met, the marriage functions as it was designed to, and both partners experience a deep sense of satisfaction in the relationship.

**WHAT STANDS
IN THE WAY OF FULFILLED NEEDS?**

People experience a number of barriers when it comes to this sequence of expressing needs and having those needs met.

Low self-esteem. Many people can focus on others' needs but not their own. They feel unworthy. Or past experience (with an abusive parent, for instance) has taught them that their needs are not important. When you ask them to identify their own needs, they don't know where to begin. They can't even acknowledge that their needs are legitimate. If you or your spouse struggles in this way, consider seeing a counselor who can help you resolve issues of low self-esteem.

Conflicting needs. It happens all the time: One part of us wants one thing while the other part wants the opposite. For example, "I need you close. However, I fear closeness because I don't want to lose my individuality." These conflicting needs have to be sorted out, resolved, or balanced so that you can send a consistent message to your spouse. If you send conflicting signals, your spouse will understandably be confused and frustrated. Counseling is often necessary to clarify a person's needs and resolve his or her inner conflicts.

Taboos. People are often taught from childhood not to express their needs, not to be "selfish," not to say, "I want. . . ." These prohibitions or "taboos," ingrained in us during childhood, can have a powerfully inhibiting effect on our adult lives.

I once counseled a taboo-ridden man who found it impossible to express his own needs. He would come into the kitchen while his wife was cleaning up, and he would just stand around. His wife would ask what he wanted, and he would shrug. Then she'd ask if he wanted X, and he'd shake his head; she'd ask if he wanted Y, and he'd say no. With luck, she'd hit on what he wanted, he would brighten, and she'd know she got the right answer. Sometimes he would call his wife from work, and he'd just hang on the phone, breathing; his wife would pose question after question until she finally got a positive response. But the man could never bring himself to simply state his needs. As you can imagine, his wife soon tired of having to play this game with him, which is why she dragged him into counseling.

If you go through life pretending you have no needs yet hoping someone will notice and meet them, you can be sure that those needs will go unmet.

Unhealthy patterns of relating. Couples run into trouble over needs when they have settled into unhealthy patterns of relating to each other. For example, one spouse always asks for his or her needs to be met while the other always provides. In other patterns, both partners try to give to each other, and no one receives; or both withhold from each other. It is often difficult for us to recognize these patterns ourselves—we're right in the middle of them. Often, it takes someone who stands outside of our situation (such as a counselor) to see them more clearly and point them out to us.

Timidity and indirect communication. Indirect communication is frequently the result of timidity—the fear of confronting an issue squarely and directly. Timid people often behave as if to say, "I won't ask you directly for what I need. Instead, I'll show you *by giving to you* what I, in fact, need, in the hope that you'll take the hint."

Jake and Emma were a middle-aged couple who came to me for counseling. They had a pattern of behavior in which he would withdraw and she would pursue. I learned that he tended to withdraw whenever she wanted him to do something. Here's how their little marital drama would play out:

Emma: "Jake, do you want to do such and such?"

Jake: (noncommittally, from behind his paper or football game or whatever) "Mmm-uhm."

Emma: "Does that mean yes or no?"

Jake: "Ahhh. Ahem! Mmm-uhm."

The fact is, Jake didn't really know if he wanted to do such and such or not, but the simple law of inertia ("a body at rest tends to remain at rest unless acted on by an outside force") dictated that he probably preferred to remain at rest. However, because his wife (the aforementioned "outside force") had suggested it, he assumed she wanted to do such and such, so he grudgingly agreed. This had become a well-ingrained pattern.

Jake didn't really want to do such and such, and Emma wasn't sure what she wanted to do. When Emma said, "Do you want to do such and such?" she wasn't trying to maneuver him into doing it. She just wanted to elicit from him some kind of preference or opinion; she hoped he would make a commitment for both of them. Instead, he just went along with her suggestion halfheartedly.

I directed Emma to say to Jake at least once a day, "I want . . ." and then to make a simple request of her husband. Through this exercise, Emma soon learned to express her needs in clear, direct terms. As Emma began communicating directly instead of indirectly with her husband, their relationship improved dramatically.

Pride. Some people feel that by stating a need, they are giving up a piece of themselves. *If I need something from you,* they seem to think, *that means I am weak. If I maintain a facade of total self-sufficiency, then I am strong.* Others feel that if someone else meets their needs, they lose control over their own lives. *I hate to receive,* they seem to think, *because then I'm in someone else's debt. I feel controlled.* It is crucial that couples develop a healthy, mutual interdependence. True interdependence will deflate excessive pride. When we admit that we do need another person, that person is in a position to meet our needs.

Throughout Scripture, God invites us to bring our needs to him so that they can be met (see Matt. 7:7; Phil. 4:19; Heb. 4:16). In a healthy relationship, both partners truly want to meet each other's needs, and both are eager to be asked.

What about My Needs?

1. List five needs—practical, emotional, sexual, etc.—that you
   would like your spouse to meet for you.

   After listing those needs, place a check mark in front of each
   need that you have verbalized to your spouse.

   Consider those needs that do not have check marks. Why
   haven't you verbalized those needs to your spouse? What
   holds you back from asking for what you need or want?

2. The sequence for getting needs met is:

   1. You must know what your need is and be able to articulate it.
   2. You must ask your spouse to meet that need in a specific way.
   3. You must be willing to make yourself understood.
   4. Your spouse must be willing and able to meet your need.
   5. You must be willing to receive from your spouse.

   At which of these steps does communication tend to break
   down between you and your spouse?

   What can you do to repair the communication process so that
   you and your spouse can effectively meet each other's needs?

   Are you willing to commit yourself in an active, daily way to
   following this sequence so that you and your spouse can
   experience greater satisfaction in the area of needs? If so,
   express that commitment to your spouse. Consider writing
   out an agreement between the two of you to focus on those
   problem areas in the sequence.

   Do you expect your spouse to read your mind and meet your
   needs without your having to verbalize them?

   What are some problems that arise between partners when
   one partner expects the other to "just know what I need
   without my having to say anything"?

   Make a commitment to verbalize your needs clearly and

openly without relying on ESP to get the message across. Ask a counselor, marriage support group, or trusted friend to hold you accountable for verbalizing your needs to your spouse.

3. Do you feel inhibited about sharing your needs with your spouse? If so, what is the source of this inhibition? (Check as many as apply.)

	WIFE'S RESPONSE	HUSBAND'S RESPONSE
My needs are too private and personal.	_____	_____
If I say, "I want . . ." I'm being selfish.	_____	_____
I don't want to impose on my spouse.	_____	_____
I'm afraid of how my spouse might respond.	_____	_____
I don't deserve to have my needs met.	_____	_____
My needs are inconsistent and conflicting.	_____	_____
I'd rather show my spouse by giving to him/her than verbalize my needs.	_____	_____
If I express needs, my spouse will think I'm weak.	_____	_____
If I express needs, I will feel weak.	_____	_____
Other _____	_____	_____

Name three specific things you are going to do this week to free yourself of your inhibition or inhibitions so that you can become more verbal and proactive in getting your needs met. Recognize that by actively asking for your own needs, you liberate your spouse to do the same. The issue is not selfishness but mutually giving to each other, which is the way God intended marriage to function.

4. Pray with your spouse regarding these needs and your mutual openness in expressing them. Express thanks to God for this person he has given you to play a vital role in meeting your needs. Thank God also for the privilege you have of meeting your spouse's needs.

14

How Can We Blend These Stepfamilies into One?

"Sure," Howard said into the phone. "No, it's no problem. I'll be right over." He hung up the phone, turned around, and almost ran into his wife. She was glaring at him, standing in his path with her hands on her hips. Howard's heart leaped into his throat and stuck there like a watermelon.

"Who was on the phone, Howard?" asked Janice, her voice hard-edged with suspicion.

"Well—"

"It was The Sponge, wasn't it?" That was Janice's term for Howard's former wife, Emily. In the four years they had been married, Howard had never heard Janice use Emily's name. It was always The Sponge—or something worse.

"Emily needs some help," Howard explained nervously. "She's got a foot of water standing in the sink, her gardener didn't show up, the front lawn's a foot high, and she's got a dozen twelve-year-olds showing up in three hours for a birthday party."

"*Whose* birthday party?"

Howard gulped hard. "Little Dwayne's."

Janice went ballistic. "Little Dwayne is her *boyfriend's* son! Let Big

Dwayne unclog her drain and mow her lawn for Little Dwayne's birthday party!"

"But Big Dwayne is picking up the cake and the party favors. Emily really needs—"

"Howard!" Janice yelled right in his face. "I've been asking you to take care of *our* lawn and *our* shower drain and *our* broken fence and *our* broken screen door for six months! There are three kids in this house—my two daughters and the baby we made together—and they don't get enough of your time. I'm your wife, and I hardly ever see you! But let The Sponge call you up—a woman you haven't been married to for six years, a woman with a boyfriend of her own, a woman who already soaks up half of every dollar you make—and you're Johnny-on-the-spot! Get this straight, Howard. I'm a *wife*. She's an *ex*. If you don't want me to be an ex as well, call her up right now and tell her you can't come."

Howard looked at her, astonished. "But I can't do that! I promised!"

"It's easy. Just call her right back and *un*promise."

"No way!"

"Fine," said Janice. "I'll do it." She picked up the receiver and started punching buttons on the phone.

"What are you doing?" Howard reached for the receiver, but Janice turned away.

"Hello?" she said into the phone. "Guess who this is. . . . That's right. . . . No, I'm afraid Howard can't come over today—or any other day, for that matter."

"Hey! Gimme that!" Howard lunged and grabbed the phone. "Em? It's me. . . . No, Janice is just clowning around. I'll be right over. Bye!" He slammed the receiver down, then grabbed the line cord and gave it a big yank. The cord came loose in his hand, leaving the modular plug sitting uselessly in the phone jack. Then he picked up the phone and threw it clattering down the hall.

"Are you crazy?" shouted Janice. "You just destroyed our telephone!"

"Don't you ever do a thing like that again!" Howard snarled, then headed for the door. Janice had never seen Howard so angry, so forceful before. Why couldn't he be that forceful on *her* behalf?

Two hours later, Howard returned home, tired and sweaty from fixing his former wife's sink and mowing her lawn. Janice and the kids were gone. There was no note.

BLENDED—OR ALL MIXED UP?

What was Howard's problem?

He was divorced and remarried, a stepfather and a father, responsible for a new family. His wife and the children in his own new family needed him, yet his former wife and, in fact, his former in-laws, and even his former wife's boyfriend and his children continued to plague him with demands. He was not legally obligated to his former wife, yet he continued to do things for her that he couldn't find time for in his own household. Why did he feel duty-bound to accede to all the demands of a family he was no longer part of?

The biggest factor, of course, was guilt. He felt responsible and guilty for the breakup of his first marriage, so he continued to allow his former wife to enter his life in ways and at times that were totally inappropriate. Unable to set healthy boundaries between his former family and his current family, Howard had brought himself to the very brink of another divorce.

As one newly initiated stepfather once put it, "Now I know why they call it a 'blended family.' I feel like someone put us all in a blender and pushed the button marked LIQUIFY!" The term *blended family* is really a misnomer. When divorced people come together and try to build new families, the result is rarely what you would think of as a nice, smooth, homogenized "blend." Instead, what you frequently have is a lot of people living together, trying to build relationships, and getting all mixed up.

A better term, perhaps, than *blended families* is *blending families,* since this term suggests that the people in this family are engaged in an ongoing process of coming together. Second families have specific issues to face—very different issues from those faced in first families. When those issues are not addressed head-on with care, commitment, and love, the result is enormous pain for the couple and for the children involved. Sometimes these tensions can even pull a marriage apart.

In chapter 12, we talked about the chronological stages of marriage. In blending families, however, the normal stages of chronological progression do not march logically from one to the next. In fact, the stages may be all mixed up. For instance, if a man in his forties with two college-age children marries a woman in her early thirties with a small child, you have a man and woman at two different developmental stages dealing with different sets of parenting issues.

There are big adjustments to make whenever two people get married, even for the first time. But in a remarriage, the number of adjustments multiplies and the size of the adjustments magnifies. The lines of relationships in blending families tend to get tangled. There are many losses and changes in every relationship that must be dealt with on an individual basis. Both partners must negotiate and balance a multitude of additional relationships at the same time, including:

- relationships with birth children
- relationships with former spouses
- relationships with new in-laws
- relationships with former in-laws
- relationships with stepchildren

Partners have to manage expectations from previous families, such as when their stepchildren critique their actions: "That's not the way we did it when Mom and Dad were together!"

BLENDING IN THE REAL WORLD

My wife and I were married in our early twenties. At that stage in our lives, we weren't dealing with loss and change. We were "kids," just out of college, and we really didn't know who we were. Now we are in our forties, and the issues we are dealing with are very different from the issues we faced in our twenties. If I were getting remarried right now, I'd be juggling a whole different set of issues—the painful loss of my first marriage, guilt about what I am doing to my kids, needs and demands of my first wife, my kids, my new wife and her kids, moving into a new home, the loss of former in-laws, scheduling time with my kids who don't live with me anymore, and on and on. The relatively minor level of stress and change accompanying a first marriage doesn't begin to compare with the massive upheaval that accompanies a remarriage.

Many couples who are blending their families get into trouble because of their expectations. We have an entire generation of young adults who were raised on a cute but grossly unrealistic television show, *The Brady Bunch*. A man with three sons marries a woman with three daughters. Sure, they have their ups and downs and just enough step-sibling conflict around which to build a half-hour script. But nowhere in this show do you find the intense dynamics that take place in real blending families. On this show, the daughters embrace this new stepfather and call him "Daddy." The boys stick up for the girls, and the girls befriend the boys. It's wonderful! And none of that stuff ever happens in real life!

Out here in the real world, where life is something that happens to you day after day and there are no commercial breaks, no reruns, and few of those tidy little Hollywood happy endings, the kids usually resent their new stepfather as an intruder and a threat. The stepsiblings often hate each other and battle each other for turf. The kids want their real parents to get back together again and often spend much of their time thinking up ways to sabotage the new marriage. To top it off, the stepdad often blows in and announces, "OK, I'm your dad now, and you've gotta call me "Dad" and respect me and do what I say." To which the kids respond, "Oh yeah?!"

Stepmothers have a rough time of it, too. They have to adjust to kids who resent them for replacing their real mom. They face especially stiff resistance from stepdaughters, who often compete with them for Dad's attention and affection. Expectations tend to be higher on step-Mom (who's supposed to be the primary manager of house and kids, even if she's employed outside the home) than on Dad (who tends to be viewed as essentially a breadwinner). Stepmothers are expected to come in and be Mom, with all the responsibilities that go with the job.

Many stepparents get tripped up by paradoxical expectations. A stepfather, for example, often finds himself presiding as the male authority figure in a household where he is, in many ways, viewed as the outsider. Mom has been taking care of her kids all by herself for several months, or even years. Yes, she has wished there were a man around the house to help her, but she was managing by herself. Now she has to share responsibility, check decisions with another person, negotiate roles, and give up autonomy. What a hassle!

When she married, she told her new husband that she wanted him to have an active role in the parenting of her children. She wanted the kids to respect his authority. But something strange happens the moment he actually assumes that role and begins to discipline the kids: Suddenly, Mom's whole demeanor changes. She is now a momma bear protecting her cubs—and he's the big bad wolf! This is just one example of the many conflicting, paradoxical loyalties that have to be sorted out in a blending family.

REDEFINING "FAMILY"

In the new marriage arrangement, Dad often has his own kids, and Mom has hers. Dad's kids are probably living with a new stepfather, and he only gets to see them every other weekend. Kids feel disloyal to their real parent if they show any friendliness to the stepparent. Kids live in one parent's house, spend holidays and weekends in the other house, and they're in, they're out, in, out, like the bellows of an accordion. What is their concept of family? It might be three people this week, ten people the next.

In a first marriage, a young couple has months or years in which to bond and build a relationship. They can get through the settling-in phase, make their adjustments, fight their battles, make up, and get to know each other without a lot of prying little eyes checking on their every movement. Couples in a blended situation don't have that luxury. They don't live in a safe, private enclosure; they live in a fishbowl. And some of those fish can be piranhas!

Partners in a blending family are thrust into family life with a bunch of strangers. They are rubbing elbows with kids, competing for the bathroom, struggling to maintain privacy, struggling to build intimacy, and jostling and jockeying for respect and control under chaotic conditions. On top of the problems at home, the couple may have to deal with the annoying, vindictive behavior of an angry, acrimonious former spouse.

The success of a blended family often hinges in large part on how supportive former spouses are. A civil and amicable divorce can help to ensure the success of a remarriage; a bitter and destructive divorce can make remarriage a living hell. When divorced parents love their kids enough to separate on good terms, they are able to support each other's house rules, support each other's authority, and avoid tearing each other down in front of the children.

THE DEVELOPMENT OF A BLENDED FAMILY

The stages of development in a blending family are different from those in a first family. These differences can be observed clearly as early as courtship.

When two previously married people come together in a dating relationship, they usually experience a sense of awkwardness that exceeds even the awkwardness of adolescence. For most previously married people, dating is ancient and dimly remembered history. Both sides are a little rusty at the rituals and rites of courtship.

Looking back over my own life, I realize that I've literally never had a single life as an adult. Marcy and I got married right out of college. I've never been in a singles group, and I wouldn't know where to go or what to do if I were single. If anything happened to our marriage at this point in my life, I would have to ask myself, "How is a man in his forties supposed to act when he's dating? Should he behave like a teenager? call a woman up, take her to the movies, and hold hands and act ginky all the time?" That's a real problem for a lot of people who find themselves back in the courtship phase after years of marriage.

This is a time when people frequently make major mistakes in reading situations and potential partners. At an unconscious level, they are eager—even panicky—to restore that old, familiar situation: a husband, a wife, kids, a home. This urgency about getting back into a family unit often drives previously married people to look at people and situations through rose-colored filters. They see a potential spouse not as who he/she really is but as a symbol of caring and nurturing. *Aha!* they think. *This time I've really, finally found the person who can support me, meet my needs, and make me feel whole again.*

As a result of this filtering and the unconscious craving to restore the comfort of a family unit, many recently divorced or bereaved people tend to jump into new relationships with both feet. The courtship phase becomes very intense and very serious—very fast. Using the stages we discussed in chapter 12 as a reference point, these two people quickly become intensely, powerfully "stuck" on each other. In their passionate attraction to each other and accelerated bonding, they forget that they need time to get to know each other.

In many cases, the sense of a ticking biological clock or that old midlife panic that says, "Life is passing me by!" only serves to super-charge the intensity of this blind passion. Both partners are also likely to be very needy, having come through the pain and loss of divorce, and they clutch at anything or anyone who can make the pain go away. Let anyone try to tell them they ought to slow down and give some thought to what they're doing, and they're likely to snap, "I'm a big boy (or girl) now, and I'm old enough to know what I want! This is the real thing at last, and we're very happy, so butt out!"

I've seen it again and again while doing premarital evaluations and counseling for churches. I would have couples take a written psychiatric evaluation, and when I got the evaluation back, it was clear that these people saw each other and themselves through a romantic halo. In reality, they were marrying right back into the very same problems and issues they "escaped" through divorce a few months earlier. The problems they had in their previous marriage would come around again—only bigger and much worse—in their next marriage, and they don't have a clue! No matter how I tried to counsel them and awaken them to their potential problems, they were just sure that I didn't know what I was talking about.

This is not to say that all—or even most—remarriages are doomed to repeat the pain and failure of the first marriages. But it happens with alarming, tragic regularity.

Another serious complication to the courtship phase of a remarriage is children: One or both partners usually have them, and kids get very uneasy when they see their parents dating. In fact, it's not unusual to see children behaving in ways that are covertly or overtly hostile to the intruding partner.

Once a couple remarries, they find themselves facing an array of difficult and complex tasks, including:

Establishing and maintaining boundaries. Remarried couples are thrown into the paradox of trying to establish safe perimeters around their relationship while being forced to maintain a lot of contact with former spouses, children by the former marriage, and former in-laws. Time must be consciously, carefully scheduled for relationship building with one's spouse and with each child. Privacy of grown-ups and children should be respected, and every individual in the family should have his or her own space.

Establishing intimacy and closeness, despite limited opportunities and many competing demands. Privacy must be planned in advance. The marital relationship is forced to fight for prominence in the many layers of relationships.

Establishing new traditions, borrowing from the backgrounds of both families. Family traditions (regarding Christmas, Easter, birthdays, vacations, and so forth) help to create a sense of identity and security in the new family. Children need to be allowed to maintain some old traditions from the previous family (providing security and continuity) while building new traditions with the present family.

Monitoring and readjusting expectations. Those in the family who are living with—or disillusioned over—their Brady Bunch fantasies need to be brought along and allowed to realize that family love and mutual acceptance takes time and many adjustments. One of the tasks of parenting in a blended family is to inject a dose of realism into the family's expectations.

STEPPARENTHOOD

Children aren't the only people in a blending family who have unrealistic expectations. Adults cast in the uncomfortable role of stepparents often feel that they should be able to jump into the situation and gain the respect, even the affection, of their new children. Relationships have to emerge and grow. Many stepparents want to become firm, respected disciplinarians immediately, or they want to take long walks in the park, hand in hand with their stepkids, or help them with their homework (and be thanked for it, warmly). In the overwhelming majority of cases, the stepchildren are just not ready for that. They're not happy about having a stepparent; they're angry! They feel that if they like this new person, they are being disloyal to their real parent, so they will do everything in their power to avoid bonding with the stepparent.

In time, with a lot of patience and a lot of pain, you can probably build a relationship with your stepchild. The key to success in the stepparent role is to take your time and not force issues.

In a blending family, children always seem to be coming and going. They spend weekends, Christmases, summers, and other times with their "other family." So it is important to maintain clear expectations and rules for children who aren't there all the time.

If the couple decides to conceive children of their own, they need to explain to the stepchildren what is happening. Kids need to be able to ask questions and express feelings. Parents and stepparents need to supply answers for questions kids are either afraid to ask or cannot articulate. For example, parents and stepparents need to reassure the existing children that a new baby doesn't mean anyone is being supplanted or replaced. No matter how many there are in the family, there's always enough love to go around.

PRINCIPLES FOR
BLENDING A HEALTHY NEW FAMILY

A blending family is a family desperately trying to find its balance. The situation is critical but not hopeless. Sometimes it's necessary to bring in outside help, such as a counselor, to work with family members together. But families can take some practical, effective steps themselves. Most of all, they need to be patient with each other and learn to communicate honestly but without hostility.

Try to Resolve Major Issues (Rules, Discipline, Boundaries, Roles, and So Forth) before the Marriage Takes Place.

In as many areas as possible, try to create clear understandings ahead of time. As a parent and stepparent, agree in advance on house rules and discipline styles. When you are in front of the kids, support each other 100 percent. If you have disagreements with your spouse on parenting issues, settle them in private. Don't let kids think they can drive a wedge between the two of you by acting up or rebelling—because if they think they can, they'll probably try it!

Place a Higher Priority on the Marriage Relationship than on Relationships with Children.

The best thing your children and stepchildren can possibly experience, especially if they have been through a marital breakup before, is to see what a good, functional, strong marriage looks like. Schedule time to be alone with your spouse on a regular, weekly basis. Allow the children to see that the two of you are each other's top priority. They will struggle with jealousy for your first allegiance, but eventually they will feel more secure in knowing that the two of you are going to stick together and give the family a firm foundation.

If You Can, Start Your New Life Together in a Neutral Location—Not His House or Her House, but a New House.

Everyone in the new family system needs to recognize that this is not the old setting, with old roles and rules. This is a new adventure, and we're all starting out fresh. It's easier to partition new territory among family members than to "rezone" old territory. You will likely need more space, as well, so that each person can have some private space.

Take Time to Negotiate Family Roles.

Have family meetings in which all members participate, express feelings, ask questions, and share ideas. Make sure no one is left out and that every member is able to wrestle openly, and without being criticized, with the question "Where do I fit into this new system?" Stepparents should lay the cards on the table and ask their kids, "How would you like me to relate to you? How do I fit in? What kind of parenting would you like me to do?" Kids should be invited to voice their questions: "Have the rules changed? How do I relate to my stepparent? Whom do I obey?" These issues should be faced directly, not left hanging.

Accept Conflict and Crises As Opportunities for Relationship Building.

Remember that intimacy is built not only during the "warm-fuzzy" times but also during the crunch times in a relationship. Family conflicts can actually become opportunities for bonding to one another if they are faced honestly and lovingly. Times of conflict force family members to face their true feelings and "get real" with one another.

Give Everyone a Chance to Blend.

Each family member will move toward acceptance of the new system at his or her own pace. The new system will seem somewhat artificial and even "weird" to some family members who cling to the memories of their "real family," the first family that no longer exists. What many family members miss most about the old family is the security (although, in a divorcing family "security" may be mere familiarity) and the sense of being valuable to the people in it. In time, the new family will provide these assurances.

Encourage Honest, Open Family Communication.

Avoid showing shock, surprise, anger, or rebuke when someone raises a question. Accept and acknowledge all feelings, even if you cannot agree with what is being expressed: "I certainly understand why you would feel that way. We're all going through a lot of changes in this new situation." When conflicts arise, meet them head-on and settle them openly.

Learn All You Can about the Issues and Problems of Blending Families.

I wouldn't recommend that any couple, no matter how well-matched they appear to be, go into remarriage without counseling. Seek a counselor with a lot of experience working with issues of blended families. For more information, contact the Stepfamily Association of America, Inc., 215 Centennial Mall South, Suite 212, Lincoln, Nebraska 68508.

Relax. You'll make it. And so will your spouse, your children, and your stepchildren. Even though *The Brady Bunch* is a myth, a blending family is for real. While the two of you, as "Mom and Dad," are not responsible for making everyone happy, your honesty, love, and patience will build the framework for a family system that is healthy and is caring for each of its members.

How Can We Blend
These Stepfamilies into One?

1. Answer the following questions individually, then discuss them together.

   What is the biggest challenge facing you in this new marriage?

   On a scale from 1 to 10, where 1 equals "No Support" and 10 equals "Total Support," rate the support you receive from your spouse in managing or resolving this challenge.

   What could your spouse do to help you better resolve or manage this challenge in your remarriage?

2. If you were divorced:

   On a scale from 1 to 10, where 1 equals "Very Hostile and Destructive" and 10 equals "Very Friendly and Supportive," how civil was your divorce?

   What steps could you take to ease tensions with your former spouse so that his/her remarriage and your remarriage could function more smoothly and effectively?

3. Discuss together what you see as the current emotional stage of your marriage:

   Stage 1: Stuck (or Stuck/Fighting)
   Stage 2: Unstuck
   Stage 3: I-ness
   Stage 4: We-ness

   Are you and your partner at the same stage? Why or why not? Explain your answer.

4. Talk together about what blended-family issues are currently impeding the progress and emotional growth of your marriage.

Look at the list below, and discuss the statements that you think apply to your marriage.

Our marriage has a lack of privacy (intrusions of children).

Our family suffers from a lack of boundaries (intrusions of former spouses and others).

Our children, or other people, are making deliberate or unconscious efforts to sabotage our relationship.

There is a confusion over roles in our family.

There is conflict between stepsiblings in our family.

The two of us are conflicting over parenting styles.

One or both of us—or our children—have unrealistic expectations about the way our family should be working.

5. **It's very easy, under the best of circumstances, for couples to reshuffle their priorities in unhealthy ways. For example, many parents and stepparents see the hurts of their children, resulting from bereavement or divorce, and they feel guilty. The children are demanding and needy, and the parents/stepparents feel guilty. The result is that the children are placed at the top of the list of priorities. Former spouses, parents, and in-laws put their demands into the mix, and before you know it, the needs of the marriage—such as the needs for intimacy and boundaries—get shoved to the bottom of the hierarchy. It is at this point that many second marriages fail.**

Be honest with yourself, and each of you list your priorities in the order in which they actually occur in your life.

Husband's Priorities

1: My relationship with _____

2: My relationship with _____

3: My relationship with _____

4: My relationship with _____

5: My relationship with _____

6: My relationship with _____

Wife's Priorities

1: My relationship with _____

2: My relationship with _____

3: My relationship with _____

4: My relationship with _____

5: My relationship with _____

6: My relationship with _____

Now, list three specific steps you will take, beginning this week, to put your priorities in their proper, healthy order— God first, then your marriage, then children, and so forth. Ask a trusted friend to hold you accountable for taking these steps.

1._____

2._____

3._____

6. List at least six activities that you and your spouse could do to get away from the house and the kids for a few hours to build some intimacy. Covenant with each other to do at least two of them per month for the next three months.

   1._____

   2._____

   3._____

   4._____

   5._____

   6._____

7. Spend time together in prayer. Pray for the new family that you are building together. Pray for the emotional and spiritual

growth of the children. Pray for wisdom to learn and grow through the pain of the past so that this marriage will stand upon a secure foundation of love and realistic thinking.

As you begin new traditions together, don't neglect the very special bonding experience of family devotions. Obtain a family devotional book from a Christian bookstore. Make sure you have a story or songs that are appropriate and interesting for the age and interest level of your youngest participant. Avoid lengthy prayers that would make family devotions a trial for short attention spans (save your long list of prayer requests for your personal devotions or for devotions with your spouse).

As you pray with your family, open your heart to God and to your kids. Ask God to build your family into a secure community of people who love, nurture, and protect each other, so that God himself will be honored when people see the way you live together as a family.

15

Why
Would You Be
Unfaithful to Me?

"Why, Stan?" asked Debi, staring at her husband through red-rimmed eyes. "Why did you do it?"

Stan looked away and shrugged. "I told you before. I don't know. I really don't know. People do things without really knowing why."

"It's not as if I wasn't available to you. It's not as if your needs weren't being met. Half the time, I pursued *you* for sex! It's not like you needed someone to talk to. I was the one who was always saying, 'Stan, you can tell me anything. Share with me, all your feelings and struggles. I want you to share deeply with me.'"

"Yes, Debi, you always said that."

"And you always said, 'I'm all right. There's nothing to share.' You were always closed to me, Stan."

"Look, Debi, affairs just happen, you know? I didn't get involved in this—" Stan paused, groping for the right euphemism—"this situation because you are somehow not adequate as a wife. You're terrific. You're terrific in bed. You try to be a good friend. It's not as if I need to go elsewhere to get better sex or to find a better listener or any of that stuff. It just happened, that's all, so stop looking for reasons. Sometimes in these . . . situations . . . there just aren't any reasons."

Stan really believed what he said. He really didn't know why he committed adultery, and he really was convinced that adultery sometimes occurs for no reason at all. But he was wrong. Every time a marriage partner strays from the marriage bed, there are reasons. The reasons may be hidden, tangled, confused, and even contradictory, but they do exist.

Infidelity deals a massive, traumatic shock to a marriage. But the wound of infidelity can be healed—if we can uncover, understand, and treat the root causes of the affair.

THE NATURE OF BETRAYAL

What is infidelity? Some people would say that it occurs only when there has been "actual intercourse." Of course, that leaves a lot of territory open to interpretation and self-deluding denial. Do kissing and touching someone other than your spouse in an intimate way *not* qualify as infidelity? Does that mean that oral sex "doesn't count"? Does it mean that two people who bring each other to orgasm without vaginal penetration didn't engage in "actual intercourse"? And what about a homosexual or lesbian affair? Or a hand up the skirt or down the blouse of a former spouse, a coworker, or an old girlfriend? Or a flirtatious comment and a bit of peekaboo with an old boyfriend? What about lunch and sexy talk with someone from the office?

A lot of people play mind games with themselves and their spouses, pretending that if they engage in this or that behavior, then it's not really infidelity. In *Private Lies,* family therapist Frank Pittman argues convincingly that infidelity is any sexually related act you keep secret from your spouse or which, when discovered by your spouse, is viewed by him or her as a betrayal or indiscretion. When he is asked, "Do you think I'm doing something wrong in this situation?" (such as meeting an opposite-sex coworker for drinks after work), Pittman always responds with, "Why don't you ask your spouse?" He goes on to suggest definitions for the terms adultery and infidelity that make it hard for us to duck and deny the implications of borderline (or over the line) behavior:

We might define adultery as a sexual act outside the marriage, while we might define infidelity as a sexual dishonesty within the marriage. Adultery may be against the law or against God's will, but infidelity is against the marriage and is thus a more relevant and more personal danger.*

Infidelity is behavior that breaks the promise of marriage and breaches the trust of marriage. Infidelity is a betrayal of the relationship. Since honesty and trust are central, essential ingredients of marital intimacy (as we saw in chapter 3), infidelity destroys the very essence of a marriage. Infidelity erects a wall of secrecy and distrust in the very place where two married souls are to be joined together.

There are a lot of common misconceptions about infidelity, and when couples come to me for counseling about one partner's infidelity, the offending partner usually articulates one or more of these misconceptions during the first session.

Affairs are good for a marriage. "A little fun on the side keeps you from getting bored at home." You really think so? Then let's reframe this statement a little and see if it still makes sense: "Lies, secrecy, and betrayal are good ways to build intimacy and togetherness in a marriage." Fact: While it's true that many marriages can and do become dull, it is not true that marriage has to be dull. Intimacy—not infidelity—makes marriage exciting.

Well, it's all out in the open now—I guess divorce is the only option. Fact: In roughly half of the infidelity cases I've worked with, the couple has found a way to use the discovery of infidelity as a wake-up call and a catalyst to a stronger relationship.

It's my wife's/husband's fault I did this. The offended partner often owns this point of view as well: "It's my fault. If I had been a better partner, my spouse wouldn't have had to go outside the marriage for a sexual relationship." Fact: We are all responsible for our own actions. No one else—not our spouse, not the other person in the affair, no one—makes us jump into the wrong bed. In order for a relationship to be healed, the person who committed the infidelity must take personal responsibility for his or her actions. This doesn't mean that both partners did not contribute to the marital problems that preceded the infidelity, only that the unfaithful partner alone chose to be unfaithful.

This affair must mean all the love has gone out of our marriage. Fact: While affairs are frequently a warning sign of deeper problems in the marriage, they usually do not signal that "the love has gone." As we saw in chapter 1, the idea that love is something that strikes two people like a bolt out of the blue then disappears without explanation, is romanticized nonsense. It's a simplistic way of looking at the commitment that is required to make a marriage work. Feelings of attraction and desire may ebb and flow, and there is a lot that two people can do to rekindle those feelings when they have begun to subside. But love—genuine, covenant-love—is always a choice that both partners can make.

Everybody does it. "All my friends have had affairs. Why shouldn't I?" Fact: Despite what you see in soap operas, daytime talk shows, and popular magazines, everybody's *not* doing it. For the past several decades, statistics and surveys have consistently shown our society to be mostly monogamous. According to those surveys, roughly half of all husbands and roughly a third of all wives have been unfaithful—and even those statistics are misleading.

Many of the affairs included in such surveys were one-time, never-repeated episodes—not lifestyle choices, as the "everybody does it" comment would indicate. Also, many who reported having extramarital affairs did so only after the marriage was clearly dying of other causes and already headed for separation or divorce. *Marriages that are otherwise intact show much lower rates of infidelity than the average.* Faithfulness is actually the norm.

Let's get rid of these misconceptions. Let's accept the truth about infidelity as our starting point, and then we can begin rebuilding a damaged relationship and make it whole and strong again. Here are some truths about infidelity:

- Affairs are deceptive and destructive, and they endanger the very existence of a marriage.
- Marriages can survive infidelity.

- While an affair involves sex, most affairs take place for reasons having little or nothing to do with sex.

- Infidelity is not normal; it is a disorder in the relationship, and it needs to be treated and healed.

WHY AFFAIRS HAPPEN

Back to Stan and Debi.

They came to me after Debi discovered that Stan had been having an affair with another woman from their church. Debi knew the other woman slightly—her name was Celeste—and was doubly surprised by Stan's choice; Celeste seemed like such a plain, uninteresting woman. Why did Stan get involved with her? Stan and Celeste had apparently become close while working on a church committee together. The affair had lasted about four months and ended when Debi overheard Stan's side of a phone conversation between them. The discovery of her husband's adultery came as a shattering revelation to Debi, and she had strongly considered leaving Stan.

Prior to this discovery, Debi had pursued Stan for affection, sex, and intimacy. She had literally begged him to discuss "deeply" (one of her favorite words) all of his feelings and thoughts. Stan, however, was emotionally closed to her and continually stated that everything was all right.

"So why, if everything was 'all right,'" asked Debi, "did you go to bed with another woman? Did you think Celeste was sexier than me? Was she better in bed? Do you think she's prettier, smarter, what?"

"Don't be ridiculous," Stan responded dismissively. "I wasn't in love with her. You know Celeste, and you know she's not even in your league. She was just . . . there."

Debi blinked. "It doesn't make any sense," she said. At that point, it didn't make sense—not even to Stan. Later, it would all make sense.

Why do affairs happen? Frequently, even those who are involved in infidelity don't understand what drives their behavior. Some affairs may involve two or more factors, and the two partners in an affair may enter into the adulterous act for very different reasons. Here are some of the reasons marriage partners stray:

235

Unplanned passion. A man or a woman may encounter a situation of temptation unexpectedly. He or she may have been the target of some other person's seductive scheme. Or unexpected circumstances may have simply thrown two people together in an emotionally and sexually volatile situation. This does not excuse either person from responsibility when sexual temptation arises. To say that an incident of infidelity was "unplanned" or "accidental" is not to say it was inevitable. Both participants in the act of adultery are responsible and have the power to choose to do the right thing.

After an initial unplanned incident, a participant often responds by experiencing enormous guilt and anxiety. He or she has violated a sacred trust, the covenant of marriage, and many people react by feeling remorseful and promising themselves and God never to do it again. They blame themselves—and rightly so. The anxiety they feel usually focuses on the fear of exposure and all the losses that might result from that exposure—plus, perhaps, a tinge of anxiety regarding the possibility that it might happen again or that a sexually transmitted disease or unwanted pregnancy might result.

In some cases, a participant in an unplanned incident of adultery may find that he or she likes it. Some people become obsessive about engaging in infidelity, as if extramarital sex were an addictive drug.

Sexual addiction. Also called "philandering," this behavior involves a series of shallow, even anonymous sexual encounters—or it may involve multiple, ongoing relationships. The philanderer feels that serial sex is the norm and that a steady stream of different sexual partners is necessary to keep sex "exciting." He or she tends to depersonalize the sex partners in these relationships, viewing them as bodies (or even body parts) rather than as human beings with souls and feelings. These individuals also tend to depersonalize their marriage partners.

Most sex addicts are men, although there are certainly female sex addicts. Philanderers have no conscience about violating intimacy because they fear genuine intimacy. They don't want to know or be known in any depth, nor do they want to be "cured" of a pattern of behavior they consider to be normal. Whether male or female, sex addicts frequently use sex as a way of asserting power over the opposite sex, and they consider a sexual episode a conquest. Philanderers are usually charming and likable, and they have perfected a set of techniques for luring people into sexual relationship with them. They frequently have nonsexual marriages and would very strongly resent it if their spouse had an affair.

Romanticism, or relationship addiction. Romantics think that life is a romance novel. They are in love with love—idealized, romantic love. Their drug is not sex but passion—lush, crescendoing, romantic emotion that carries the relationship addict away on strains of violin music. They always believe that "this moment will last forever" and that this relationship (whichever relationship it happens to be at the time) is finally "the love of a lifetime." Relationship addicts go from partner to partner, not so much because they are sexually promiscuous, but because they always believe that the next encounter will be with Prince or Princess Charming.

Just as most sex addicts are men, most relationship addicts are women. The "perfect match"—a pairing that takes place over and over again—is the sex-addicted man and the relationship-addicted woman. They are a symbiotic couple: She feeds his lust, and he feeds her romantic fantasies while exploiting her sexually. When it's over, the relationship addict is left with guilt, regret, self-directed anger, and an enormous sense of being used. These feelings last until the next time the violins begin to play. . . .

Revenge. An affair is sometimes used as a way of getting even with one's husband or wife for some perceived insult or injury—including infidelity. Revenge affairs often take place near the end of a marriage that is clearly on the rocks, sealing the fate of a relationship that might otherwise have been salvageable if either partner had tried to save it.

Midlife crisis. Many affairs happen when one or the other partner reaches a point of dissatisfaction with marriage, career, and life in general. He or she feels that life is passing by too quickly and many of life's more exciting experiences have still not been tasted. A "grab for the gusto" mentality sets in, supercharged by the fear that "maybe I'm losing my virility" or "maybe I'm losing my attractiveness." In an effort to prove that he or she "still has what it takes" and to reduce the anxieties of this transitional stage in life, the individual initiates an affair.

A classic example of this type of affair is found in 2 Samuel, chapters 11 and 12, where King David gets involved in an adulterous affair with the wife of one of his top military leaders. It occurs when David is at a midlife transitional stage—and it leads to disaster, exposure, murder, and judgment in David's life.

Midlife is an extremely dangerous time for a person suddenly to decide to have an affair. The vast majority of divorces among couples married twenty-five years or more are the result of infidelity. Decades of accumulated trust, happy memories, family relationships, and the respect of one's children can all be flushed away for the sake of a casual, meaningless (and often awkward and unpleasant) sexual encounter. If you see yourself heading in this direction, save yourself and your family a lot of agony and get counseling—fast!

Dysfunctional marital arrangements. Sometimes one spouse turns a blind eye to the other spouse's serial infidelities. In some cases, one partner doesn't like sex. Obviously, this person should seek therapy to heal the emotional issues that hinder the normal enjoyment of his or her sexuality. In all too many cases, however, the partner who doesn't enjoy sex—to avoid being bothered by the other partner's needs—allows (or even sends) the other partner outside the marriage to get those needs met.

In other arrangements, both partners behave sexually toward each other, but one of them uses extramarital sex either because of a sexual addiction or to maintain emotional distance from the spouse (fear of intimacy). The nonadulterous partner allows the other partner's behavior either out of fear of losing that partner or because he/she also desires emotional distance, or because he/she has bought the partner's argument that "some people just have a high-powered sex drive, and a monogamous relationship isn't enough to satisfy it."

Frequently these arrangements are made in silence; both sides know what's going on, but neither side talks about it—a case of mutual denial. But sometimes these arrangements are actually arrived at through discussion and negotiation. The couple may work out a verbal arrangement between them whereby one (or both) partners are permitted to carry on affairs, often with certain conditions thrown in ("Never bring a woman into our house" or "You can be with a man when you're away on a business trip but never in town where someone we know might see you").

Those who enter into such arrangements—either silently or by agreement—fail to understand how unhealthy and self-destructive such behavior can be. The risk of one partner's bringing a disease to the marriage bed is only a small part of the danger of these arrangements; the greater harm comes from the psychological and spiritual damage of maintaining a marriage relationship with denial, indeterminate boundaries, and the repression of normal feelings (such as anger, anxiety, and jealousy). It is impossible for true intimacy to grow under such conditions.

Unfulfilled expectations. Couples enter into marriage with both spoken and unspoken expectations. In fact, most people are not fully aware of all the expectations they harbor regarding marriage and their spouses. If these expectations go unsatisfied, the relationship begins to deteriorate, and the unsatisfied partner may choose to go outside the marriage to seek satisfaction. These unfulfilled expectations are usually not of a sexual nature; the unsatisfied, unfaithful partner may be seeking intimacy or someone who will listen and offer emotional acceptance and affirmation. Sex is merely a component of a much larger emotional picture.

Attention getting. Some partners, feeling ignored, may use an affair as a way to get attention. In such cases, the goal (whether conscious or unconscious) is exposure, not secrecy. The unfaithful partner will usually find ways to leave clues and hints so that the affair will be "accidentally" discovered by the other partner.

Looking for excitement. Some partners get bored with each other or with their lives and simply go looking for excitement—not just the excitement of sex but the excitement of taking a risk.

Some people who feel a lack of sexual desire or whose spouse is sexually unavailable will seek excitement outside the marriage. Sometimes a person who has trouble becoming aroused in marital sex finds that the danger of extramarital sex, along with the adventure of experiencing sex with a new partner, stimulates greater arousal and sexual excitement. Also, the fact that adultery is sinful contributes to the excitement; as we saw in chapter 11, many people are brought up with the unhealthy view that sex is sinful—and therefore, the more sinful the act, the sexier it is. In counseling, these individuals can often be helped to see that sex is clean and good and that wholesome sex is the best sex of all.

Utilitarian affairs. Some affairs are strictly business. People will sometimes allow themselves to be sexually used in order to gain a job, a career advancement, or some other favor. Properly viewed, most utilitarian affairs are really nothing more than a form of prostitution.

In some cases, sexual favors are extorted from another person, as when a boss sexually harasses an employee because he has the power over her job and her paycheck. Though individuals who find themselves in such situations still have the power to say no to harassment (and they definitely should say no), those who say yes should be viewed more as victims than as perpetrators. A person in desperate need of staying employed may see the sexual infidelity as a smaller problem than losing his or her job, and the boss who takes advantage of such situations deserves the larger share of the blame.

Exit affairs. Sometimes when a partner makes a decision to leave the marriage, he or she will initiate an affair. An exit affair may be a premature "shopping trip" for a new spouse, or it may be a way of announcing to one's spouse (and even oneself), "This marriage is over. I'm taking my sexuality elsewhere." For people who have difficulty verbalizing feelings and confronting issues, having an affair—then allowing the other partner to find out about it—is sometimes used in place of face-to-face communication.

Clearly, people have affairs for all kinds of reasons, and none of those reasons are particularly logical or healthy. There were reasons for Stan's infidelity, even though Stan himself didn't know and couldn't articulate what they were. It took a lot of digging and probing in therapy before he and Debi were able to understand what had taken place inside—and outside—their marriage.

HOW TO RESPOND TO INFIDELITY

A couple of times during counseling, Debi suggested a frame for Stan's behavior: "the midlife crazies." Each time she raised that phrase, Stan rejected it. He liked to picture himself as a careful, logical thinker. He didn't do anything that was "crazy." As our sessions unfolded, however, it became clear that Stan—who denied having any problems or anxieties, who virtually denied having any emotions at all!—had been carrying a great emotional burden even before the affair.

Stan was a worrier, and he tended to "own" all the problems and issues in the home—that is, he felt personally responsible for everything that happened in the family. He had always been reasonably but not spectacularly successful in his sales career, but his industry had gone into a slump and sales were down. As a result, he was chronically anxious about finances, though he never confided his concerns to Debi. He also worried about communication problems and conflict between Debi and their preadolescent daughter and about Debi's apparent emotional neediness—a neediness she never talked about but which she seemed to expect Stan to take care of. She was generally unhappy but would not suggest anything Stan might do to make her happy. She always seemed to want something from him—a level of sharing, an emotional connection, a depth of affection—that he could not deliver, and he was very upset about it.

So, at age forty-eight, Stan was beginning to feel like a failure. He was financially troubled at a time when several of his friends were bragging about how their smart investments were going to enable them to take early retirement. His family life was troubled and punctuated by conflict. He felt that he was inadequate as a husband since he was unable to meet his wife's emotional needs. He was worrying about his own mortality and even his virility. He thought about all the experiences that had passed him by in life—including the experience of "sowing some wild oats" (he and Debi had married young, and both were virgins on their wedding night). He had begun to wonder what sex with another partner might be like.

Stan didn't realize it, but he was in typical midlife crisis.

Then one day, after a church committee meeting, Celeste asked if Stan could give her a ride home. During the drive, she talked about how difficult her life had been since her husband died of cancer two years before. Stan felt tongue-tied and awkward, wishing he could think of something to say that might be helpful and supportive. As she was getting out of the car, however, Celeste thanked him for being a good listener.

Stan went home with a strange, indefinable feeling inside. Somehow, without really knowing what he had done, he had managed to be emotionally supportive to a woman—something he had not been able to do for his own wife. He went home and, in response to Debi's questioning, told her a few superficial details about the committee meeting. He did not mention driving Celeste to her house.

Two weeks later, another committee meeting—and again he gave Celeste a lift. Again she talked about how unhappy her life had been since her husband passed away. She made one comment that stuck in Stan's mind: "It's so hard getting into that big, empty bed every night." In Stan's mind, it almost sounded . . . well, like an invitation. Those words continued to roll around in Stan's mind for days.

Two weeks later, another meeting, another ride home. This time, Stan stood by her front door for a few minutes, talking a little, listening a lot. Celeste invited him in for coffee. He said, "No, thanks, I really ought to be getting home." But instead of leaving, he kept talking and listening another few minutes. He knew Debi wasn't really expecting him for a while—the meeting had ended early. When Celeste invited him a second time for coffee, he accepted—though he never did get that cup of coffee.

When Debi accidentally discovered the affair, she suffered a shock much like that of bereavement. She entered the five-stage grief process that most people experience with the loss of a loved one: denial, anger, bargaining, depression, acceptance.

When she first overheard Stan talking to Celeste on the phone about their relationship, her initial reaction was denial. Not *her* husband! Surely she had misinterpreted what he was saying! Even after she confronted him and he admitted the affair, all she could say to herself was, "This can't be happening! Stan would never do this to me!"

Then—understandably—she became angry. Extremely angry, in fact. The details of what she did and said are better left undescribed.

Interspersed with her bouts of anger were bouts of bargaining—bargaining with Stan ("What can I do to make sure you never do this again?") and bargaining with God ("Please, God, make this situation and these feelings go away! Can't it be like it was before? Can't things be as if this horrible thing had never happened?").

Depression had settled over Debi by the time she and Stan came in for counseling. Her depression was a bleak, black aura of mingled sadness, hopelessness, anger turned outward ("How could you do this to me, Stan?" and "How could you allow this to happen to me, God?"), and anger turned inward ("What did I do to bring this on? How could I have been so stupid?").

She was, it seemed, a long way from the acceptance stage.

How should a couple respond when an affair is discovered? An incident of infidelity does not have to destroy a marriage; in fact, the honesty and caring required to save a marriage can actually cause a relationship to emerge from this horrible experience stronger than it was before.

The restoration of the relationship depends on both partners' making emotionally healthy, honest, loving choices in the aftermath of the infidelity. Trust has been broken and can only be rebuilt by patient effort, honesty, and love.

If You Are the Offending Partner

Confess the affair to your spouse. "But," you may say, "my spouse doesn't know. Wouldn't it be better for me to just end the affair, make sure it never happens again, and not say anything that would hurt my spouse?" That's not only cowardly, it's bad for the marriage. You build a healthy marriage on intimacy and honesty—not secrets and lies.

An affair is usually symptomatic of deeper problems in the relationship that need to be brought into the open, addressed, and resolved. If you fail to confront the core problems in your marriage, you will probably find that, despite your good intentions, the infidelity will not stop. Either you will end up going back to the affair, or you will become involved in a different one. The issues that led you into the wrong bed are still there, waiting for you at home, unresolved and unhealed.

Face the problem. Face the truth. Face your spouse and settle the matter.

It's probably advisable that you confess to your spouse in the presence of a pastor or counselor. (Marriage counseling is a foregone conclusion.) Avoid making excuses, using euphemisms, or minimizing the seriousness of your conduct. Above all, avoid blaming anyone but yourself for your actions. Admit that you are responsible, not your spouse or the person with whom you had the affair. It's time to own your own actions and beg your spouse for mercy and forgiveness. Nothing less than abject remorse, repentance, and contrition will do.

Expect your spouse to be angry and hurt. Expect tears and shouting. Expect probing questions about issues you would rather not discuss. Expect questions such as, "Was she sexier than me?" or "What kind of sex acts did you do with him?"

Be honest. Be humble. Accept every accusation and indictment that is hurled at you. Defend nothing. Don't retaliate. Don't counteraccuse. Don't do anything but accept the responsibility for your actions.

If You Are the Wounded Partner

If your spouse is confessing to you, you need to listen. Avoid acting or speaking rashly. Seek help from a pastor or counselor. Make sure you obtain answers from your spouse to the following questions:

- Is the affair still going on?
- Are you going to end the affair immediately?
- Are you willing to be honest and open with me in working through the reasons this happened?
- What is the significance of this affair to you? Was it a casual fling—or is it a romantic entanglement?
- What decisions have you made about our marriage?
- How do you think the children will be affected by these decisions?

As you talk with your spouse, carefully monitor your own thinking. Expect to experience strong emotions and distorted perceptions.

Thoughts will occur to you which may fill you with a sense of panic, pain, dread, despair, hopelessness, or rage. You'll be bombarded by such thoughts as, *I'll never be happy again,* or *My entire marriage has been a lie,* or *God can never untangle the mess my life has become.* Be aware that these feelings and the crisis of this situation will eventually pass. Yes, this is a horrible moment in your life—one of the worst you have ever experienced or will experience—but you will come through it.

If you have just discovered your spouse is having an affair, try to remain calm. You may want to get the help and insight of a pastor or counselor before confronting your spouse. But make no mistake: You must confront your spouse about his or her infidelity.

When confronted, your partner may (1) deny the affair, (2) admit the affair but defend himself/herself, (3) admit the affair but blame you, (4) admit the affair but blame someone else, (5) refuse to talk about it, or (6) throw himself/herself completely on your mercy and beg forgiveness.

If your spouse becomes defensive or—worse—offensive, refuse to accept any particle of blame or shame for the affair. This was not your choice, and you are not to blame for your spouse's infidelity.

If the affair is ongoing, make it clear to your spouse that it must end right now. You may want to insist that your spouse get on the phone in your presence and end it on the spot. Don't accept a plea that, "I need some time to get out of this." If your spouse doesn't want to lose you, he/she should be willing never to see or speak to the other person again, period. Force your spouse to make a choice, and don't compromise.

Express your hurt and anger—but avoid doing so in a destructive or violent way. Express the fact that you want something positive to come out of this—a closer relationship, not greater distance. Remember: The safer your spouse feels, the more likely he/she will be to be open and truthful with you. If your spouse feels threatened, he/she may "edit" the truth as a self-protective measure.

Feel free to express any curiosity or questions you have about the affair. Intimacy has been broken by your partner's lies and secrecy. You have a right to some information. Let your partner explain and apologize.

Understand that you probably see everything—including your marriage relationship—more clearly than your spouse, whose perceptions are still in the haze of unreality that is a part of being unfaithful. The greater weight of deciding the fate of the marriage probably rests with you, at least for now. Resist the temptation to punish or exact revenge. Resist the temptation to reject or shame your spouse. Don't threaten a "revenge affair" of your own.

Above all, pray. Ask God for wisdom, peace of mind, serenity, and a spirit of love and forgiveness so that the marriage can be healed.

A special word of caution: If you find that your spouse has been involved in a series of affairs or multiple simultaneous affairs, it is important that you realize that your partner is probably extremely self-centered and not a likely candidate for repentance and permanent change. Individuals who are inclined to engage in multiple affairs tend to be very good at conning other people, including their spouses, into getting what they want. As marriage partners, these individuals are very bad risks. You should not attempt to deal with a philandering, multiple-adulterous spouse by yourself; you need the help of a counselor who understands the unique psychological dynamics of these individuals.

Normally, I would avoid suggesting divorce if you are willing to work to restore the marriage. Philandering spouses, however, are in a category by themselves. Staying married to a person who is virtually incapable of being truthful, faithful, and monogamous can be very destructive.

REPAIRING THE RELATIONSHIP

As you work through the process of understanding the problem and restoring the relationship, allow emotions to flow freely. There will be many strong feelings, and they will be overwhelmingly painful. They will subside at times, then come on with full force once again, hours or days later. Expect ups and downs.

Take inventory of your relationship together. Ask yourselves: How did we get to this place? Where is God in our relationship now? Are we finally being fully honest with each other, or are we still holding back? Are there secrets that still need to be uncovered, feelings that still need to be expressed?

Avoid blaming each other. Both partners should take responsibility for their own actions and their own neglect of the relationship, but the offending partner should remember that no one else is to blame for his or her infidelity. One partner may have to admit that he became too busy with his career or that she allowed communication and intimacy to deteriorate, but that does not excuse the other partner's affair.

Trust will need to be rebuilt very patiently, piece by piece. An offending partner may say, "You're just going to have to trust me when I say it will never happen again." But that's nonsense. Trust is not a light switch that you can click on. Trust is something that is built up slowly over years of experience—and which can be destroyed in a few moments by a single act of unfaithfulness.

Trust is a commodity that is spread out over the various compartments of one's relationship; there is sexual trust, emotional trust, financial trust. If your spouse discovers that you have been lavishing gifts and favors on the person with whom you had an affair, expect him or her not to trust you with credit cards and checkbooks for a while. If you made your liaisons during business trips, expect your spouse to check in on you frequently and unexpectedly every time you're away. If your affair grew out of an emotional bond of friendship with someone at work or at church, expect your spouse to demand that you sever your opposite-sex friendships.

Expect to make a lot of changes in your life in order to rebuild the trust that you have broken by your bad choices. This is not a matter of your spouse's trying to punish you; these are just the natural consequences of an act of infidelity. If you want to rebuild your marriage, be prepared to accept those consequences.

You can, however, negotiate solutions to some of these problems of broken trust—solutions which will, over the long haul, enable you to rebuild trust and intimacy in your marriage. For example, your spouse may say to you, "After what you did on that trip to Chicago, I just can't see how I can possibly allow you to take business trips anymore."

A positive response might be: "I understand how you feel, but my job requires me to travel. So let's find a way for me to put you at ease and help you know that you can trust me when I'm gone. I'll give you my itinerary so that you know when I'm in business meetings and when I'm on my own. I promise that when I'm not in meetings, I'll be in my hotel room. Anytime you feel anxious or just want to check in on me, call my room, and I'll be there. I won't even leave to go down to the restaurant—I'll get room service for every meal. Every moment of my free time on the trip, I'll be in my room, by the phone, accountable to you. The moment I begin to feel tempted in any way, I'll call you immediately, and we'll talk about it."

Throughout this restoration time—which will be a matter of years, not weeks or months—concentrate on relationship building through specific activities:

Plan to do acts of caring for each other so that you can experience again the feelings of affection and support you felt for each other before the affair. Set aside a special weekly night for these caring acts, and make specific requests of each other: "I'd like you to take me out to dinner tonight." "Give me a back rub in front of the fireplace before we go to bed." "Please do the dishes and put the kids to bed for me tonight."

Remember the good times. Get out picture albums or the wedding videos. Share positive memories and rebuild the emotional ties that once bound you so intimately together. Relax together, making room for those old feelings to come back.

Talk about things you never talked about before. Share childhood memories. Share feelings you've kept hidden. Share fears and hopes. Don't avoid the subject of the affair, but purge the emotions on an ongoing basis. Don't let feelings or thoughts build up inside; allow them to flow between you.

Mutually commit yourselves to a lifestyle of uncompromising honesty. No more lies or secrets, even in the smallest matters. Become totally transparent to each other. Nothing rebuilds trust and intimacy like truth.

Face sexual issues squarely. Expect to have problems with sex for a while since the act of sex between you and your spouse will inevitably arouse mental images of the affair. Be patient with each other. If sexual dysfunction becomes persistent, seek professional counseling.

Forgive again and again. Hurt like that cannot be forgiven once and for all. Memories and emotions will continue to recur, and anger will unexpectedly recur, red-hot and stinging, even months or years after you thought you were finally healed. Remember that forgiving doesn't mean condoning, nor does it mean you don't hold your partner accountable. Forgiveness and accountability go hand in hand. Adultery is wrong, a violation of your relationship, but you are choosing to release your spouse from condemnation for his/her wrongdoing. For your own sake as much as for your partner's, you are going to let go of anger and bitterness, and you are going to get on with your life and your relationship.

Symbolize a renewed commitment. Consider making a meaningful gesture or ceremony to mark a new beginning in your relationship together—a renewal of your wedding vows, a new ring ceremony, a second honeymoon, a communion service. Mark the event with photos, and hang the photos on the wall of your home. As you forgive, make sure you never forget the new beginning of your love and intimacy together.

Monitor the emotional needs of your children. Your children may or may not be aware of the infidelity, but even the youngest of your children will know that something is wrong in the family. Be aware of your children's feelings during the time of crisis after the infidelity has been revealed. They are likely to experience many feelings: insecurity, fear, anger, sadness, distrust, and so forth. Grown-ups often fail to realize that children frequently feel as betrayed or unloved by an unfaithful parent as the betrayed partner feels. In the aftermath of an affair, young children and teenagers become more susceptible to depression, suicidal impulses, and regressive behavior (thumb sucking, bed-wetting, rebellion, night terrors, petty crimes, running away, vandalism, and arson).

If you feel you have little motivation to reconcile with your spouse, consider your children: The crisis you are going through right now will have a profound effect on the shaping of their attitudes about men, women, marriage, honesty, and infidelity. Before this crisis, they lived in a world of relative trust, comfort, security, and family unity; their world may now be fractured and disfigured, but it can still be mended if you are willing to do what it takes to heal the family. It is also within your power to dramatically warp the outlook of your children and affect their futures negatively as well.

Children of adulterous marriages are much more likely to become adulterers themselves. They see their parents' dishonesty, secrecy, lack of intimacy, and lack of self-control, and sometimes they emulate it. Looking at their parents, they see one who is wounded, sad, hurt, ignored, disregarded, and treated as unimportant. Then they see the other parent, the adulterer, the one who breaks promises, who deceives, who acts irresponsibly, who gets to "play" and have a good time and who may even seem to get away with it. With which parent do you think the child is going to choose to identify?

Some children, particularly those who have experienced extreme emotional pain and humiliation as a result of a parent's infidelity, react against the unfaithful parent and grow up to be extremely moral and faithful. But all too many children grow up and adopt the philandering, self-centered ways of the irresponsible parent.

How much should children be told about the infidelity of their parent? They should not be burdened with information or emotional content that is beyond their years or emotional development. If they have been exposed to some of the conflict between their parents, they should be reassured that both parents are working on a problem between them, that the problem will be solved, and that none of the conflict is the fault of the children. If the child is upset, the parents should soothe and pray with the child and reassure the child of their love.

Finally, start over with each other. Don't try to restore the old relationship. Focus on building a new relationship on a foundation of total openness, vulnerability, availability, and intimacy. That is the caring, courageous choice that Stan and Debi made. It was a long journey— and their journey is still continuing. They had a lot of painful issues to address, a lot of tears to shed, and a lot of secrets to uncover. It was hard for Debi to learn to forgive and to trust again. It was hard for Stan to learn to be open about his feelings and his deepest thoughts. But in the process, these two people discovered depths to their relationship that they had never before realized could exist.

"I can't say that I'm thankful for the infidelity that brought us to this point," Debi says today. "It still hurts too much to think about it. But I'm thankful for everything that has happened since. For the first time since we said our marriage vows, Stan and I are really together—and I'll always be thankful for that."

What about you? If infidelity has broken your marriage relationship, you have the option of turning this crisis into an opportunity. You can replace the badly functioning, broken relationship with something new, lasting, and wonderful. A marriage that has been restored, rebuilt, and transformed is well worth the effort and pain it takes to do so. As the Scriptures say, "Two are better than one, because they have a good return for their work: If one falls down, his friend can help him up. But pity the man who falls and has no one to help him up!" (Eccles. 4:9-10). I urge you to begin a new adventure of love and intimacy together—and God bless you on your journey.

Why Would You
Be Unfaithful to Me?

1. What do you consider to be infidelity? Place a check beside the following acts that you rate as "unfaithful." When you have gone through the list, have your spouse go through the exercise also.

	WIFE'S RESPONSE	HUSBAND'S RESPONSE
My spouse makes a business call at the office of an old boyfriend/girlfriend.	_____	_____
My spouse gives a hug and a kiss to several opposite-sex coworkers at an office party.	_____	_____
My spouse makes an appreciative, almost flirtatious comment about my best friend's appearance in my presence.	_____	_____
My spouse makes an appreciative, almost flirtatious comment about my best friend's appearance when I'm not present.	_____	_____
My spouse goes dancing with someone he's introduced to while on a business trip. Nothing else happens.	_____	_____
My spouse watches a sex-laden R-rated movie, starring his/her favorite sexy film star, one night after I go to bed; he/she doesn't tell me about the movie.	_____	_____
My spouse meets an "old flame" for coffee and reminiscing after work. Afterwards, they shake hands, say, "It was really good to see you again," and part company.	_____	_____
My spouse makes a business call on a prospective client in the client's home. The client "comes on" to my spouse—an obvious attempt at seduction—and my spouse exits the situation but does not tell me about it afterward.	_____	_____

	WIFE'S RESPONSE	HUSBAND'S RESPONSE
My spouse has a secret opposite-sex friend. They have been meeting for years—not for sex, just to talk, sometimes holding hands or hugging. But it's not really an affair—more of a friendship. My spouse does not discuss it with me.	_____	_____
My spouse insists on a one-week separate vacation every year. I don't know what takes place on those vacations—my spouse says, "Everyone's entitled to just one week away a year, no questions asked."	_____	_____
My spouse talks to an old boyfriend/girlfriend once a week on the phone. This person lives five states away, and my spouse hasn't seen this person in ten years.	_____	_____
My spouse flirts with almost every opposite-sex person he/she meets. My spouse says it's just his/her personality: "I'm outgoing and fun loving, that's all."	_____	_____
While I'm out of town, my spouse accompanies an opposite-sex friend to dinner and a concert. Nothing else happens.	_____	_____
My spouse makes a business call on a prospective client in the client's home. The client "comes on" to my spouse. My spouse sees that this person is needy and lonely. To push this person away would make him/her feel hurt and rejected, so my spouse engages in sex—not so much an act of passion, but really an act of mercy, kindness, even politeness. At least, that's how my spouse later explains it to me when confessing.	_____	_____
My spouse and I have a huge fight. My spouse storms out of the house and drives away. The next day, my spouse comes home and remorsefully confesses to having had a "quickie" revenge affair with someone he/she met at a bar. It was a meaningless act, only intended to get back at me for the argument, and it will never happen again.	_____	_____

	WIFE'S RESPONSE	HUSBAND'S RESPONSE
My spouse, who is bisexual, occasionally engages in sex acts with same-sex partners. My spouse explains that this is not infidelity and I should not be jealous because these are not "affairs" with opposite-sex partners.	_____	_____
My spouse engages in sexual touching and fondling with another person, but does not engage in actual intercourse. It only happens once.	_____	_____
My spouse has been exchanging annual Christmas letters with an old flame for the past fifteen years.	_____	_____

After both of you have rated these statements, compare your answers. How are your attitudes on infidelity similar or different? On statements where your answers differ, discuss why each of you responded as you did.

2. **Based on your responses to question 1, do you see that you have two standards of faithfulness and fidelity—one for yourself and one for your spouse?**

   Do you see areas in which your standards need to change and become more consistent? Explain your answer.

   In view of the insights you have gained from this exercise, are there changes you need to make in your lifestyle or behavior? Explain your answer.

3. **Now, you and your spouse read the following questions separately, thinking through the answers or writing them in your journals.**

   Are there aspects of my sexual behavior that interfere in any way with my relationship with God? With my relationship with my family?

   Do sexual or romantic thoughts interfere with my ability to perform effectively in my workplace, my church, or my home?

   Do I think about sex more than I would like to? Are there aspects of my sexual behavior that are beyond my power to control?

Do I feel empty or ashamed after experiencing sexual fantasies or sexual activity? Do I use sexual thoughts or sexual activity to avoid certain feelings or problems in my life?

Is there an opposite-sex person in my life, other than my spouse, who makes me feel special and whom I am unwilling or unable to tell my spouse about?

Does my sexual behavior cause me to violate my conscience, ethical principles, or beliefs? Does my sexual behavior cause me to risk my job, my health, or my financial security?

Do I "channel-surf" TV or flip through reading material in search of sexually stimulating material? Do I seek out sexually stimulating material in stores, in video shops, on cable TV, or via my computer?

Has an important relationship in my life ever been endangered, damaged, broken, or compromised as a result of my sexual behavior outside of that relationship?

If your answer to any of the above questions is yes, you are probably either involved in or at risk for an affair. You should strongly consider obtaining professional counseling to resolve the issues that are placing your marriage relationship at risk.

4. Do you trust your spouse? Why or why not?

   Does your spouse trust you? Why or why not?

5. Think of three secrets about yourself that you have never shared with your spouse. What effect do you think these secrets have on your level of marital intimacy?

   Would you be willing to share those secrets with your spouse at this time? Why or why not?

   How do you think your spouse would respond if you shared them?

   If your spouse shared these exact same secrets about himself/herself with you, how would you respond? Would you still love your spouse?

   Having answered the last question, do you now feel more safe and comfortable about sharing your secrets with your spouse so that intimacy can be enhanced?

6. On a scale from 1 to 10, where 1 equals "Totally Closed to Each Other" and 10 equals "Completely Transparent to Each Other," rate the level of intimacy that exists between you and your spouse.

What steps could you and your spouse take right now to become more open, vulnerable, and intimate with each other?

Where Do We Go from Here?

NASA's space shuttle is the most complex machine ever constructed. In order for a space shuttle to perform its job safely and effectively, every interlocking system and subsystem—from its three powerful main engines, each generating 375,000 pounds of thrust, to its high-tech zero-gravity toilets—must function as designed. Most important, each system and subsystem must function cooperatively with all the other systems. When one system fails—even a seemingly minor one—disaster can result.

That's exactly what happened on January 28, 1986, when the space shuttle *Challenger* leaped off the launchpad and clawed its way into the chilly Florida sky. What no one knew was that a dirt-simple piece of space technology—a circular rubber seal—had become brittle in the freezing temperatures of the predawn morning. The heat of the solid rocket booster caused the brittle rubber seal to rupture, allowing blowtorchlike gases to escape, firing straight into the thin hull of the huge main fuel tank. Just seventy-three seconds into its flight, that accidental blowtorch burned through the tank wall, igniting the fuel. The space shuttle exploded about nine miles above the ground, killing seven astronauts and shutting down the entire U.S. space program for two years.

What happened? Leading up to the spectacular fireball and explosion were a lot of little errors, neglected warning signs, and minor oversights. The government commission investigating the disaster determined that many warnings from engineers had gone unheeded, that quality-control measures had gone slack, that communication between various parts of NASA had broken down, and as a result, the decision to launch the shuttle on such a freezing cold morning when the rubber seals were brittle was a seriously flawed decision.

A marriage is much like a space shuttle. The relationship between a husband and a wife is incredibly complex; and many of its systems and subsystems must interlock and mesh together, or major breakdowns can occur. Warning signs must be heeded, and problems must be corrected quickly. Quality control is a must in such areas as intimacy, boundaries, trust, expectations, and sexuality. Communication channels must be wide open, clear, and free of distortion. Leadership roles must be designated thoughtfully, and conflict must be managed carefully.

If all these systems are not working correctly and functioning together, if a marriage becomes brittle at the points of pressure and stress, if important warning signs are ignored, the entire relationship can rupture and blow sky-high. But how do we juggle all the complexities of a marriage and keep it aloft? How do we successfully mesh all the components, systems, and subsystems of a marriage so that a relationship can truly soar?

THE "MAIN ENGINE" OF MARRIAGE

Love is the "main engine" of a marriage. Love drives and propels the marriage, but the love we're talking about isn't passion or romance or sexual attraction. As we saw in chapter 1, authentic, Christlike love—the only kind strong enough to support a marriage relationship—is a commitment, a decision, an act of the will. It is covenant-love, rooted in loyalty and faithfulness to a promise.

There are many forces which, over the years, will put a strain on the relationship. There are external stresses and internal conflicts—and romantic-love (eros) and friendship-love (phileo) are not strong enough to withstand those forces. Romantic-love and friendship-love only last as long as the person you love is lovable. But in marriage, you can expect to encounter many situations in which your spouse will not be very lovable at all! And believe it or not, there are times when you're not so lovable yourself!

When things temporarily turn not-so-lovable, many people throw up their hands and divorce each other. If they understood covenant-love (agape), rooted in a promise, their marriage could hold together through the crisis. Eventually, both partners would become lovable again, they would grow emotionally, spiritually, and relationally through the crisis, and their bond of intimacy would become all the stronger. Unfortunately, all too many couples conclude that the love is gone, so they pull the "eject" lever and bail out of a marriage that could have been saved—if they had understood what love is all about.

This is why I say that love is the "main engine" of the marriage; covenant-love, based on a commitment of the will, keeps the relationship moving forward to more intense levels of intimacy. If a couple does not understand how to love through an act of the will instead of through mere emotion, the marriage will be more likely to abort and crash to the ground.

THE "HEAT SHIELD" OF MARRIAGE

The space shuttle is covered with protective ceramic tiles. These tiles shed the heat of reentry and protect the crew from destructive outside forces. Every healthy marriage has a similar "heat shield"—or rather, a series of heat shields. These protective buffers in a marriage are called boundaries.

As we saw in chapter 2, boundaries draw clear, healthy distinctions around the relationship. Boundaries form a protective zone; we do not allow parents, in-laws, friends, acquaintances, and other influences to cross certain lines into our marriage. An emotionally healthy couple is comprised of two people who have left their respective families and have established clear physical and emotional out-of-bounds lines between themselves and their childhood families and between themselves and the rest of the world.

Sexual boundaries protect a marriage from the "heat" of infidelity; when both partners understand that certain behaviors and certain people are clearly out-of-bounds, the marriage is secured against the risk of sexual intrusion.

But boundaries also draw clear, healthy distinctions within the relationship—boundaries between one partner and the other. It is our separateness that allows us to fully enter into a close and permanent bond with another person. Though the goal of a healthy marriage is intimacy—an emotional, intellectual, and spiritual bonding so intense it borders on fusion—each partner must also maintain his or her own uniqueness and individuality. That is what boundaries are for.

Boundaries keep some things out while keeping other things in. The boundaries around the relationship shield both partners from the "heat" and destructive "friction" of the world, of parents, of any and all forces that attempt to intrude and damage the relationship. Boundaries within the relationship protect each partner from taking too much heat from the other. Each partner must be able to say to the other, "This is who I am as opposed to you. These are my thoughts, my feelings, my desires, my goals."

Boundaries—the heat shields of marriage—are a critical component of the system. With strong, secure boundaries, the vehicle of marriage can soar. Without this heat shield in place, a couple can burn up in the atmosphere of stress, conflict, and infidelity.

THE "LIFE-SUPPORT SYSTEM" OF MARRIAGE

Astronauts have to breathe. A space shuttle without a life-support system is not going to get very far. In a marriage, the life-support system is something we call trust. Both partners need to know that it is safe to "breathe" in the relationship; that is, it is safe to be intimate, open, and vulnerable with each other.

Individuals whose ability to trust was damaged in childhood have some issues and emotions to be examined through counseling. Old wounds must be flushed out and dealt with so they can no longer hinder the present relationship. The partner who is haunted by fears of engulfment or abandonment needs to come to a place where it is emotionally possible to experience genuine intimacy within the strong, protective enclosure of love, boundaries, and mutual trust. In order for trust to grow, both partners must commit (or recommit) themselves:

- to a reaffirmation of their wedding vows
- to a lifestyle of uncompromising truthfulness
- to both giving and receiving trust
- to making and keeping promises

The commitment of a promise is foundational to trust in a marriage. Like the oxygen supply in a space shuttle, a promise guarantees that the things we depend on for our survival will be there when we need them. A promise looks to the future and overcomes the unpredictability of tomorrow, enabling us to feel secure—enabling us to trust.

When we make and keep promises, we declare ourselves to be reliable and unchanging, even in the face of unpredictable events and circumstances. As we generate trust in the relationship, we remove fear and anxiety so that the relationship becomes strong, healthy, and durable. The life-support system of trust, discussed in chapter 3, makes life possible in a marriage and is one more system that makes it possible for the relationship to move forward.

THE "MISSION" OF MARRIAGE

Anytime a space shuttle launches, it follows a "mission profile." The entire flight has been planned in order to achieve certain goals and expectations.

Marriage, too, has a mission profile. Both partners in the relationship have goals and expectations. Some are conscious, spoken expectations. But many of the expectations we have of our spouses are unspoken expectations:

"If he loved me, he'd just know what kind of lovemaking I want."

"After twenty years of marriage, I shouldn't have to tell her what makes me mad. I'll just sulk until she figures it out."

Unspoken expectations are dangerous. The mission profile of a marriage—both his expectations and her expectations—should be brought out into the open and negotiated verbally and clearly. An emotionally healthy couple continually seeks to bring hidden expectations out of hiding. This is done by carrying out the following:

- setting aside regular time for discussing issues and communicating openly about mutual expectations

- practicing good listening habits; listening receptively rather than defensively. Good listeners seek creative ways to meet the emotional needs the other person expresses. Poor listeners seek to evade or deflect those needs.

- using "I" statements when expressing needs: "I need more time to myself," not, "You need to go away and leave me alone."

- writing out a mutually negotiated "Contract of Expectations," expressing such matters as mutual faithfulness and support, spiritual expectations, emotional expectations, sexual expectations, and practical expectations (chores, children, finances, and so forth)

As we saw in chapter 4, when we go through the process of actually articulating and negotiating our expectations, we begin to see that some of those expectations are not realistic or reasonable. So we discard some expectations, modify others, and attempt to mesh our expectations with those of our spouse. This keeps our "mission" on course, flying straight and true on a stable flight plan.

THE "GUIDANCE SYSTEM" OF MARRIAGE

Like the guidance system of a spacecraft, our human brains collect data, analyze and sort that data, and enable us to use that information to stay on course and respond to emergencies and new situations. In a general sense (as you may recall from chapters 5 and 6), the brain can be viewed as consisting of three main divisions:

- The Survival Brain (made up of the brain stem and the limbic system, centered beneath the cerebral cortex)

- The Storehouse Brain (the right hemisphere of the cerebral cortex)

- The Logical Brain (the left hemisphere of the cerebral cortex)

Each division of the brain plays a unique and crucial role in marriage communication and relationships. When our mental "computer" is programmed with accurate perceptions and information, we tend to respond appropriately in various situations, and our relationships stay on course. But if the programming of our brains is flawed, our responses to various situations in marriage will also be flawed.

What is our programming? It is what I call the maps, symbols, filters, frames, and postures (or, for short, our mental images) that we have accumulated in our storehouse brain. These powerful symbolic images, which are stored at a level below our conscious awareness, cause old emotional issues, old hurts, and old struggles to recur again and again in our relationships. They create distorted impressions of our partner and generate suspicion and wariness, which damage trust and inhibit intimacy.

We use our mental maps in order to know how to respond to a given situation. That's fine as long as our map is accurate, but if it is distorted, our map will lead us off course. We may think we know what our spouse is thinking, what his/her motives are, why he/she is doing this or saying that; but that is just our map, and the map could be inaccurate. The less accurate our map is, the more likely we are to shoot off-course and get lost in our relationships.

Our maps tend to magnify isolated actions and incidents into powerful, emotional symbols. If your spouse absentmindedly turns his/her back on you while you are speaking, it probably only means he/she was momentarily distracted. But if your mental map tells you to be wary of the possibility that your spouse is disrespectful and uncaring toward you, then the simple act of turning around may be received as a powerful symbol of rejection in your mind.

As a couple's relationship develops over time, their mental images take on definite shape. If they allow authentic covenant-love to decline, if they begin to lose their desire to deepen intimacy and understanding of each other, they may allow the distortions in their mental images to harden into deep misconceptions. Instead of actually seeing each other, two marriage partners may begin to see only the stereotypes and caricatures they have allowed to build up in their minds. They begin relating to each other on the basis of false impressions and assumptions.

In order to make sure that the guidance system of your marriage is functioning properly and giving you realistic information on which to base your decisions, behavior, and responses, you should do the following:

- Seek to understand and monitor the workings of your unconscious, symbolic mind. For example, if you become angry over something your spouse says, ask yourself, "Is my anger proportional to what my spouse actually said, or am I overreacting? And if I'm overreacting, why? What is my map of this situation? How am I filtering and framing it? What symbols does this situation arouse within me?"

- Take an emotional "reality check." Before responding to your spouse, pause to get in touch with your feelings and to understand what has triggered those emotions.

- Recognize that your spouse also has maps, symbols, filters, and frames. Your spouse may not be so much in conflict with the real you as with a mental symbol or caricature of you.

- Accept the fact that both you and your spouse have unresolved feelings and issues from childhood. If those issues are serious and difficult to deal with, consider obtaining counseling.

- Make a commitment to grow in genuine intimacy with and understanding of your spouse—not a mental or symbolic caricature of your spouse but the authentic reality.

THE "COMMUNICATION SYSTEM" OF MARRIAGE

A successful spaceflight depends on good communication. So does a successful marriage. A space shuttle needs to remain in constant contact with Mission Control in Houston; a married couple needs to remain in constant contact with God. Astronauts need to be able to communicate effectively and clearly with each other; so do marriage partners. All the various systems and subsystems of a shuttle—radar, telemetry, flight controls, computers, power systems, main engines, maneuvering engines—need to communicate with each other and integrate with each other for smooth and successful performance; all the various systems and subsystems of a marriage need to cooperate and harmonize as well.

So communication is crucial to maintaining forward motion in a marriage. We have to be aware of how communication styles vary between men and women and from individual to individual. As we saw in chapter 7, women and men come from different worlds and they communicate in very different ways. The same words mean different things and are used to accomplish different purposes.

Clear communication is also crucial in the negotiation and apportioning of leadership roles in the relationship. As we saw in chapter 8, leadership is not a matter of "Who controls?" but of "Who serves—and how?" Leadership in marriage should be reciprocal and can take the form of initiating sex, planning meals, earning money, budgeting the family finances, planning vacations, and so forth. In many areas of the marriage and family life, each partner can play to his or her personality strengths. The husband can lead in areas where his gifts, talents, and abilities are strongest, and the wife can lead in her areas of greatest strength. This way, instead of competing with each other, the partners complement each other.

Clear communication is also crucial in the realm of conflict management. Conflict is inevitable even in the best of relationships. In fact, a certain level of dynamic, creative tension should be welcomed in a healthy relationship so that both partners will be challenged to learn, change, and grow. Handled in a healthy and mutually loving way—in an atmosphere of covenant-love and trust and with an awareness of the way our mental images affect our feelings and responses—conflict can lead to resolution, understanding, and deeper intimacy. Handled poorly, with communication that is either closed down or distorted, conflict can easily destroy a marriage.

In a healthy relationship, both partners learn to disagree, negotiate, and achieve resolution. As discussed in chapter 9, each partner stays in the present while discussing the issues and avoids the temptation to dredge up old issues and old wounds to use as ammunition. By continually monitoring and resolving communication problems while they are small, healthy couples keep emotional pressures from becoming explosive—and destructive.

In times of conflict, healthy couples think Win/Win. They seek each other's benefit while avoiding the doormat role. Instead of approaching every issue from an "I win, you lose" stance, they achieve creative solutions to conflict that make everybody a winner.

MISSION ACCOMPLISHED!

Every space mission has a set of goals, and the success of that voyage can be measured by how close it comes to achieving those goals. We tend to forget that marriage has a goal, too. We assume that marriage is just about two people coming together, making life less lonely, and—we hope—staying together for life. But there's more to a good, healthy marriage than that.

A healthy marriage has a sense of direction. In a healthy marriage, there is always someplace new to go, some new adventure to experience, or some new uncharted territory to explore. A healthy marriage is a marriage with a goal. That goal is not more sex or more money or more status or a bigger car or house. The goal of a healthy marriage is intimacy, and the success of a marriage can be measured by how intimately connected the marriage partners become.

Intimacy, as we saw in chapter 10, is the intersection at which two human souls connect. Intimacy in all its sparkling facets—emotional, intellectual, aesthetic, sexual, creative, and spiritual—is the fulfillment of Genesis 2:24: "For this reason a man will leave his father and mother and be united to his wife, and they will become one flesh." When you reach that level of intimacy with your spouse, you can say, "Mission accomplished! Objective achieved!"

Intimacy takes place in an atmosphere of safety (trust) and honesty (vulnerability). A sense of safety and trust is created by covenant-love and by promises that are made and kept. When we feel safe with our spouse, we are free to become honest and vulnerable, sharing those aspects of ourselves that we do not share with any other human being. The deeper we move into intimacy with each other within the safe, enclosing boundaries of marriage, the more we truly know each other. And that is our mission in marriage, our goal—to know and be known as fully as any two people can know each other.

That's our mission. That's the destination of a spiritually, emotionally healthy couple.

How long have you been married? A year? ten years? twenty? fifty? No matter how many years you have known that person at your side, there are mysteries to be explored and surprises to be discovered. There are depths of intimacy ahead of you and your partner that neither of you has yet imagined! And that is your mission: To explore new worlds of intimacy, to discover new depths and new realizations, to boldly go where no married couple has ever gone before!

So take off on this adventure together. But along the way, continue to monitor the systems and subsystems of your relationship. Make sure your commitment to love and promise keeping is rock solid. Be truthful in everything; be trusted and trusting. Create a zone of safety around your marriage. Safe within that zone, revel in the excitement and joy of fully knowing and loving this incredible life partner God has given you.

Where do you go from here? Deeper into intimacy. Deeper into each other.

Godspeed on your journey together!

Where Do We
Go from Here?

Evaluate where you are in the following areas of your marriage, using a scale from 1 to 10, where 1 equals "Very Satisfied" and 10 equals "Very Dissatisfied."

1. Where are you on your mission toward intimacy with your spouse? (1 equals "Sitting on the Launching Pad"; 10 equals "Mission Accomplished!")

    What one action will you commit to this week to help build intimacy with your spouse?

2. How satisfied are you with the level of committed covenant-love you demonstrate toward your spouse?

3. How satisfied are you with the level of committed covenant-love your spouse demonstrates toward you?

4. How would you describe the present state of the boundaries between you and your spouse? (1 equals "No Boundaries/Enmeshed"; 10 equals "Too much Separation/Isolated")

5. How satisfied are you with the security and appropriate boundaries around your marriage, protetcting your marriage from intrusion by the outside world (including parents and in-laws)?

6. How satisfied are you with the way and extent to which your spouse meets your needs?

8. How satisfied are you with the level of trust that exists between you and your spouse?

9. How satisfied are you with the amount, openness, and clarity of communication between you and your spouse?

10. How satisfied are you with the frequency, quality, and mutuality of sexual expression between you and your spouse?

11. How satisfied are you with the way leadership roles are negotiated and apportioned in your marriage?

12. Place a check next to the biggest roadblock to intimacy in your marriage?

	WIFE'S RESPONSE	HUSBAND'S RESPONSE
Practicing covenant-love (chapter 1)	_____	_____
Receiving covenant-love (chapter 1)	_____	_____
Dealing with in-laws (chapter 2)	_____	_____
Maintaining my individuality in the marriage (chapter 2)	_____	_____
Establishing healthy boundaries around the marriage (chapter 2)	_____	_____
Trusting my spouse (chapter 3)	_____	_____
My spouse's lack of trust (chapter 3)	_____	_____
Understanding and being understood by my spouse (chapter 4)	_____	_____
Understanding my feelings and my responses to my spouse (chapter 5)	_____	_____
Recurring conflicts (chapters 6 and 9)	_____	_____
Communicating with my spouse (chapters 4 and 7)	_____	_____
Leadership issues (chapter 8)	_____	_____
Managing and resolving conflict (chapter 9)	_____	_____
Experiencing intimacy (chapter 10)	_____	_____
Sex (chapter 11)	_____	_____

	WIFE'S RESPONSE	HUSBAND'S RESPONSE
Adjusting to change in the relationship (chapter 12)	_____	_____
Adjusting to changing emotional needs (chapter 12)	_____	_____
Getting my needs met (chapter 13)	_____	_____
Dealing with stepfamily issues (chapter 14)	_____	_____
My own infidelity (chapter 15)	_____	_____
My spouse's infidelity (chapter 15)	_____	_____
Other _____	_____	_____

After identifying the current biggest problem area in your marriage, take another look at the chapter or chapters indicated for that problem area, then list below three actions you intend to take this week to begin changing and healing that problem.

If possible, ask your spouse, a counselor, a pastor, or a very close and trusted friend to hold you accountable for making those changes in your marriage. Ask that person to pray with you and for you during the week and to check in with you next week to see how you did.

Renew this commitment from week to week. As you make progress in one area of your marriage, identify and work on a different problem area and ask for prayer and to be held accountable.

It might be helpful to keep a journal or diary of your feelings, progress, setbacks, and accomplishments as you work through the various issues of your marriage. Set a target date—say, a year from today or your anniversary or New Year's Day—and go over your journal and the written exercises you've completed in this book. Odds are, you will have made noticeable, significant progress in your relationship—progress that will encourage you to continue your journey toward deeper and richer intimacy with your spouse.

BIBLIOGRAPHY

Bader, Ellyn, and Peter Pearson. *In Quest of the Mythical Mate*. New York: Brunner/Mazel, 1988.

Bagarozzi, D. A., and S. A. Anderson. *Personal, Marital, and Family Myths*. New York: Norton, 1989.

Beck, A. T. *Love Is Never Enough*. New York: Harper & Row, 1988.

Beck, A. T., and C. Emery. *Anxiety Disorders and Phobias*. New York: Basic, 1985.

Bellah, R. N., R. Madsen, W. M. Sullivan, A. Swidler, and W. M. Tipton. *Habits of the Heart*. New York: Harper & Row, 1985.

Bowen, M. *Family Therapy in Clinical Practice*. New York: Aronson, 1978.

Bradshaw, John. *Bradshaw on: The Family*. Deerfield Beach, Fla. : Health Communications, 1988.

Clinebell, H. J., Jr., and C. H. Clinebell. *The Intimate Marriage*. New York: Harper & Row, 1970.

Covey, Stephen. *The Seven Habits of Highly Effective People*. New York: Simon & Schuster, 1989.

Curran, Dolores. *Traits of a Healthy Family*. New York: Ballantine, 1983.

Decker, Bert. *You've Got to Be Believed to Be Heard*. New York: St. Martin's, 1992.

Fisch, R., J. H. Weakland, and L. Segal. *The Tactics of Change*. San Francisco: Jossey-Bass, 1982.

Friedman, E. H. *Generation to Generation*. New York: Guilford, 1985.

Gray, John. *Men Are from Mars, Women Are from Venus*. New York: HarperCollins, 1992.

Haley, Jay. *Uncommon Therapy*. New York: Norton, 1973.

Hendrix, Harville. *Getting the Love You Want*. New York: Harper & Row, 1988.

Hoffman, L. *Foundations of Family Therapy*. New York: Basic, 1981.

Jones, Dan. *Words for Our Feelings*. Austin, Tex.: Mandala, 1992.

Kaplan, H. S. *Disorders of Sexual Desire*. New York: Brunner/Mazel, 1979.

Kaplan, H. S. *The New Sex Therapy*. New York: Brunner/Mazel, 1974.

Lederer, W. J., and D. D. Jackson. *The Mirages of Marriage*. New York: Norton, 1968.

McGoldrick, M., and E. A. Carter. *The Family Life Cycle*. New York: Gardner, 1980.

Neuer, Werner. *Man and Woman in Christian Perspective*. Wheaton, Ill.: Crossway, 1991.

Paul, J., and M. Paul. *Do I Have to Give Up Me to Be Loved by You?* Minneapolis, Minn.: Compcare, 1983.

Pittman, Frank. *Private Lies*. New York: Norton, 1989.

Sager, Clifford. *Marriage Contracts and Couple Therapy*. New York: Brunner/Mazel, 1976.

Satir, Virginia. *Conjoint Family Therapy*. Palo Alto: Science & Behavior, 1967.

Smedes, Lewis B. *Mere Morality*. Grand Rapids, Mich.: Eerdmans, 1983.

Subotnik, Rona, and Gloria Harris. *Surviving Infidelity*. Holbrook: Bob Adams, Inc., 1994.

Tannen, Deborah. *You Just Don't Understand*. New York: Ballantine, 1990.

ABOUT THE AUTHOR

Licensed psychologist Dr. James Osterhaus has been working with families and married couples for twenty-three years. He holds a Ph.D. in counseling psychology from American University and has taught other counselors in graduate schools at Denver Seminary and the University of San Francisco. He was the director of the Community Presbyterian Counseling Center in Danville, California, for several years before establishing a private practice at the Counseling Center of Fairfax, Virginia.

Osterhaus's other books include: *Counseling Families: From Insight to Intervention* (Zondervan, 1989); *Building Strong Male Relationships* (Moody, 1993); *Bonds of Iron* (Moody, 1994); and *Family Ties Don't Have to Bind* (Nelson, 1994).